# Goldfish Varieties and Tropical Aquarium Fishes

# Goldfish Varieties and Tropical Aquarium Fishes

## A Complete Guide to Aquaria and Related Subjects

ʊ

BY

## WILLIAM T. INNES

FORMER PRESIDENT OF THE AQUARIUM SOCIETY OF PHILADELPHIA

ʊ

*Second Edition*

ISBN 978-1-4341-0385-7

Published by Waking Lion Press, an imprint of The Editorium

Waking Lion Press™, the Waking Lion Press logo, and The Editorium™ are trademarks of The Editorium, LLC

The Editorium, LLC
West Jordan, UT 84081-6132
wakinglionpress.com
wakinglion@editorium.com

# CONTENTS

## AUTHOR'S PREFACE

There is perhaps no other means of bringing so complete a bit of Nature into our very homes as that afforded by the aquarium. Here we have opportunity for the student, the artist, the scientist and for those who simply love pets. Modern research, by the discovery of a few simple principles, has enabled us to absolutely reproduce the conditions of aquatic Nature, so that now we may have, at first hand, an intimate knowledge of much of that mysterious life of the water-world. Through the glass of the aquarium we have a window where that which we see is only limited by our own capacity for observation.

Although interest in aquaria has undergone a great awakening in the past few years, the public in general is still ignorant of the correct principles of aquarium management, and of the wonderful accomplishments of the breeders of fancy fishes. In addition to the extraordinary goldfish forms there are now available for our purposes over 300 other kinds of aquarium fishes. These, with other aquatic animals and a wide range of plants give us a great wealth of material from which to choose.

It is the aim of the author and the publishers to present in simple yet comprehensive form a practical digest of all available information on the subject. This, it is hoped, will be of real value to the intelligent aquarist and at the same time give the general public a clearer idea of possibilities under proper management, so that an aquarium will no longer be merely something which must be perpetually re-stocked with fishes, but an endless source of pleasant and profitable observation.

The illustrations used are, in nearly all cases, either drawn or photographed from life, thus establishing records which should be of value for present or future reference.

In the preparation of this volume the author has received valued assistance from leading specialists, breeders and general experts including the distinguished head of the United States Bureau of Fisheries, Dr. Hugh M. Smith. Special acknowledgment for generous co-operation is tendered Dr. E. Bade, Mr. Franklin Barrett, Dr. Herman Burgin, Mr. Wm. H. De Nyse, Mr. Richard Dorn, Mr. Henry W. Fowler, Mr. Joseph Froelich, Mr. Frank J. Myers, Mr. Wm. L. Paullin, Mr. W. A. Poyser, Mr. Fred. Schaefer, Dr. C. H. Townsend and Mr. Charles E. Visel. Mr. W. L. Brind should receive credit for his assistance in the preparation of the list of Exotic Fishes, his knowledge and specialized technique as a translator proving of particular value.

*Chapter One*

———

# The Freshwater Aquarium

## AQUARIUM MANAGEMENT

The principles involved in successful aquarium management are really simple, and if applied success is bound to follow. The common goldfish is a very hardy pet, and with proper handling should live from ten to twenty years. Yet we hear of numerous failures, and there are many who would like to keep an aquarium but refrain from doing so because of two erroneous ideas: first, that goldfish are delicate; second, that an aquarium requires frequent cleaning. The main causes for failure, in the order of their importance, are:

Overcrowding
Overfeeding
Sudden temperature changes
Lack of proper plant life
Insufficient lighting.

**Overcrowding.** A great many unscrupulous and short-sighted dealers, in order to increase sales, recommend the use of more fish than should properly be put into an aquarium of given size. The beginner also wishes to have as many fishes as possible, so that this is one of the greatest difficulties to overcome. The proper rule is this: ONE INCH OF FISH TO ONE GALLON OF WATER. That is, in a ten-gallon aquarium of the usual oblong shape, well planted and in a good light, one could successfully keep ten one-inch fish, or five two-inch or two five-inch fish. Successful aquarists adhere to this rule, and for some of the fancy and more delicate varieties, even more water per fish is allowed. The beginner will do well to do likewise and disregard all advice to the contrary. If already stocked with too many fish, some of them should be disposed of or a larger aquarium secured. Should the fish get into poor condition from overcrowding it will be difficult to save any of them.

**Gasping.** When the fishes persist in coming to the top and gasping air, it is usually a sign that they are overcrowded or that the water has become bad from some kind of decomposition. The trouble should be quickly found and remedied before the fish become seriously affected or perhaps suffocate. A partial change of water or the removal of some of the fish will usually improve matters. Sometimes the condition is produced by a dead snail or mussel, or again from the decomposition of uneaten food.

**Overfeeding.** Many people kill their fish by kindness. Whenever the fish seem hungry they are fed. This is a very great mistake. In

Nature the food is scarce and difficult to get. Therefore the fish have to exercise themselves in procuring it. In the small confines and artificial conditions of the household aquarium, less food can be properly digested, for fishes, like men, suffer from indigestion, but with quicker and more fatal results. Fish should never, on any account be fed more than will be consumed at once. (This does not apply in raising young fish.) If any food is left after five minutes, they have been overfed and the surplus should be removed with a dip-tube. (See Chapter on Aquarium Appliances.) In summer or at any time when the water is at 60 degrees or higher, it is allowable to feed daily. Should the water range from 55 degrees to 60 degrees, every other day is sufficient, and when it is from 40 degrees to 55 degrees, feedings separated by about three to six days, will keep them in good condition. An exact scale is difficult to establish, partly because fish, under one year of age, can assimilate more food than old ones, and partly because the temperature in an aquarium varies at different hours in the day. The foregoing scale will give a very good working basis, to be followed with a certain amount of personal judgment. Let it be said there is practically no danger of starving a fish, the errors being almost altogether on the other side. A correspondent once wrote the author that she kept a fish for seventeen years, and in that time had fed it on rice wafers once a week only. The matter of feeding fish is a difficult point to correctly impress on the mind of the general public. When the fish swim coaxingly to the near side of the aquarium it is a great temptation to feed them whether it is their meal time or not, but those who love their pets will do them a far greater kindness by depriving them until the usual feeding hour.

**Changing the Water.** If for any reason it becomes necessary to change the water, there is one very important thing to keep in mind— *do not subject the fishes to any sudden change of temperature, either higher or lower.* This is one of the most frequent causes of sickness and eventual death.

With the foregoing conditions carefully observed and carried out there should be no need to change water except at rare intervals, when the aquarium gets dingy looking or overcrowded with plants. Experienced aquarists replant about once a year, occasionally adding water to make up for evaporation.

The fish are stimulated and probably benefited by changing a small part of the water every few days. From one-fifth to one-tenth of the total volume should be sufficient. If the aquarium is in proper condition and not overcrowded, even this slight changing of water is not necessary. However, it can do no harm and may do good.

In cases of overcrowding, a partial change of water should be made daily, the amount depending on the degree of overcrowding. Here, again, a little personal judgment should come into play.

A sprinkling pot is excellent for adding water to the aquarium. The small streams oxygenate the water well and do not disturb the contents of the aquarium.

If running water is used, a very tiny stream will be sufficient. Fish used to running water when placed in still water should at first be given ample room.

**Plant Life.** Fish live by absorbing oxygen, and they give off carbon dioxide as the waste product of their chemical life. Plants, under the influence of light, do the exact opposite, so that what is poison to one is life to the other. This explains why healthy plants are so desirable, and accounts for the phrase "balanced aquarium," because there is a self-maintaining interchange established.

Still water takes up a certain amount of oxygen from the air. The fishes, however, consume more oxygen than can be supplied in this manner, and if oxygen-liberating plants are not used the fishes become restless, come to the surface to breathe the air, and may finally die of suffocation unless the water is changed.

The term "balanced aquarium" is not accurately descriptive, as an exact balance is never maintained. In practise we always endeavor to have the oxygenating element the more active, since any excess of oxygen goes off harmlessly into the air, while an excess of the poisonous carbon dioxide cannot be quickly taken up by the plant life. A more correct term might be "reciprocating aquarium."

**Aquarium Plants.** Different plants have varying powers of producing oxygen. It is therefore well to bear this in mind when making a selection for planting. Purely ornamental plants are desirable only after a fully sufficient quantity of the oxygen-producers have been provided. In the order of their oxygenating powers we would name, Anacharis, Vallisneria, Sagittaria, Nitella, Bacopia, Fontinalis, Potamogeton, Ludwigia and others, which will be more fully described later.

**Light.** As just stated, plants require light in order to do their work. Select for the aquarium a place close to a window with a good, strong light, preferably one where it will get about two hours of direct sun a day. In hot weather one should be careful not to overheat a small aquarium in the sun. A range of between 50 and 75 degrees F. is safe.

Green water is caused by the presence of a microscopic form of vegetable life suspended in the water. Their growth is usually promoted by a combination of too much direct sunlight and a large number of fish in the aquarium. There are several ways of clearing the water. First change it, add a few fresh-water mussels, cut down the light by use of tissue paper or other means, take some fish out of the aquarium. To clear the water chemically, add one grain by weight of permanganate of potash (dissolved) to each gallon of aquarium water. This will turn the water first a lavender, and then a brownish color for a few days, after which it will clear up. Unless the original conditions are changed, however, the water will soon again become green. Before using this chemical remove all snails and mussels. Goldfish can withstand the strength of the solution recommended, and probably be benefitted if suffering from any form of fungus. (See Chapter on Diseases.) Other fishes do not stand this chemical so well. Green water, while unsightly, is not unwholesome. On the contrary, a sick fish is often cured by being transferred to a tank of green water. Live daphnia will clear water in a few days.

**How to Know When the Fishes are Sick.** The first signal of distress in most fish is the drooping of the dorsal (back) fin. This fin should be carried stiff and upright. When the fish is sick its movements are sluggish and it often seeks a quiet corner in which to hide. In some of the fancy varieties the dorsal fin is so overdeveloped that the fish even in health has not sufficient strength to hold it erect. When such fish are ill their fins become more or less stiff, losing flexibility. Fins should be clear and clean-cut. When they become thick-looking, opaque, lined with red veins, overcast with red, blooshot at base of fins, or ragged and split, the fish is in need of attention. (See Chapter on Diseases.) Another sign of poor condition is thinness of the body. The excrement of fishes in health is usually of a dark color. When it is pale, dotted with gas bubbles, and of slimy appearance, the fish is apt to be out of condition.

**Sick Fishes.** It is always safer to remove an affected fish from its fellows. If the trouble is a contagious one, the aquarium or tank should be thoroughly disinfected, not overlooking the plants in this matter. For all practical purposes they can be sterilized by placing for one hour in a permanganate of potassium solution, 3 grains by weight to the gallon of water. Satisfactory results will also be given by dipping plants for a few moments in concentrated lime water. Either of these methods should be applied to all new plants introduced into the aquarium, especially those collected from the wild, or from aquaria of doubtful condition. In case of an aquarium becoming contaminated it can be disinfected by dissolving in it permanganate of potash to the strength already indicated, allowing it to stand from two to three hours, first removing all mussels, snails and fishes. In changing back to clear water again it will do no harm if a little of the permanganate solution remains.

Unless newly acquired fishes come from a source beyond suspicion it is a grave risk to introduce them at once into an established aquarium of healthy fish. They should first be quarantined and carefully observed for about two weeks, this being particularly true of imported goldfishes. They may already be inoculated with diseases only in process of incubation, but which will nevertheless develop.

**Chemical Depletion of Water.** Constant absorption of minerals from the water by plants and fishes makes a condition which should be provided for. This can be done by the occasional addition of salts. Make a mixture of three parts of evaporated sea salt (Turk's Island Salt), and one part Epsom salts. About once in two or three weeks a level teaspoonfull to 20 gallons of water will prove beneficial. Usually the fishes will greedily swallow these salts as they sink to the bottom, which acts as a mild cathartic with them.

The decomposition of plants, etc., sets up an acid condition in the aquarium, which is not good for the fish and which causes most of the crumbling noticed on the shells of snails. Ten drops of lime water to the gallon of aquarium water will neutralize any ordinary acid condition, but a better method is to keep a small piece of Plaster of Paris in the aquarium. In dissolving, it neutralizes the acid, but as it only dissolves under acid conditions, there is no danger of getting the water too alkaline. If the Plaster of Paris dissolves quickly it is a sign of pronounced acid condition. We would call two weeks a short time in which to dissolve a piece half the size of a shellbark in a 20-gallon aquarium. Pieces of gypsum will perform the same function, but more slowly.

Pieces of coral, sea-shells, etc., look out of place in a fresh-water aquarium, and many of them are sufficiently rough to injure the fishes if they chance to be knocked against them.

**A Word to Beginners.** It is much the better plan to start with a few fishes of the hardier varieties until the rudiments of aquarium keeping are well understood. If one can keep common goldfishes in perfect health and experience practically no losses, then it is time to branch out into the more varied and interesting breeds. Some beginners, having more enthusiasm than experience, lose valuable fishes at the start and turn away in disgust from a fancy that, if properly understood, would have afforded them many hours of pleasant recreation.

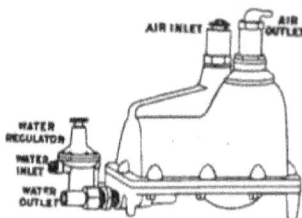

FIG. 1. *Air Pump*

**Aeration.** In Nature there is always sufficient plants or air surface to keep the fish well supplied with oxygen, but in the aquarium, particularly on dark days when the plants give off little oxygen, it is impossible to keep the fish from coming to the surface without the help of some artificial means. This is best accomplished by means of compressed air liberated at the bottom of the aquarium. As the air passes through the water there is sufficient oxygen absorbed to keep the fish always in good condition. This is also very helpful to the fish at night.

There are many varieties of pumps that can be used for this purpose, but the cheapest and most satisfactory are those which are operated by water power. The type known as "beer pumps" are the best. These operate on a very simple principle, having a minimum of working parts and therefore little to get out or order. Air is forced out of an air-chamber by the entrance of water. When the air is all expelled, an internal float stops the supply of water and starts a siphon working which empties the pump preparatory to the next filling. As this operation takes about a minute it is advisable to have a small storage tank for the air to pass through in order to equalize the flow. A very small stream of air running through the aquarium will keep the water sweet even though the aquarium is somewhat overcrowded. Overcrowding, however, is not to be encouraged at any time.

The air should be liberated in as small bubbles as possible. Liberators are made especially for this purpose, but a good home-made plan is to place a piece of bass wood or other open grained wood in the end of a tube to force the air through it. In case the liberator becomes clogged up, allow it to dry out for a day or two.

An air pump may also be used to operate a filter for the aquarium or to make a fountain without the use of water other than that already in the aquarium. (See Chapter on Aquarium Appliances.)

**Scavengers.** Nature has supplied us with means of getting rid of most of the harmful offal and decomposition in the aquarium. These con-

FIG. 2. *African*          FIG. 3. *Japanese*          FIG. 4. *Red Ramshorn*
THE THREE BEST FRESHWATER AQUARIUM SNAILS (*Life size*)

sist largely of those species of snails that do not attack the plants. Among the best known, most satisfactory and easily obtained are the large Japanese snails (*Viviparous malleatus*), the so-called African paper shelled

snail (*Lymnaea auricularia*) and the red variety of the European Ramshorn Snail (*Planorbis corneous*).  These are all active in eating vegetable
growth from the glass or particles of food which the fish have not taken,
and in no case will they injure any of the aquarium plants.  The Japanese
snails are very interesting in that they bring forth fully developed young
about the size of a pea.  These snails are male and female, but a female
once impregnated seems, like a queen bee, to remain fertile for the
remainder of her life.  The right horn of the male is somewhat the longer,
this serving a sexual purpose.  These snails are quite long-lived and grow
to the size of a large walnut.  Another snail resembling the Japanese
species is the Potomac snail.  This has two brown stripes on a horn-
colored background running with the spiral.  It is quite attractive and is
frequently sold as the Japanese snail, but it is sluggish and should not be
crossed with the Japanese.  The latter can be identified by the slightly
raised keels showing on the last spiral.  The paper shelled snail is very
prettily marked with brown spots on a horn-colored background, and is
an extremely rapid breeder, but is of short life.  The young hatching
from the spawn of these snails make a food regarded by the fish as a
delicacy, as is evidenced by the fact that none of these snails ever get
beyond the early stages of development if kept among the fish.  It is
therefore apparent that to breed these snails successfully they need to
be kept by themselves until the young are about half grown.  With the
Japanese snails no such precaution is necessary, as the young are furnished with a fairly hard shell at the time they emerge.

The European Red or Coral Snail (*Planorbis corneous*) is a recent
introduction and is unique on account of the bright red coral color of
the body.  When seen in the sunlight this snail is quite an added attraction to the appearance to an artistic aquarium, and is an active worker.
The snail is easily bred if the young are kept away from fish.  In breeding snails in small aquara or receptacles it is desirable to give them some
extra food.  Rice wafers, powdered fish food of almost any variety, lettuce leaves dried and powdered, boiled oatmeal or raw cream of wheat
will serve the purpose.  Eggs are deposited on plants and glass, and do
best at from 70 to 80 degrees Fahrenheit.

To those interested in identifying species of native snails we would
recommend a very excellent work published by the State Department of
Public Education at Albany, N. Y., entitled "A Monograph on the Snails
of New York State," by H. A. Pilsbry.  The book is profusely illustrated
in color and to all practical purposes covers the species east of the
Rockies.

The frog tadpole has been used by many as an aquarium scavenger,
but its value is of considerable doubt.  They dash about the aquarium

in an aimless manner, keeping the water stirred up and the natural sediment agitated. Furthermore, they soon learn to eat fish food and, after that step in education, they refuse to consume the less desirable particles found in an aquarium occupied by fish.

Another scavenger is the fresh water mussel. The chief value of the mussel is to keep down the vegetable growth which causes aquarium water to turn green. Mussels are equipped with a sort of siphon arrangement,

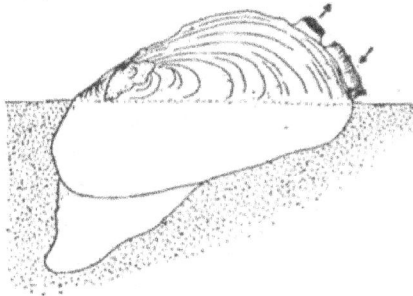

FIG. 5. FRESHWATER MUSSEL, SHOWING WATER INTAKE AND OUTLET; ALSO "FOOT" WITH WHICH THEY BURROW AND TRAVEL

by which they suck in water in one opening and eject it from another. In the few moments which they hold the water they extract from it the floating vegetable organisms. Two or three mussels should keep a ten-gallon aquarium free of green water. Care should be taken to occasionally see whether the mussels are living, as they decompose very rapidly and spoil the aquarium water. This can be done by tapping lightly on the shell and seeing whether they respond by closing.

A curious but useful scavenger is an eel-like fish called the Weatherfish. Varieties are native to Europe and Asia. They are freely imported

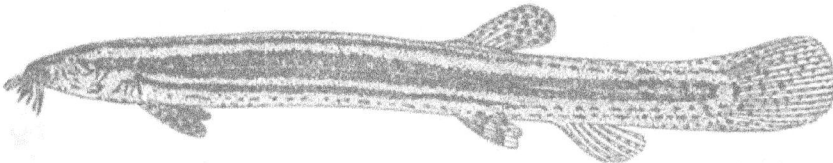

FIG. 6. THE WEATHERFISH (*Cobitis fossilis*)

and inexpensive. When not scouring the aquarium bottom for bits of decomposing matter, they sometimes burrow into the sand, leaving only the head exposed, producing a quaint appearance. In their special occupation as scavengers they employ a method which is both effectual and interesting. The dirt and top sand are taken in the mouth and rapidly shot out through the gills. Any particle of food considered edible is automatically separated from the bulk of the dirt and swallowed.

Another scavenger fish is the Sacchobranchus fossilis. This fish has a head like a catfish and an elongated body like an eel. Both of these scavengers are harmless to other fish, but should not be used when over five inches long as they stir up the water too much.

Goldfish keep the sand loose and in good condition by picking it up in their mouths, but most other aquarium fishes do not touch it, which allows it to cake and become permanently dirty. The Weather-fish is most excellent to introduce with such fishes, even a single small one keeping the sand in a large aquarium loose on the top.

**Aquarium Covers.** It is a popular idea that a free access of air to the aquarium is essential to the welfare of the fishes, but this is not so, particularly if there is a liberal plant growth. A glass cover, raised about a quarter inch, promotes a more luxuriant growth of plants, keeps the surface of the water free of dust or bubbles, prevents objects from accidentally falling in the aquarium, keeps the fishes from leaping out and our friend the cat from fishing in. Wire gauze, properly secured, will serve the latter purposes.

With tropical fishes the glass cover should rest directly on the aquarium or jar, with no intervening space. This keeps the water a few degrees warmer. Furthermore, there are a number of tropical fishes which can leap through a very small opening. This they are most apt to do when newly placed in an aquarium or otherwise disturbed. Our wild native fishes have an increased tendency to leap as the breeding season approaches, this characteristic being shared in by the single-tail goldfish.

## PLANTING

Planting is usually done directly in the sand or grit. Some aquarists prefer planting in miniature pots so that when it is desired to clean the aquarium it will not be necessary to uproot the plants. In potting plants in this manner a few pebbles should be placed in the bottom of the pot and then a layer of soil, preferably from the bottom of a pond. Spread the roots well into the soil and then cover with about one-half inch of sand, so that the earth cannot become free and cloud the aquarium water. As a rule, it is not advisable to use any soil in planting the aquarium itself.

The first operation in planting an aquarium is to see that the sand or grit is thoroughly clean. This can only be brought about by a long and thorough washing. After the water runs clear from the sand, spread the bottom of the aquarium to a depth of, say, half an inch. Next fill with about two inches of water. Now take the roots of Sagittaria,

Vallisneria, or other rooted plants, and spread them out well. (See chapter on Plants.) After the proper arrangement of plants is made, add from an inch to two inches of sand and pebbles, being careful not to completely cover any of the leaves. Now fill the aquarium and with a slender stick lift up any leaves which have been held down by the sand. After the leaves have been brought into an upright position, take hold of them and pull upwards until the crown of the plant comes just to the surface of the sand. Aquatic plants with crowns seem to do better if the crown is not quite covered. The crown is the point from which the leaves put out.

Care should be taken in planting not to allow the leaves to become even partially dry. This can be accomplished by frequent sprinkling, and the work should be completed as rapidly as possible.

Bunches of Cabomba, Anacharis and other plants, can be added last. These need to be weighted down with bits of lead or tin wire. In filling the aquarium it is a good plan to place a piece of paper in the center of the aquarium and let the water strike on this. By this method the plants will not be seriously disturbed. The use of a watering pot for filling will also prevent any serious disturbance of the planting. The aquarium should be allowed to stand at least a day before the fish are introduced; but a week would be better, so that the plants may become active in time to be of real use to the fish.

The use of pebbles only in the bottom of an aquarium is not to be recommended, because particles of food may fall between the stones where neither the fish nor snails can reach them, and the decomposition thus set up is liable to foul the water.

**Testing Aquaria.** Before putting plants or sand in the aquarium it is well to test its tightness. More often than not the larger sizes leak after removing or standing dry. These leaks can usually be corrected in a few days by filling with very muddy water, stirring it occasionally.

**Fish Globes.** Ignorance is responsible for most barbarity, and one of the commonest forms of both is the keeping of fishes in globes. The globe is in every way opposed to the correct principles of aquarium-keeping. When it is filled, the air surface of the water is extremely small in proportion to the bulk of water. The convex form acts as a lens to perpetually focus light into the eyes of the fish. Even the side light of a straight-side aquarium is known to be less desirable than top-lighting in an opaque tank. What then must be the effect of a focused side-light? A proper plant growth in a small globe is almost impossible. All of these evils are multiplied by the apparently universal over-crowding in these little prisons, and by the frequent pollutions of the water by overfeeding. As these globes are the cheapest form of aquarium, it seems as though they are destined to remain with us, but the public could be educated in the rudiments of handling them—not to overcrowd nor overfeed, nor fill to the top, nor stand in the summer sun; and to establish growing plants. If this point can be reached it is a step to the abandonment of the "globe" for a real aquarium, where the chances of success are so much greater.

**Removing Dust and Scum.** When the aquarium has no cover glass or when there is a considerable decomposition of old plants there is sometimes a scum formed on top of the water. To remove this tear a piece of newspaper to the width of the aquarium. Float the paper at one end of tank, lifting by one edge and draw quickly over the length of the water. Repeat once or twice with fresh paper.

**Algæ and Confervæ.** Should the plants become completely covered with algæ or "moss" try introducing a considerable number of small snails. The large Japanese variety are not always suitable for this, as they are unable to crawl on the smaller leaves. If this fails, remove and destroy the plants, thoroughly disinfect the aquarium in every particular and replant. Do not allow quite so much light in the future.

There is a very long, hard confervæ about the thickness of horsehair which grows into matted masses. This is quite a pest when once established, as it soon fills the aquarium and enmeshes young fish which usually die before being rescued. The only way to get rid of this is to take up all plants, go over each carefully and see that no single thread of the confervæ is left. If the smallest bit remains the growth will soon be as bad as ever.

Fig. 7. Prizewinning Scaleless Telescope Goldfish
*(Reduced one-quarter)*

This fish won the Diploma of Honor in 1907 as the best fish (any class) owned. Although no special attention was paid to "broadtails" at this time, there were quite a number of them, this being a good specimen.

FIG. 8. PRIZEWINNING VEILTAIL MOOR (*Reduced one-third*)

This is considered to be one of the finest black goldfishes ever bred. The short, deep body, the sail-like dorsal fin, the large, clear eyes, the broad flowing tails, the velvety black color combined with good lines and style make this remarkable fish a pattern which we might hope to equal but hardly to surpass.

*Chapter Two*

———

# Goldfish Varieties

## THE GOLDFISH

There are two root-stocks from which the goldfishes of to-day have originated. Both are members of the carp family. The European gold-fish, *Carassius carassius*, has never been developed into any of the fancy forms except by crossing with cultivated types of the Asiatic stock, *Carassius auratus*. The Orientals, principally those of Korea, China and Japan must be given credit for first establishing, by selective breeding, the goldfish as an ornamental pet as well as for the incredible lengths to which they have gone in fixing fancy breeds. Of this more will be said later.

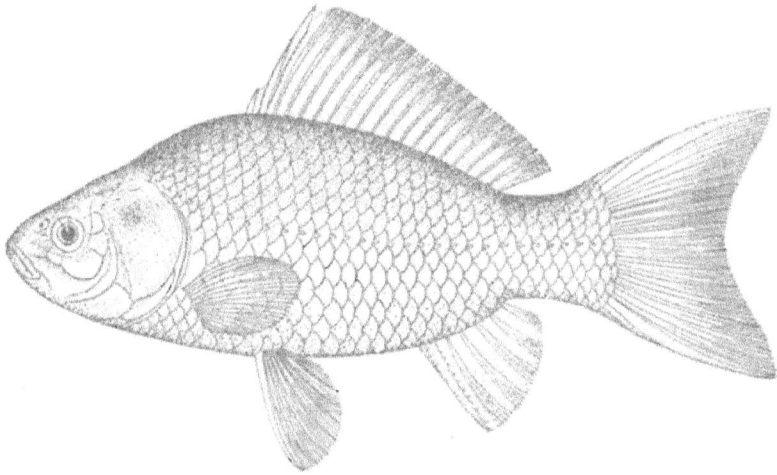

FIG. 9. THE COMMON GOLDFISH (*Carassius auratus*)

Although a common American goldfish has been described by at least one writer, no such division properly exists. Those sometimes found in American waters are invariably from escaped or liberated stock from one of the two varieties mentioned, or from their hybrids.

The normal color of fishes of both root-stocks is of a silver-gray or olivate hue, but with a strong natural tendency towards albinism, which produces occasional specimens of a yellow or golden color. By selective breeding the colors have become fairly well fixed, although in the scaled varieties the color is still at first carp-like, turning to gold, white or black, as a rule, in from three to eight months. Instances are quite common where they live to an old age without ever turning, so strong is the tendency among goldfish to revert to the ancestral stock.

The common Goldfish being closely related to the original stock has most of its characteristics. It is very hardy, can withstand extremes of temperatures if brought about gradually, can remain out of water for several hours when kept moist, is easily tamed and is a prolific breeder. The body is rather long and flattened on the sides. The head is short, wide, and without scales. Names of the different fins should here be carefully noted, as they are frequently referred to in other parts of this work. The Dorsal Fin (on back), the Caudal Fin (the tail) and the Anal Fin (small fin nearest tail) are all single in the Common Goldfish. The Pectoral Fins (nearest head) and Ventral Fins (nearer lower centre of body) are paired.

Under pond culture they will, in several years, reach a length of 16 inches and live for eighteen years or more.

COLORS IN GOLDFISHES. In color the fish varies from a smoky drab or olive to metallic red, yellow, white or partially black. Indeed a combination of all these colors is not infrequent, once the first carp-color is gone. The more prized colors in common goldfishes are deep red (called "gold"), white (called "pearl") and a combination of the two.

The smoke-colored fishes are known as silverfishes, their color and metallic lustre somewhat resembling tarnished silver. Breeders call them "uncolored," because they have not yet turned to one of the more desirable colors. Goldfishes of the metallic or "scaled" type are liable to change color at any time, the least liable to turn being the white or pearl fishes. After the first change from "silver," the rule is to progress towards a lighter color. That is, from black to red or from red to white. Exceptions are very rare. It will also be found that the lighter colors are the more persistent in breeding, and as these are considered the least desirable, it is well to avoid light-colored fishes when it comes time to select breeding stock. Even when darker-colored breeders are used, the fancier is frequently disappointed by having a large proportion of the young develop light colors.

Black is a color which for some unknown reason is confined almost exclusively to the telescope goldfish. In breeding telescopes it not infrequently happens that the abnormal eye development never takes place. These fishes may develop any or all of the color peculiarities of their parent-stock except that of being black. In the breeding of fancy goldfishes any freak combination of characteristics seems liable to occur, but the writer has never seen a good black fish without telescope eyes, although he is told by a reliable authority that there was one a number of years ago.

We have referred to "scaled" goldfishes. There is another division not known to the general public but which plays a highly important part in the goldfish fancy. This is the "scaleless" variety. These fishes are really not without scales, but the scales are of such transparent character that they are scarcely observable to the eye. However, they usually show with moderate distinctness in a clear photograph. Scaleless fishes do not have the metallic sheen of the ordinary goldfish. The colors are more refined and present a far greater range of variety. The most important difference is the presence of blue and lavender tints among scaleless fishes. Among the scaled fishes these are not found. A further account of these colors will be found in the description of the Calico Telescope on page 31 and in the chapter on judging Goldfish Competitions, page 43.

Another important peculiarity of the scaleless type is that they never go through the period of being silverfish, but at the age of about six weeks commence to develop their permanent colors. Their first color is white, sprinkled with small, black specks. A good idea of the final color may be had in ten weeks, although as elsewhere remarked, the very finest of the calico colors are not fully apparent under two or three years. Scaleless fishes have a charm of refinement distinctly their own and make most interesting inmates of the aquarium. So transparently scaled are some specimens that at the breeding season it is often possible to tell females by seeing the eggs through the translucent walls of the belly. The main objection to the scaleless goldfish is that the ribs or rays of the fins are rather weak. Soon after the fins have attained a high degree of development the fish is no longer able to hold them in a position where they will show to advantage. In the majority of instances the dorsal and caudal fins (hereafter in this work popularly referred to as "tails") commence to droop and sag in from two to three years, while the scaled fish often maintains an admirable stiffness of fins for a long life. This we would call ten years in a highly-bred fish. Questions are frequently asked regarding the length of life of fancy goldfishes, but these are always difficult to answer satisfactorily. A large proportion die under the age of 6 weeks. Of the remainder there are quite a few which do not develop rapidly, always remaining the "runts" of the batch. A few of these drop off from time to time during the winter, but in the early spring months they, and all other weak fishes, go rapidly, so that very few of the undersized fishes are left by the first of May. Those passing this period are generally good until the next spring, when the death toll is rather heavy again, but a fair number pass it successfully and they are likely to live several years more to an age of from four to six years. Anywhere from six to twelve years can be considered a long life for a fancy goldfish, although well authenticated instances exceeding this are known.

EARLY VARIATIONS. In breeding single-tail fishes together in which there is no known double-tail stock, one will sometimes find a fish with the lower lobe of the tail double, making it a reasonable supposition that this was the first "break" in form away from the common stock. This is called a "tripod tail." The next higher development is the "web-tail" in which both tails are fully formed but joined at the top edge instead of being completely divided. From these early "breaks" have been developed the fully divided tails, double anal fins *et cetera*.

By careful selective breeding, types have become fairly well fixed, but the goldfish has a strong tendency to revert far back to ancestral types, in form as well as color, often to the annoyance of the breeder. One of the most interesting things about a spawning of goldfishes is the tremendous variety in the young. In a lot of a thousand young scaleless fishes there may not be two alike, and none may resemble either parent. That this, however, is not always so is a self-evident fact, else selective breeding would be without results.

The accomplishments of Oriental breeders seems only to be limited by the scope of the imagination. Through the most patient efforts, not only of a lifetime, but of several generations of a family, such changes have been wrought in form and color that some of the breeds do not seem to even distantly resemble the common goldfish. That this is so is often evidenced by the fact that strangers to the fancy on first seeing a collection of highly developed fishes *want to know what they are*. An amusing incident illustrating this point occured in the preparation of the present volume. The engraver who made the plate for the goldfish design on the outside cover billed the publishers with "One Cut of Butterfly"! Those outside the fancy sometimes seriously refer to the fins of fancy specimens as "wings." Among fanciers a high dorsal fin is often referred to as the "sail."

When it is borne in mind what a considerable period of time must have been necessary to bring about these strange breeds, it is not surprising that racial ideas and characteristics should, to a certain degree, be expressed in them. The Telescope Goldfish was originated in China and undoubtedly bears a resemblance to Chinese art. It has a sort of beautiful ugliness, a deliberate grotesqueness, intended first to shock and then excite curiosity. The wonderful range of colors, too, suggests the art of the Chinese—that race which continues to-day to lead the world in the clever use of color. The Japanese Fringetail Goldfish is another expression of national art. It is the very embodiment of that aesthetic elegance and grace so well understood by the Japanese people. America has not been without its logical contribution. Here in this vast melting pot it is our desire to bring forth combinations of the best from the old worlds, to which is added a touch of individuality of our own. Although we have made several other combinations in crosses, the most important is the beautiful Scaleless Fringetail. European aquarists have not as a rule developed fancy goldfish breeding to the point it has been carried in America. Their interests, particularly among the Germans, are centered in tropical fishes, in which specialty they easily lead the world. In the Veiltail Telescope, the most important breed in this country, American breeders have virtually created a new class, although none of the separate points are of our own development. We have combined the short body and long fins of the Japanese Fringetail with the Chinese eyes, and colors. The broad, square tails seem to come from the Chinese side, but so far as we know they did not especially breed for this point nor for length in connection with it.

It is believed that the first cultivated goldfishes came from Korea, that country from which even ancient China borrowed ideas, education and arts, but so little is known of this that we have to take our facts as we now find them. That there have been and are breeds of goldfishes in both China and Japan which have never been sent out is well attested by travelers to-day and by a book published in Paris in 1780, by de Sauvigny. This remarkably illustrated work shows many of the varieties in color. The only known copy in the United States is in the Academy of Natural Sciences, Philadelphia, where it will be shown those interested.

The easiest characteristic to fix in a breed is the lengthening of the body and fins. This brings us to a description of the first of the fancy goldfish varieties or breeds.

## THE COMET GOLDFISH

The Comet has been referred to as the Japanese Comet because it is probably a "sport" from Japanese stock. Japanese experts have assured us the breed is not recognized in their country and certainly no considerable numbers of them have ever been imported from there. The first of the long single-tail breed appears to have been originated in the ponds of the Fish Commission in Washington in the early eighties. Mr. Hugo Mullertt either secured some of this stock or later originated a strain of his own. At any rate, he was the first to place them on the market in quantity. The Comet is long of body and fins, the tail in particular being very free-flowing. In movement this fish is the most graceful of all the fancy goldfishes and it can swim with great rapidity when necessary. This activity has made it easy for the fish to revert to its ancestral tendency to leap out of the water. Aquaria containing Comets should be covered by a screen, particularly in spring. The Comet makes the most beautiful and generally satisfactory pond goldfish where a decorative effect is desired. They are perfectly hardy over winter in a deep pool or where they may burrow in leaves or soft mud. The type breeds quite true to form and many thousands of them are raised annually for

FIG. 10. THE SCALED COMET

the trade. A few years ago there was a wonderful strain of scaleless comets of deep, oxblood red color. Unfortunately this was lost and present-day breeders with scaleless stock that could be so crossed as to produce scaleless comets find it more profitable to utilize their spare time and energy in propagating other breeds.

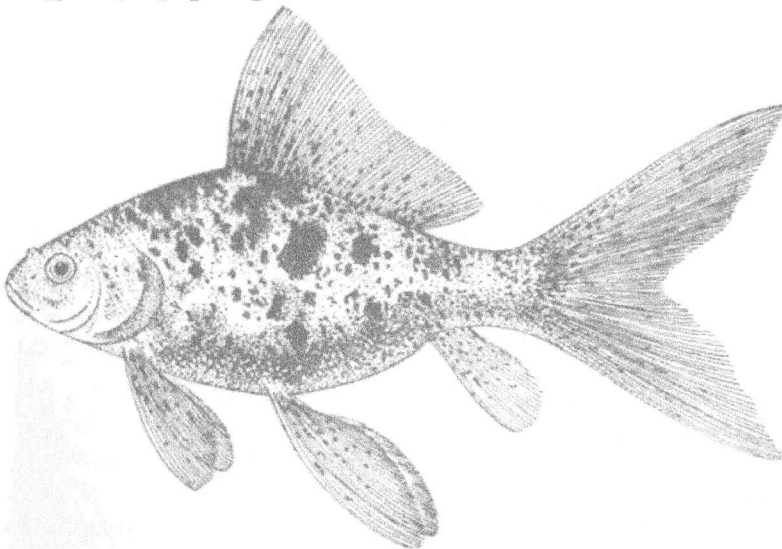

FIG. 11. THE SHUBUNKIN

## THE SHUBUNKIN

One of the more recent introductions is the Shubunkin. This is simply a transparently scaled, highly mottled, common goldfish. All breeders of fancy stock occasionally get fish which are known as "sports" which have reverted back in form, but not in color to the original type. The Japanese have now fixed them as a breed, and export a fair number of them. They are of the most striking variation in color, and make a hardy, attractive aquarium or pond fish. The colors most sought after are blue backgrounds, sprinkled and mottled with dark red, brown, yellow and black.

The Japanese stock has quite short fins, but those bred in America are a little more developed in this respect, the illustration showing the American style.

## THE FANTAIL GOLDFISH

This is no doubt the early type of double-tailed goldfishes and is the kind most frequently met with in pet shops. Enormous quantities of them are annually raised in Japan, China, United States and Germany. Being long of body, with fins not highly developed they make good breeders and

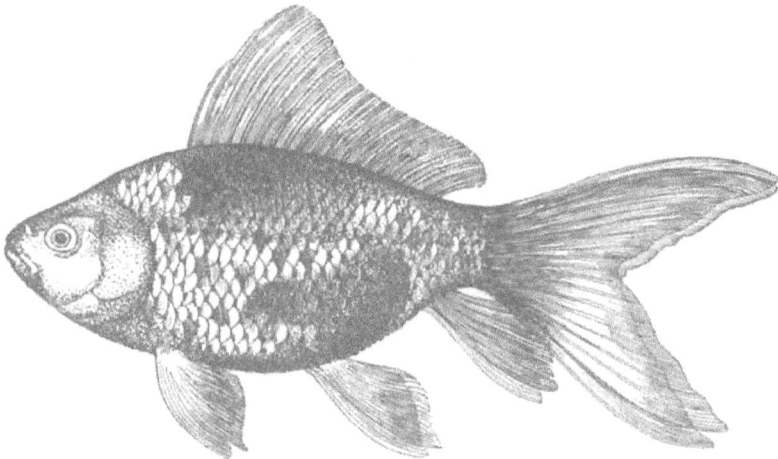

Fig. 12.   The Fantail

agile swimmers. This means that in the contest for life they are able in most cases to hold their own with the hardy single-tailed variety. Since the price for "fantails" is considerably in advance of that for "commons," it would seem a better commercial venture to invest a little more money at the start for "fantail" breeding stock. However, none should go into the raising of fish of any kind as a commercial enterprise without first obtaining actual experience in a smaller way.

The anal fins, as well as the tails, should be double and clearly divided.

## THE JAPANESE FRINGETAIL GOLDFISH

In point of pure elegance there is no breed of goldfish equal to the Japanese Fringetail. Our illustration is taken from a sketch of the fish, made by its owner, Mr. Franklin Barrett. A few words regarding this,

FIG. 13. THE JAPANESE FRINGETAIL (*Veiltail or Broadtail style*)

the best-known individual fish that has ever been owned in this country, might be of interest. The Japanese Imperial Government sent a collection of its best goldfishes to the World's Fair at Chicago in 1893. Only a few of them survived the journey and still fewer lived through the Exposition. These had fallen into a diseased condition and were given to Mr. William P. Seal. He cured them and later sold this one, now known as "The World's Fair Fish," to Mr. Barrett, for a comparatively small consideration. At that time the fish had not developed the wonderful qualities which have made it famous. It was one of those cases where "blood will tell."

Regarding this fish as a type of perfection that could not be improved upon, the Aquarium Society of Philadelphia had a drawing of it made from Mr. Barrett's sketch and used as a society emblem. The society later had the fish struck on its medal. It lived to an age of about fifteen years, and was the father of many fine specimens.

The characteristic points of the Japanese Fringetail are brought out in the illustration. The body is short, rounded and chunky, with short head and flat eyes. The lower fins are long, pendant and delicately lace-like, and are all paired. The dorsal fin is as high as the body is deep. It should be carried erect, producing the effect of a sail as the fish moves majestically through the water. As in most other varieties, the deeper colors, both in scaled and scaleless specimens, are the more highly prized. Scaleless fringetails, an American production obtained by crossing Japanese Fringetails with Chinese Scaleless Telescopes, are exceedingly refined in appearance.

The illustration shows the tubercles on the gill plate and pectoral fins, indicative of the male sex.

### THE JAPANESE NYMPH GOLDFISH

The Nymph is virtually a single-tail Fringetail. The anal fin and tail are single. The latter, instead of drooping, should be carried out

Fig. 14. The Nymph

straight, and well spread. This fish is usually a "sport" from fringetail stock. Although seldom deliberately bred, fine specimens are very attractive in an aquarium and are often retained by fanciers. In their active movements as well as in points of conformation they make a pleasing contrast with the double-tailed varieties. One of the principal features is the dorsal fin, which should be large and carried quite erect, as described for the Fringetail. The body requirements are also the same.

## CHINESE TELESCOPE GOLDFISHES

This most curious fish is either of Chinese or Korean origin, but was undoubtedly brought to its highest stage of development in China. The name correctly implies its chief peculiarity—projecting eyes. These make

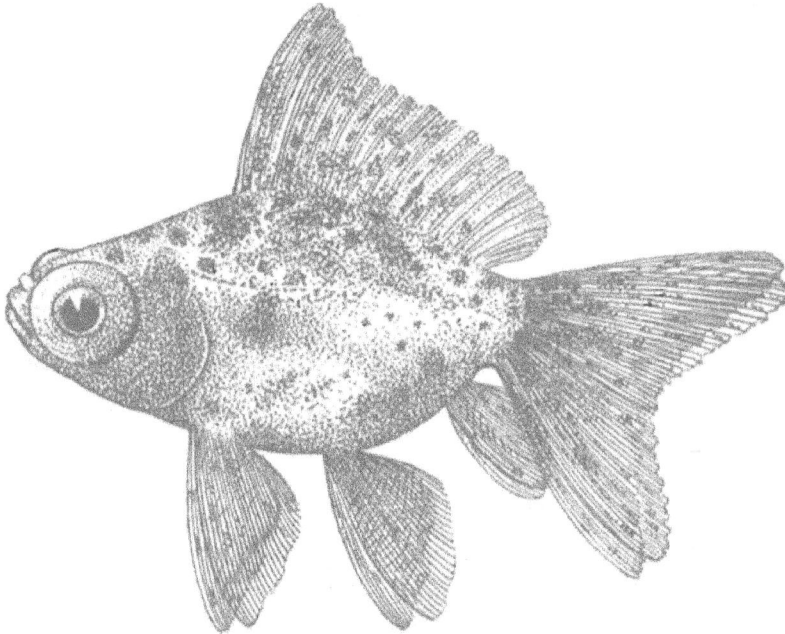

FIG. 15.   EARLY STYLE CHINESE TELESCOPE

a very weird appearance, and almost without exception produce a shocking impression on being seen for the first time. So perverted or educated do our tastes later become that we find our admiration increasing in proportion to the degree of malformation attained in the fish. Telescope eyes vary in shape and in direction. The majority of them are spherical or conical. Tubular eyes are rare and highly prized, but any form is considered good so long as they are large and stand out far from the head. Most telescope eyes point in the same direction as normal eyes, but some point forward. This is unusual. The Celestial Telescope has still more peculiar eye formation. This is described under its own heading.

One point in common between all telescope goldfishes is that in the early weeks of life the eyes appear entirely normal. Until they actually start to "develop eyes" at anywhere from two months to even two years, it is impossible to tell whether or not they will become telescopes. The usual development period, however, is from three to five months. Should they pass ten months without turning, they may be safely called Japanese fringetails. Many such fishes that have come from telescope stock are used to breed to telescopes to produce telescopic young. This is usually successful in the first generation, but it has a tendency to spoil the breed by gradually reducing the size of the eyes. Telescope fishes of the present time are, for the most part, considerably inferior in point of eyes compared with the stock of fifteen years ago, due mainly to breeding too exclusively for short bodies and long fins. Type characteristics in any kind of breeding can, like liberty, only be maintained at the price of eternal vigilance.

FIG. 16. CHINESE SCALELESS TELESCOPE (*Dorsal view*)

## THE CHINESE SCALELESS TELESCOPE GOLDFISH

As before stated, "scaleless" is somewhat of a misnomer, the fish being transparently scaled, making the scales difficult to detect. We use the word "scaleless" in its accepted popular sense.

Fishes of this general division are divided into two color classes—plain scaleless and calico. The plain scaleless is red, white or a combination of the two. Red in scaleless fishes is quite different from that in scaled varieties, being more of an ox-blood color, producing a highly refined appearance. In scaleless fishes the bodies do not have a metallic lustre. The colors seem as though they had been laid on by the delicate hand of a water-color artist. These fishes have white fins. During the first few months the roots of the tails are usually dark, but this gradually disappears.

The Calico Telescope is the consideration of first importance, not only in this group, but among all fancy goldfishes in America. Its name is suggestive of its coloring, but the colors are by no means in geometrical arrangement, as they are in the fabric. Red, yellow, brown, gray, black, blue and lavender are laid in fantastic blotches and spots over the body, usually on a lighter background. Many small dots of black are sprinkled over the body and fins. In extra fine specimens red dots will also appear in the fins. The color chiefly sought is blue, and the more blue, the more valued the fish. Probably every American breeder of scaleless telescopes has an ambition to breed a solid blue fish with high-class body and fins. A few solid blues have been produced, but the other required points were woefully lacking. Calico Telescopes of the higher order seldom find their way into the pet shop, the price effectively keeping them out. This is true of most of the finer fishes. Public taste in these matters is not sufficiently educated to warrant dealers in taking the risk of carrying the more highly developed, and therefore more delicate, specimens in stock. It must be noted, however, that the past few years has witnessed a gratifying development of general interest in the better aquaria and fancy fishes of all kinds.

## THE SCALELESS VEILTAIL TELESCOPE

While it is true that some of the early Chinese scaleless importations had broad tails and medium length bodies, it is highly probable that none of them equaled in short bodies and long fins the present American standard type. We crossed Japanese Fringetails with scaleless Chinese Telescopes, thereby producing two new varieties which have become permanent—Scaleless Japanese Fringetails and Scaleless Veiltail Telescopes. Both have been bred for broad-tail qualities (veiltail), and may be considered an American variation. The characteristic points of the Scaleless Veiltail Telescopes are the same as those for the body and fin formation of the Japanese Fringetail and the eyes and coloring of the Chinese Telescope. The coloring almost always tried for is calico, but if a fish fails in this and

FIG. 17.  PERFECT CALICO VEILTAIL TELESCOPE

still retains the other characteristics of the breed, it is considered a good fish.  A perfect calico veiltail telescope is the acme of perfection which most American breeders have in mind as their highest goal.

## THE CHINESE CELESTIAL TELESCOPE GOLDFISH

For a long time an erroneous belief existed that the peculiar eyes of the celestial goldfish are produced by placing the young in jars which were lighted only from a small slit in the top.  Although this variety is difficult to breed, it has been done several times in the United States.  No peculiar contrivances of any kind were used.  At the usual period of about ten weeks they developed ordinary telescope eyes in the regular way. Later they gradually turned towards the top of the head as shown in Figs. 18 and 39.

If any such peculiarity had been produced by mechanical means, it would not be reproduced in the offspring.  By some Orientals the Celestial Goldfish is considered sacred on account of its constant heavenward gaze, and is accorded a place in their temples.

Fig. 18.  The Chinese Celestial

The Celestial Telescope is the most difficult of the imported gold-fishes to rear or to keep alive in the aquarium.


## THE JAPANESE BARNACLED GOLDFISH

Barnacled goldfishes are so rare that the majority of leading fan-ciers have never seen them.  They were first imported from Japan in 1897, soon disappearing from view.  Although no new stock is known to have been imported, the peculiar characteristic has recently made its appearance again.  Whether these fishes are inheriting from the original imported stock, of whether they represent an independent "break," such as the Japanese breeders utilized in starting the breed, it is impossible even to surmise.  The scales are raised sharply in the center, presenting regular lines of dots along the sides of the fish.  These should not be confounded with fishes suffering from dropsy.  In the latter case the scales stand from the body at the outer edge. Otherwise the fish has the characteristics of the telescope fish.

## THE CHINESE MOOR TELESCOPE GOLDFISH

The Moor is a most striking breed of the goldfish, its intense, velvety black color forming a rich contrast for the more gaily colored specimens in the aquarium. The intense blackness extends to every part of the fish except the under side of the belly. This shades off to a blue-gray or a slight golden tint. In the latter case the fish is likely to eventually turn

FIG. 19. YOUNG CHINESE MOOR (*Veiltail*)

gold. This is not certain, nor is the blue-gray a guarantee against turning, although it is less likely to do so. Breeders have not found that the greatest percentage of blacks is produced by using two blacks, but by crossing a deep red scaled fish with a black. A good Moor with the body and fin development of the Fringetail, is a very choice fish, and is always in demand. The accompanying illustration, made from a very fine yearling fish, does not give a full idea of the intense black color of the original. Some of this had to be sacrificed in order that the drawing might show all details of the fish. Our photographic illustration of a veiltail Moor, on page 18, will give a better idea of the color.

## THE JAPANESE LION-HEADED GOLDFISH

In point of grotesqueness and the amazing accomplishments of breeding fancy goldfish, probably nothing surpasses the so-called Lionhead. It is often remarked that the name is not particularly appropriate, but seems to have become established. "Buffalo-head" would be a much more descriptive and appropriate name. There are three strong characteristics to this fish. The first is a thick growth over the gill plates and head somewhat resembling a large raspberry. The second is the entire absence of dorsal fin, and the third is the extremely thick, short body. The growth on the head seldom commences before the age of six months

FIG. 20. THE LIONHEAD, OR BUFFALOHEAD

and sometimes never appears. It is well developed in two years and increases in size as long as the fish lives. After the head growth has become quite thick it is advisable to keep the fish in running or other well oxygenated water. The mechanical difficulty of breathing is considerable and unless there is plenty of oxygen the fish is liable to suddenly expire when in apparently good condition. The tails and anals should be double, but defects in these points are not considered serious if head and body are good. The colors are the usual pearl and red of the common goldfish. A few transparently scaled specimens have been produced by crossing with transparently scaled fish of other breeds. One or two Lionheads in a mixed aquarium add considerably to the variety. It was believed by some that the absence of dorsal fin was the result of its being extracted by Japanese breeders while the fish was young. This has been proven a gross error for the same reasons stated in paragraph on Celestial Telescopes.

## THE ORANDA

In the opinion of the writer an Oranda was originally a Lionhead with a dorsal fin—in other words, a Lionhead which did not come true

FIG. 21.  THE ORANDA

to form.  However, it is recognized as a variety and is accorded a place in goldfish shows.  The fins and body are usually longer than in the Lionhead.

## THE CHINESE TUMBLER GOLDFISH

Among other breeds of Chinese goldfish never popularly known in America is the Tumbler.  The peculiarity of this fish is that of somersault gyrations comparable to those of tumbler pigeons, caused by the spine curving backwards.  A fish performing in this manner is occasionally seen in a hatching of any short-bodied stock, and is usually killed to relieve it of the misery of existence.  We cannot imagine that a breed of this sort would ever become popular in this country, for it would be too suggestive of troubles we already have in fishes caused by internal derangements, chiefly of the swimming bladder.

In addition to the few specimens seen in this country, a similar fish is described by de Sauvigny.

## THE CHINESE EGGFISH

A few of these fishes were imported some years ago, but have never become generally known. So far as America is concerned the breed is temporarily lost. This fish, as its name correctly implies, has a rounded

Fig. 22. The Chinese Eggfish

white body resembling an egg. The absence of dorsal and anal fins enhances this effect very much. The tails are bifurcated and decidedly drooping. This fish would form an almost dazzling contrast with a Veil-tail Moor Telescope. The breed is recognized in Europe.

## CHINESE LETTERED GOLDFISHES

It has been claimed that in some instances the Orientals have succeeded in breeding fishes marked with Chinese letter characters on the sides. In strongly mottled stock such a design might accidentally appear, but from our knowledge of goldfish breeding traits we do not believe any definite color pattern could be deliberately produced. It is much more probable that the fishes have been cleverly stained by the use of oxalate of iron or dilute hydrochloric acid.

## THE METEOR, OR TAILLESS GOLDFISH

In breeding for long-tailed fishes a strange perversion sometimes occurs in the form of a tailless fish, the other fins being well developed. The anal is single. Some of these have recently been bred together, and

FIG. 23.  THE METEOR

by a few generations of selective breeding the type has become quite well fixed. At first regarded as a mere freak, the Meteor has been accorded a place in a number of competitive exhibitions. A specimen such as illustrated can swim better than would be imagined, and makes quite a streaming effect passing through the water.

# Chapter Three

---

# Judging Goldfish
# Competitions

## JUDGING GOLDFISH COMPETITIONS

Among aquarium soceites there is a certain demand for competitive exhibitions of goldfish varieties. The difficulties of making satisfactory awards are considerable, due in part to varying ideas as to what constitutes standards of perfection. To reduce this difficulty to a minimum the Aquarium Society of Philadelphia instituted a series of conferences of leading fanciers in order to establish a satisfactory and uniform scale of standards. The diagrams shown herewith represent a composite of the best ideas obtainable. The majority of leading societies have adopted them as a whole.

The "point system" of judging, as it is called, is too slow and laborious for use on an entire large exhibition. The two or three best fish, selected on general appearances should be set aside from the others and judged independently by three judges, on points. The totals are then averaged and awards made.

In those classes requiring double anal fins the fish is penalized three points for having only one.

In the fringetail classes the tails must be fully divided to receive consideration.

The longtail or fringetail group is divided into two classes, the veiltail and the ribbontail. These are sometimes called "broad-tail" and "swallow-tail" or "cut-out-tail." In the veiltail the centre of each tail is indented or forked less than one-third of its total length. The swallowtail is cut in to one-third or more. The diagram on page 43 will plainly show this.

The making of these classes has caused some confusion. The author believes that fishes of these two types and those on the difficult dividing line should all take their chances together. The division was undoubtedly made as an expediency in order to make more awards and thereby please as many people as possible. So far as can be determined, no such divisions of fin shape have ever been recognized in China or Japan, and the same was true here until the period of 1910-12, when it became a conspicuous fact that nearly all winners of competitions were of the broadtail type. Those not possessing stock of this style became dissatisfied, and in order to appease them, a class of the old-style fish was definitely established. While the veiltail is the more difficult to handle and to breed, it is accepted as the standard to be striven for. The word "veiltail" is adapted from the German Schleierschwanz, and is more truly

FIG. 24.  AQUARIUM EXHIBITION, PHILADELPHIA

Horticultural Hall, one of the two permanent buildings from the Centennial Exhibition forms, with its magnificent setting of tropical vegetation, an ideal background for the National Exhibition of Aquarium Fishes held annually in October. Upwards of 15,000 interested visitors attend in three days, including many enthusiasts from distant points. Public exhibitions in other large cities are also remarkably successful.

FIG. 25. MEDAL OF THE AQUARIUM SOCIETY OF PHILADELPHIA
(Exact size)

The first medal offered by an American Aquarium Society. It is awarded annually for the best fish owned and the best fish bred by a member; also for distinguished achievement or services in the advancement of aquarium study.

descriptive than "fringetail," a word more apt to describe the split and ragged ends of the fins of a fish out of condition.

In competitions goldfish are divided into the scaled and "scaleless" classes, the latter being transparently scaled. The scaled fishes are colored gold (metallic red) silver (metallic drab or smoke) pearl (metallic white) and moors (blacks). The first should be of a deep shade of red. The second is a transitory color and varies but little. As a color value it ranks low. The pearl is a grade higher, but light colors in general are not favored. Moors should be a deep, purple-black, free from the appearance of a white scum. These blacks are never completely black under the belly. It is at this point that they usually begin to turn red, which is liable to happen to a moor at any age.

"Scaleless" fishes are divided into red, white, mottled and calico. The preferred shade of red is of the deep, oxblood color. White ranks lowest. Mottled is a combination of red and white, while the highest prized is the calico, a combination of all the colors in finely divided spots. In this class the all-important color is blue or lavender, the deeper the better, and also the more the better. The ideal calico has a body background of blue, red and white, over which is a sprinkling of fine black dots. The black dots and some red ones are also freely distributed over all the fins, which are otherwise white in these and all "scaleless" fishes. The highest development of this color seldom occurs under the age of from two to three years.

In the opinion of the writer, societies should avoid too frequent competitive exhibitions. They promote discord and tend to develop professionalism. Those truly interested in the development of the fancy will be willing to bring out their fish without thought of reward other than giving pleasure to their friends and the public.

## OFFICIAL CHARTS

### Showing Ideal Figures of the Principal Goldfish Varieties, Together with Valuation Points

Copyrighted by Franklin Barrett

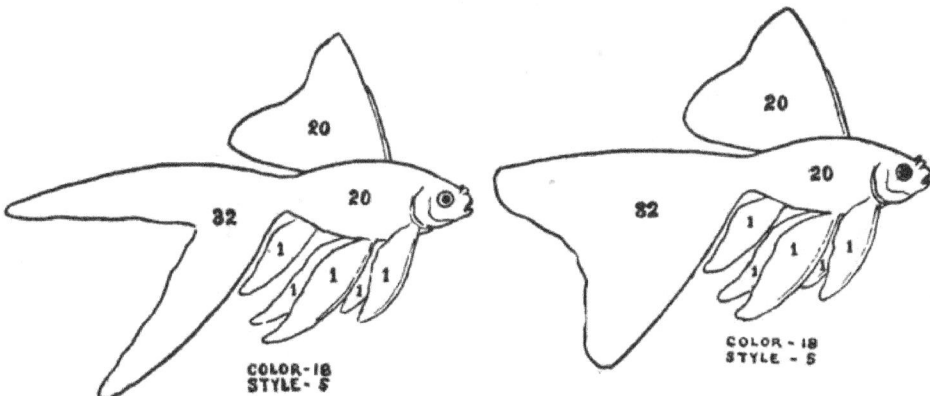

FIG. 26. SWALLOWTAIL COMET      FIG. 27. VEILTAIL COMET

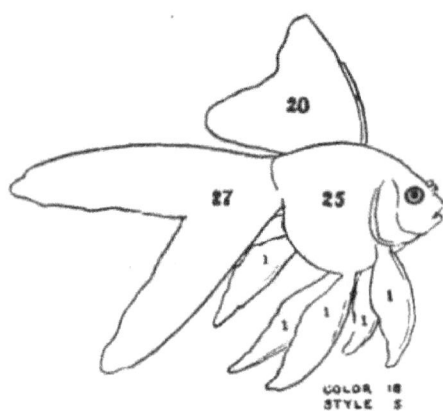

FIG. 28.  SWALLOWTAIL NYMPH

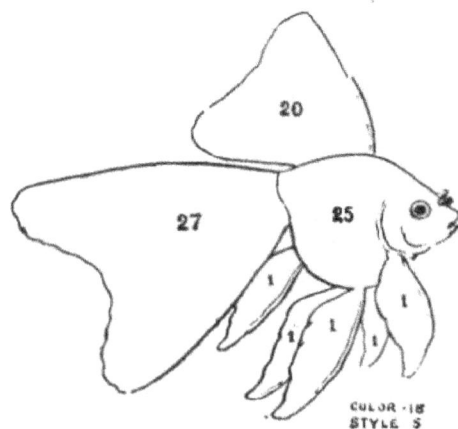

FIG. 29.  VEILTAIL NYMPH

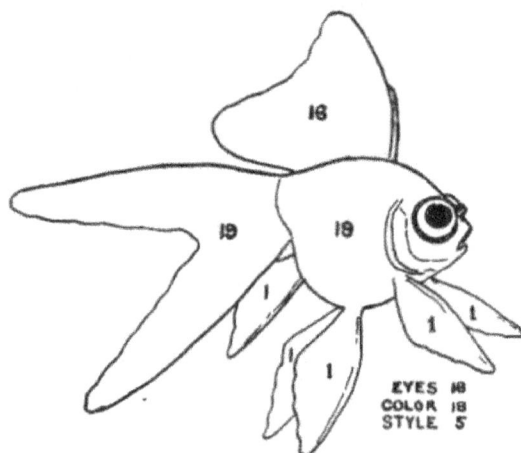

FIG. 30.  SWALLOWTAIL TELESCOPE NYMPH

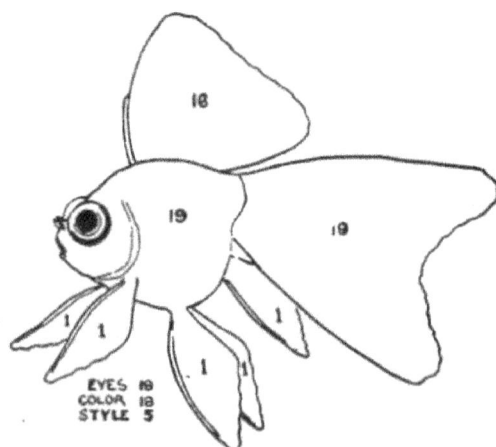

FIG. 31.  VEILTAIL TELESCOPE NYMPH

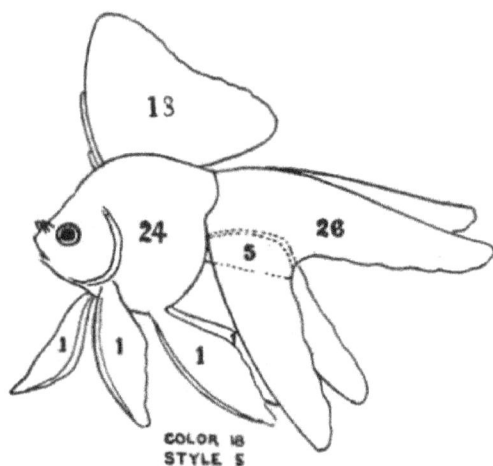

FIG. 32.  SWALLOWTAIL JAP. FRINGETAIL

FIG. 33.  DORSAL VIEW, SWALLOWTAIL
JAP. FRINGETAIL

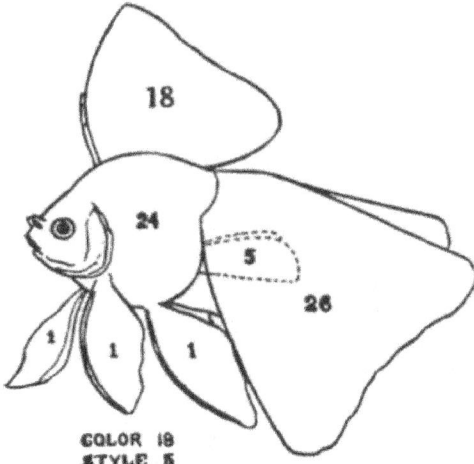

FIG. 34. VEILTAIL JAP. FRINGETAIL

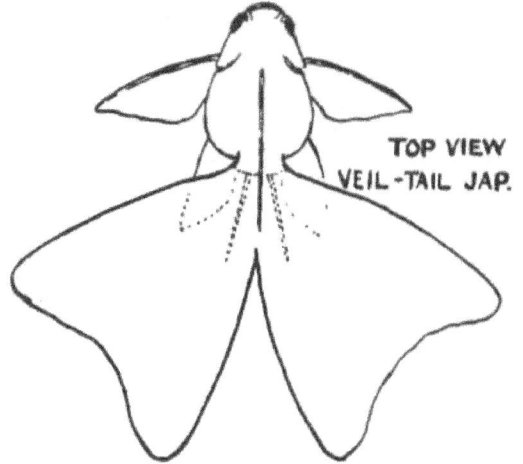

FIG. 35. DORSAL VIEW, VEILTAIL JAP. FRINGETAIL

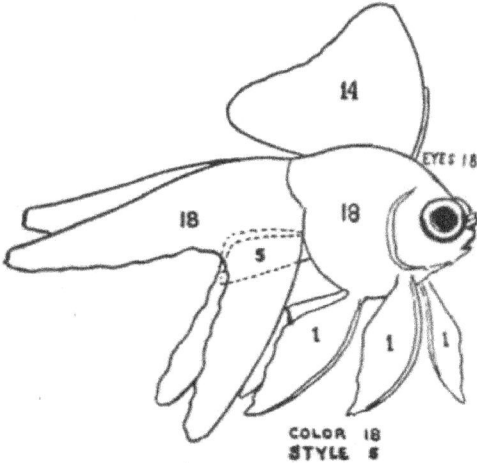

FIG. 36. SWALLOW-TAIL TELESCOPE

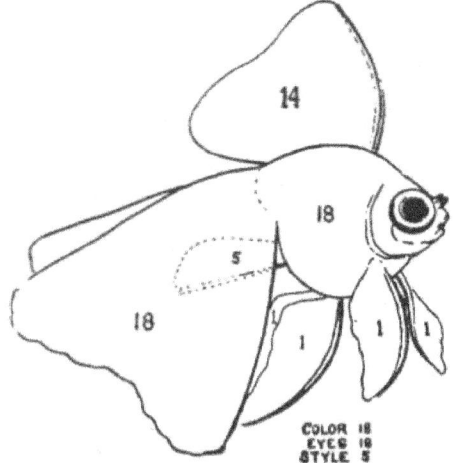

FIG. 37. VEILTAIL TELESCOPE

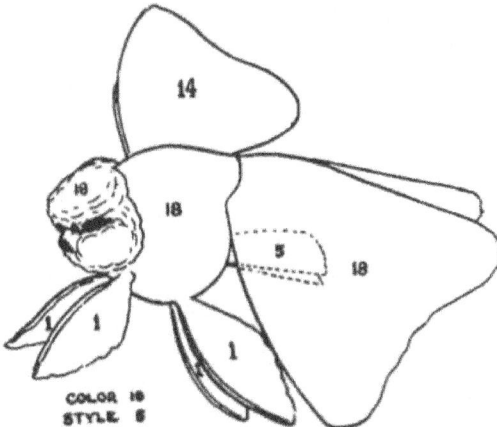

FIG. 38. ORANDA

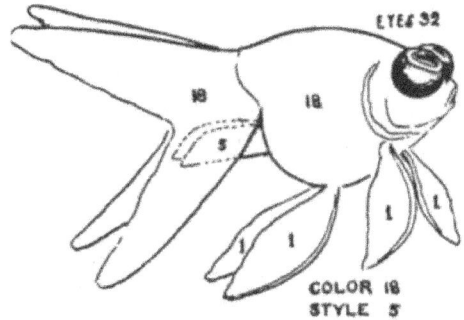

FIG. 39. CELESTIAL

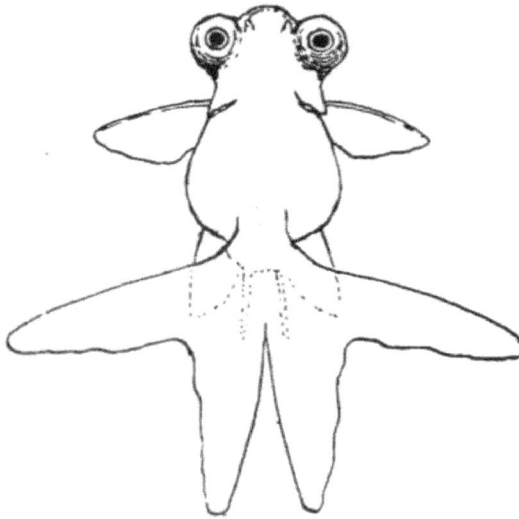

FIG. 40.  DORSAL VIEW, CELESTIAL          FIG. 41.  LIONHEAD

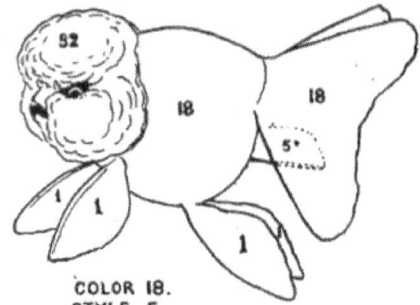

## TABLE OF POINTS FOR ALL CLASSES

|  | Body | Tail | Dorsal | Fins | Color | Double Anals | Style | Eyes | |
|---|---|---|---|---|---|---|---|---|---|
| Telescopes .......... | 18 | 18 | 14 | 4 | 18 | 5 | 5 | 18 | 100 |
| Japs ............... | 24 | 26 | 18 | 4 | 18 | 5 | 5 | | 100 |
| Nymphs ............. | 25 | 27 | 20 | 5 | 18 | | 5 | | 100 |
| Comets ............. | 20 | 32 | 20 | 5 | 18 | | 5 | | 100 |
| Telescope Nymphs ... | 19 | 19 | 16 | 5 | 18 | | 5 | 18 | 100 |
| Celestials ........... | 18 | 18 | | 4 | 18 | 5 | 5 | 32 | 100 |
| Shubunkins ......... | 10 | 10 | 10 | 5 | 60 | | 5 | | 100 |
| | | | | | | | | Head | |
| Lion Heads ........ | 18 | 18 | | 4 | 18 | 5 | 5 | 32 | 100 |
| Orandas ........... | 18 | 18 | 14 | 4 | 18 | 5 | 5 | 18 | 100 |

*Chapter Four*

———

# Propagation of the Goldfish

## SEX IN GOLDFISHES

The chief indications of a male fish ("buck") in the breeding sea-son—about January till August—are the small tubercles appearing on the gill plates. These are a little smaller than pin-heads and the fish must be viewed at a certain angle in order to see them. (See illustration on page 27 and lower photograph on page 56.)

The female fish ("roe") is usually shorter and fuller of body, par-ticularly when carrying spawn. The spawn as a rule is more on one side of the fish than the other, so that in looking directly down on the fishes' back it may be found to be curved to one side. After spawning is over this deformity often remains. In a female which has spawned the vent is always a little protuberant. The eggs can often be seen through the translucent skin of females of the scaleless type.

Early in the year the young males will begin swimming after the females, following close to the vent. Without observing any of the fore-going rules the sex may often be told in this way.

## BREEDING

The breeding of fancy goldfishes is one of the most fascinating of diversions. There are many difficulties to be encountered and even the oldest fanciers sometimes have new troubles to face. Goldfish, possibly more than any other creatures, draw their characteristics from far-removed ancestors. Or again they may become a counterpart of either parent. This makes a considerable element of uncertainty, since the characteristics of their preceding stock has for the most part contained a great deal of variety, due, no doubt, to experimental crosses. This produces a most interesting and sometimes annoying variation in a lot of young goldfish. As the fish gets beyond the small fry stage the breeder becomes intensely absorbed in daily observation of points of form, color and size as they appear.

The percentage of fancy fish coming true to type is usually small. Ten per cent. of fish to pass the critical inspection of the fanciers' eye is not considered bad. Besides these about fifty per cent. of the batch will come true, but will be qualified by slight defects. The balance may be anything at all, single-tail fish from double-tail parents being the principal disappointment. These percentages are averaged from general breeding, but are liable to wide variation. Sometimes there is no fish in a hatching to approach the quality of either parent; sometimes a large percentage is better than both parents. If a strain is carefully watched for several generations and no fish varying from the desired type is allowed to breed, the percentage of young coming true can be kept very high.

The beginner should get his first experience in breeding the more hardy varieties—the comet, for instance—but this stage passed he should select none but the best breeding fish out of known good stock. The best time to purchase new stock is in September and October, preference being given to the larger fish about seven months old. At this period the dealer-fancier is usually willing to sell off some of his larger old fish. These are more showy than the young, but should not be selected as breeders. In fact, none but the expert fancier who knows well what he is about should purchase any fish over one year old.

The fish often show signs of breeding early in the year. As previously stated the young males will start "driving" the females. If this is observed before March, the sexes should be separated, as early spawns are not to be desired, unless one has very special facilities. If the spawning can be delayed until May, results will be more satisfactory. The reasons for this are that the harmful long cold spells are less likely to occur and that living food can be obtained with more certainty. Spawning may be delayed by separating the sexes and by keeping the fish in cool water.

As spawning time approaches the fish should be well fed on nourishing food. Finely chopped earthworms, carefully rinsed, are excellent. Live daphnia are even better. When the breeders have been selected they should be placed togther by themselves. If possible there should be three males to one female. This insures a higher percentage of fertilized eggs than if only one male is used. If the definite results of a certain cross are wanted then use only one male. A second female not spawning should never be present, as she will devour the spawn.

Papier maché tubs are very nice for spawning in, but seasoned wood tubs or tanks will do. The aquarium may be used, or the spawning net shown on page 231.

Should there be no spawn after the fish have been together several days, remove about a quarter of the water daily and replace by fresh. This is very stimulating. Some intimation of an approaching spawning may be had by the fact that the males occasionally "drive" the ripe female for several days before the spawning takes place. This usually increases in intensity the evening before, and when spawning is in full swing it develops into a wild chase punctuated by short periods of rest. So vigorous is the swimming at this time that fishes with large fin development generally have their fins torn and frayed. Males with shorter caudal fins (tails) are the more rapid swimmers and their fins become less torn. As these are usually also the young, vigorous males they are to be preferred for breeding purposes. Spawning usually starts at daybreak and lasts till middle afternoon. It may be repeated every few weeks until the first of August, but the first spawn of the season is the largest.

Goldfish deposit their eggs preferably on floating aquatic plants, and these should be freely provided (first making sure they contain no snails or other enemies to fish eggs). The best are water hyacinths (with as large roots as possible) and bunches of myriophyllum. The female will swim over the plants and drop the eggs. As they fall the male passes over and fertilizes them by an ejection of spermatic fluid. They are of a mucilaginous character and adhere to the plants. The eggs are about one-sixteenth of an inch in diameter and are of a pale, amber hue. The fish drops from ten to twenty eggs at a time, and after short intermissions repeats the operation. A complete spawning of a medium sized female runs from five hundred to one thousand eggs. Large fish not infrequently spawn over three thousand. This refers to the first breeding of the season. As previously remarked, subsequent spawnings are considerably smaller. As the plants become covered with eggs they should be removed from time to time, allowing a few minutes for the last deposit to become fertilized. These plants should be removed to enamel trays about 4 inches deep and 12 to 20 inches in diameter, containing clean water of the same temperature as breeding tank. If more convenient the fish may be removed after spawning and allow the eggs to hatch where they have fallen. One of our leading breeders makes an egg-trap composed of a number of bunches of myriophyllum, secured together in a radiating circle, like the spokes of a wheel. About 10 bunches are used. The tinfoil is removed from each and tied again with thread. The same thread is carried half an inch to the next bunch and so on until they are all arranged on a string, which is then knotted together in the form of a circle. The fishes spawn in this with their heads to the centre, and as the eggs are discharged in the direction of the rays of plants, the chances of the eggs finding a lodging place in them are very good. Such a circle need not be removed until well filled with eggs. Some females eat their own spawn, so removal of eggs is safer if hyacinths or small bunches of myriophyllum are used. No snails should be present, as they eat the eggs. However, after the eggs have hatched the snails should be used to eat the infertile ones. These appear on the second day to be milky white and later become covered with large balls of fungus. The fertile eggs are of a pale amber color and are not easily seen. This fact together with the marked prominence of the infertile eggs often gives the beginner the idea that the eggs are all bad. He is generally surprised, therefore, to see what a large number hatch.

FIG. 42. TELESCOPE GOLDFISHES SPAWNING

This unusual photograph shows two females spawning on a ring of Myriophyllum. The smaller fishes are the males, in vigorous pursuit. Males do not average of smaller size than the females, but the younger ones are the more active and fertilize a higher percentage of eggs than do their elder brethren.

FIG. 43. GOLDFISH EGGS (*Slightly magnified*)

Being of a pale amber color, goldfish eggs are very difficult to photograph as they actually appear. The one beneath the arrow gives a more correct idea than any of the others, but the general distribution of eggs on Hyacinth roots is shown in a characteristic manner.

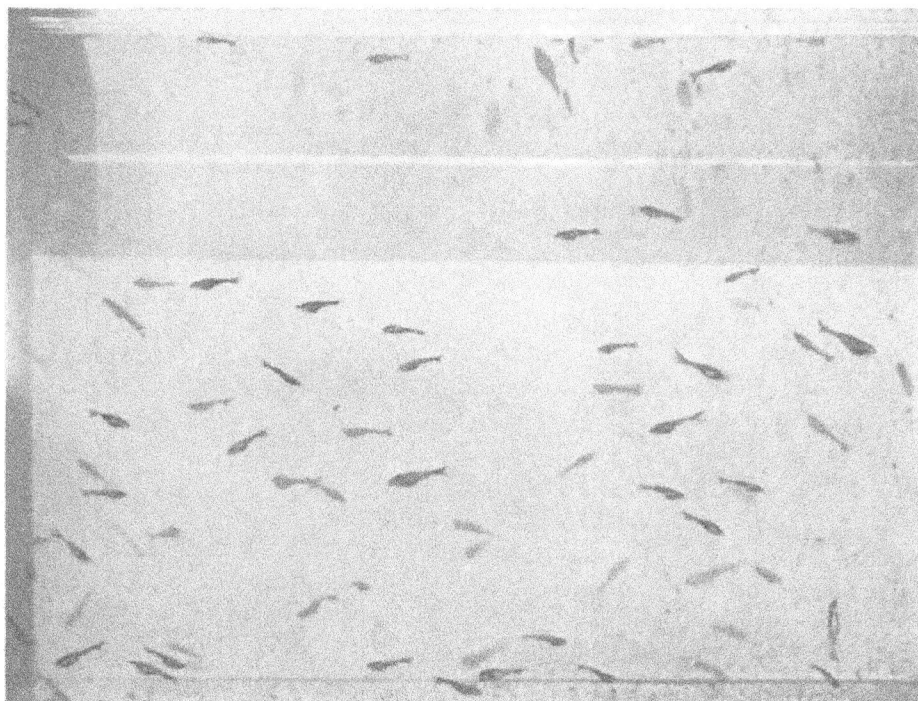

FIG. 44. GOLDFISH AT TWO WEEKS

The abdominal yolk-sacks have been absorbed but the stomachs protrude in a way to show that plenty of small living food has been provided.

FIG. 45. GOLDFISH AT SIX WEEKS

At this period they have come to look like fishes. From this point until late Fall they eat at least their own bulk daily, and the bodies in fancy stock will continue to deepen.

FIG. 46. TELESCOPE GOLDFISH AT TWELVE WEEKS

They have now attained their body form and started to develop telescope eyes. In the scaleless varieties the colors have largely appeared, but among scaled stock the young at this period remain "uncolored." By this time the breeder has usually selected the best specimens to hold for the following year. These should be placed by themselves in ample room. When the supply of live food is limited, they are the ones which are favored.

FIG. 47. PRIZEWINNING TELESCOPE

FIG. 48. PRIZEWINNING SCALELESS TELESCOPE

GOLDFISH OVER ONE YEAR OLD, FULLY DEVELOPED

The development of the embryo under the microscope is plainly observable and is extremely interesting. The hatching time is from three to fourteen days, according to temperature. At a temperature ranging from 70 to 75 degrees Fahrenheit they should take from four to five days. This is considered to produce stronger fish than a slow hatching. The hatching trays and young fish should be kept in a light place and, if possible, where they may be protected from a temperature below 60 degrees. Goldfish at any age should be partially protected from the direct glare of the sun, so that they may at will go into the sun or shade. A few sticks to form a rough lattice over the tray or tub will do very well. In case of rain the sticks, unless already weatherbeaten, should be removed, as water from new wood is injurious. If the fish are in a position where they get only about two hours of morning sun, no protection from light need be considered. Goldfish do not prosper in too much heat, and temperatures above 85 degrees, even temporarily, are to be avoided if possible. Fish under eight weeks old can stand more heat than can older fish.

When the alevin or newly hatched embryo bursts from the egg it is a very weak creature. It appears a mere thread with a pair of eyes at one end and small lump in the centre. This is the umbilical sack and serves as subsistence for the first few days. At first the alevin can only swim by a few jerky motions, and has the power of sticking wherever it touches. At the age of one day they are to be found hanging on the plants and the sides of whatever receptacle they are in. In from two to three days they are swimming freely. When the umbilical sac has been absorbed, which is in about three days, the babies will need some food which has been previously prepared. The first natural food is a large variety of microscopic animals known under the general heading of infusoria. These are present in all exposed water which has stood a few days, but in order to have sufficient for fishfood it is necessary to have conditions favorable to their culture. This consists mainly of vegetable decay. Dried and powdered lettuce leaves or duckweed, sprinkled thickly on the water produce good results in a few days, kept in a warm place and a subdued light. Also a quantity of hay over which boiling water is poured will soon produce the creatures. A low-power microscope or cheap magnifying glass should be employed in this work. (See page 140). After the culture is apparent and the fish are swimming freely, occasional dips of culture water should be put in with the young fry. Sometimes the infusorians can be found freely in standing pools, particularly where the water is not very clean, and where there are no daphnia or other crustaceans. One species, *Brachionus rubens*, sometimes occurs so thickly that the surface of the water appears to be covered by a thin, rusty scum. Small pools about a cattle yard are particularly favorable, but, of course, if the water is very dark it should be used sparingly. This sort of food should be used for about ten days to two weeks. Illustrations Nos. 93 to 96 show types of this living food, but one does not need to be very particular as to the exact form. In general anything alive that is too small to be well seen by the naked eye, but which is visible under a magnifying glass, will answer the purpose. Collection can be made with nets of fine bolting cloth. If green water can be had, some of it should be put in with the young fish. It contains vegetable matter of value to very small fry. After the fry have noticeably increased in size they should be fed young daphnia which have been screened through a fine wire tea strainer. As size increases, feed full size daphnia. (See page 130.)

While the fry are being fed on infusoria, however, no daphnia should be introduced. The daphnia, as well as the small fish feed on infusoria and are more skilled than goldfish in catching them. Where daphnia have been for a few hours, no infusoria can be found, so thoroughly do they clear the water of them. In other words daphnia and goldfish up to the age of about ten days for the fish are competitors for the same living food.

Contrary to previous theories numbers of our leading breeders now use a drip of water in the tanks with young fish over one month old. In many cases this plan seems to produce remarkable growth. The use of an ordinary drain in this connection is inadvisable, particularly if outdoors, as a heavy downpour of rain is liable to carry off the small fish. If the tank used has a drain pipe a large wire guard covered with cheesecloth will answer the purpose, but the cloth should be renewed occasionally, as the water rots the fabric. If fish are in a tub a good drain can be made by placing a 2-inch strip of stiff felt around the outside edge. Secure the felt in position by securely wrapping a cord around it as close to top of tub as possible, allowing the felt to stand about one inch above sides of tub. This will not only secure the young fish, but will prevent the loss of any daphnia by overflow.

Best results are had in raising fish out doors, but one invites catastrophe by placing them out in the first warm spell of Spring unless it is possible to again bring them indoors promptly on the arrival of the cold spells sure to occur in the Spring of our Eastern climate.

In instances where it is not possible to secure living food for raising young fish they may be started on rice flour, yellow of egg forced through bolting cloth or fishfood reduced to a powder and sifted through cheesecloth. As they increase in size an excellent diet is the paste from boiled oatmeal after straining through muslin or cheesecloth. Powdered shrimp or codfish as described on page 129 can be added to the oatmeal to advantage.

Whether fed on living or prepared food, young goldfish should be fed very liberally. This is essential to securing large strong fish of good constitution. They eat almost constantly. It is better to feed several times daily than to put in a whole day's supply at one time. With prepared food it is liable to foul the water with long standing and too many daphnia introduced at one time exhaust the oxygen in the water. This lack of oxygen retards growth and may produce suffocation.

As the fry develop in size the more nearly perfect specimens should be selected from the others, given more room and the best of the food. It is much better to concentrate on raising a few fine specimens, and to succeed in this requires plenty of room for each fish. This point cannot be dwelled upon too strongly. Even many expert fanciers fail to get the best results on account of trying to raise too many young in a given space. At the age of six weeks they should have at least one gallon per fish, three gallons at nine weeks and six gallons at twelve weeks and over. This rule is for fishes which are growing. Small fry should be dipped out with a spoon and never poured. Rough handling kills them almost instantly.

For some unknown reason certain individual fishes grow very much more rapidly than others. These larger ones monopolize the food and sometimes eat the smaller. They should therefore be sorted according to size several times in a season.

## WINTERING GOLDFISHES

In outdoor ponds where there are plenty of dead leaves and soft dirt, the hardier varieties of goldfish will survive the winter. The ice should be broken to admit air. This air space also tends to prevent deeper freezing. If a few warm spells occur it will do no harm to feed the fishes very lightly when the ice entirely melts. This should not be done oftener than once a week.

If one has insufficient aquarium or indoor pool space to keep the stock of fine fishes over winter, tubs will be found good, especially those of papier maché. Occasional partial changes of water will prove beneficial, particularly in concrete tanks.

Winter is the natural resting period of goldfishes and at this time they do not require much warmth nor food. Their food at this time, however, should receive careful attention. They need a certain amount of fresh animal food, and as the usual form (Daphnia) cannot generally be had in winter, substitutes are of value.  This is taken up in chapter on Fishfoods, page 130.

Transparently-scaled white or nearly white fishes need more warmth than the others, as cold causes them swimming bladder trouble.

# Chapter Five

# Wholesale Breeding

## WHOLESALE BREEDING

With the rapidly growing demand for aquarium fishes there is no reason why, with the proper facilities, one should not make a comfortable living from the breeding of goldfishes and other fancy kinds. Good water, plenty of room, moderate taxes, ample shipping facilities and thorough experience in fish culture are all prime requisites. Climatic conditions must be carefully considered. The weather should be settled by May 15 and continue moderately warm until early October. Localities where the nights are cold or the days excessively hot are not suitable. States in the same temperature belt as Maryland and Virginia are particularly advantageous, although it is by no means to be said that success cannot be had elsewhere. Farmers in many localities are turning otherwise unprofitable land both into goldfish and foodfish ponds. In the latter branch several of the State Fish Hatcheries are giving encouragement and practical help.

It is not necessary to have an expensive establishment in order to succeed, but certain natural advantages, besides those already mentioned, are of importance. If one has a good spring, clay-bottom soil and ground that lends itself readily to a series of pools that will drain from one to another, a start can be made with reasonable chances of success. Our figure number 49 will give a good general idea of an inexpensive layout. The water runs from springhouse to a tempering pond, where the water becomes more heated by the air and sun. It also absorbs oxygen, for in this element spring water is apt to be lacking. Where no tempering pool is used it is advisable to arrange small waterfalls if there is sufficient drop. Even 2 or 3 inches is better than none. From the tempering pond the water is run through a series of sluices into the rearing ponds. As the fishes develop, some will grow much more rapidly than others. In order to prevent them from devouring their smaller fellows, they must constantly be sorted out, particularly in the first several weeks. These larger ones can be placed to advantage in the two long pools shown in illustration, using one side for choice grades with good fin development, color, etc., and the other for single-tails or fish with blemishes.

As a final use for the water it can be placed to advantage as shown in a large pond for the propagation of daphnia or other live food. The fish pools should be drained in the winter in order to expose the bottoms to the action of frost, thereby killing lurking insect enemies. We have shown an outlet on the daphnia pond, but ordinarily this is not to be emptied. By draining it the stock of live food would not be entirely lost, but many daphnia eggs would be carried away and consequently it would take longer in the spring to develop a stock large enough for practical use. If possible it is a good plan to have two or more daphnia ponds, so that one may be

FIG. 49. FARM BREEDING PONDS, SHOWING DETAIL OF SLUICE AND GUARD

replenished while the other is being drawn from. The bottom of daphnia pools should be prepared with a substantial layer of dead leaves and manure of any kind. Later in the season when this has all disintegrated, a new supply should be occasionally added. Any decomposing vegetal or animal substances will do. If a prowling cat has met accidental death by shooting, its carcass placed in the daphnia pond will give quite an impetus to the production of live fish food. For aesthetic reasons it would be well to weight the carcass down with stones.

The plan of this system of pools does not call for running water, but only to admit it as needed. It will be seen that an overflow is provided to carry off the surplus from the tempering pond, this finally discharging into the natural brook from the spring, or into any other place capable of carrying it off.

By this plan of having one pool drain into another, instead of discharging into a general overflow, we have an added chance of saving fishes in case of an overflow or accident to the sluices.

Unless a spring is known to be thoroughly dependable at all times, the possibility of securing water from other sources should be considered in the beginning, particularly as most establishments of the kind now being described are constructed only on clay bottoms, where a certain amount of water is sure to be lost through seepage.

If the soil has no natural clay bottom, the hole should be dug 6 inches lower than the intended depth of pool, say 20 inches in all. Now mix pure clay with water in a mixing box and spread on bottom and sides to a depth of 6 inches. To secure the sides in this manner they will have to slope gradually. It is better to make the sides of cypress boards and puddle the clay in back of them. These had best be sloped at a slight angle, about 2 inches to a 14-inch board. Even when soil is mostly of clay, there is often serious loss of water near the top on account of the more porous earth.

One very important consideration in all outdoor ponds or pools is the possibility of serious loss through freshets. Not only does the pool itself have a tendency to overflow in a protracted downpour, but drainage from higher portions of ground is liable to sweep over low ponds. The latter danger can be overcome by having ample trenches dug on the sides exposed to such risk, and seeing that they in turn drain off where the water will do no harm. In regard to direct overflow it is a good plan to have extra screened outlets in each pool at a point a little higher than the regular outlet, which is of course also screened according to the sizes of fishes contained. Another point is to have a safety factor by not filling to within 3 inches of the top. That is to say the regular drain should be placed at that level. The importance of the danger of flood in a system of this kind cannot be emphasized too strongly, and unless the point is carefully provided for in the beginning, trouble is bound to ensue, and *serious* trouble.

An advantage of the tempering pool is that fishes can be kept in it over Winter. Fishes bring better prices in the latter part of the Winter, and one of the serious problems of the wholesaler is how he shall carry a large stock where it will be kept in good condition and will be available. If the spring has a good flow, the tempering pool can be kept comparatively free of ice and fish can be caught as wanted all Winter.

With the use of ground-level ponds the snake, frog and rat have good chances of enjoying the luxury of feeding upon goldfishes, unless the vigilant breeder adopts effective means of keeping these pests under control.

As stated in the former chapter, it is advisable to provide shade for the fishes. Trees at the right places would be beneficial but this cannot often be arranged. Aquatic plants, particularly water-lilies, are to be recommended. Plant life in a clay-bottom pool should be strictly limited to a few species, as some plants once obtaining a foothold can only be eradicated with the greatest difficulty. The plants to be used are Giant Anacharis, Myriophyllum, Cabomba, Ludwigia and Water Cress. All of these are desirable and furthermore find ready sale. Cyperus such as shown in illustration may be kept in pots.

**Specially Equipped Breeding Establishment.** A more elaborate and considerably more expensive establishment is shown in our figure 50, consisting of greenhouse, indoor and outdoor concrete pools and all accessories going to make up a modern commercial fish-breeding plant. The tanks are 26 inches deep on the outside surface and are not sunk into the ground. This avoids the expense of so much excavating and makes a height which ordinarily cannot be scaled by rats, snakes or frogs. Tanks had best be covered by frames of screening, but these will sometimes be warped or placed on carelessly, thereby giving these particular enemies an opportunity. Let us repeat that galvanized screening should be scrubbed with a stiff brush and water before placing over any kind of fish container. The acid-flux used in making galvanized wire is extremely fatal to fishes, and unless precaution is taken, the first rain on new screening will wash the free acid among the fishes and cause wholesale deaths. Uniform size of compartments has several advantages, among which is interchangeability of screens or covers. Allowing 6 inches for the thickness of bottom will leave an inside depth of 20 inches, but under ordinary circumstances they should not be filled beyond 14 to 15 inches. With the outside tanks this gives a safety margin of several inches before a heavy downpour of rain causes the level to rise to the screened safety overflows one inch from the top. It also catches practically all of the rainwater of the season, which is excellent for the fishes. If the water becomes high it can be siphoned off from the bottom until original level is reached. The advantage of being able to fill up, if necessary, to 19 or 20 inches in an inside tank is that at certain seasons the greenhouse capacity for fishes is

taxed to the fullest.  At such times the extra volume of water for the
storage of fish stock will be keenly appreciated.  An economy of space can
be effected by building wooden tanks to stand over the section marked
"Breeding Ponds" in figure 50, thus making two rows here instead of
one.  The wooden tanks should be somewhat narrower than the lower
concrete pools.

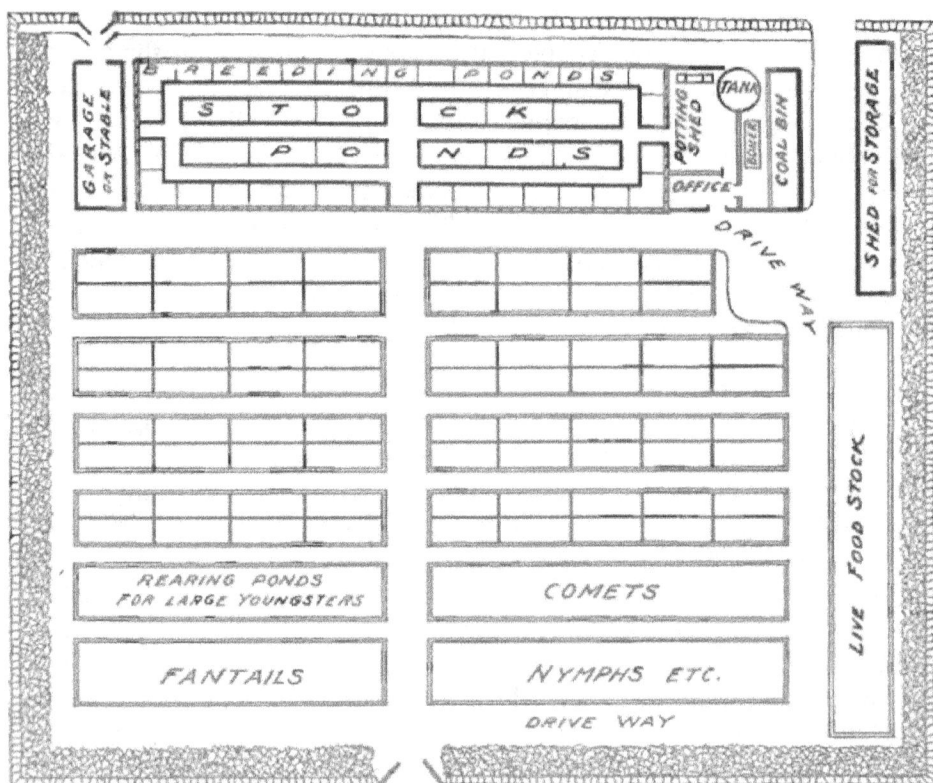

FIG. 50.  WHOLESALE BREEDING ESTABLISHMENT, SHOWING GREENHOUSE AND
OUTDOOR CONCRETE TANKS

Goldfishes are hatched in the greenhouse from February until April.
The young, as stated in the previous chapter, should not be placed out
until the weather is settled, but there is a magic about outdoors which puts
growth and vitality into the fish which the cunningest devices of temperature, plants, food, aeration, etc., cannot successfully imitate in the greenhouse.  There has been much speculation as to why fishes do not do as
well as might be expected in greenhouses.  The author suggests that the
water is too dead, owing to lack of evaporation, the atmosphere being
already charged with dampness.  Evaporation produces cold.  The cold,
oxygenated water drops to the bottom, thereby setting up a beneficial cir-

culation of re-vitalized water. Also there is more microscopic life falls on the water outside than indoors. A partial renewal of water in indoor tanks is undoubtedly beneficial and is one means of at least partially securing that freshness of water which we have outdoors. Those handling fishes in wholesale quantities in greenhouse or other large indoor pools usually maintain a small spray of running water. This should in no sense be of sufficient quantity to be regarded as running water, but merely enough to add a trifle of freshness and oxygen. Stock accustomed to actual running water is liable to suffocate when placed in an ordinary aquarium. Retail dealers are not always conscientious in this matter. In order to carry a large stock in a small space they have to resort to a liberal use of running water. They dip fishes directly out of such tanks to sell for use in household aquaria, knowing full well that the chances of survival are poor. It is by no means impossible, or even difficult, to accustom such stock to still water, but the change should be brought about slowly. Frequent partial changes of water at first, gradually increasing the length of time between them, will accomplish the result.

Some years ago Mr. Wm. P. Seal devised a fish-breeding house of a somewhat different character from the ordinary greenhouse, and the idea has been generally accepted as correct in principle. The structure is long and narrow, with solid roof. The lighting is from window sashes in the sides, these being swung or pivoted so as to admit the air in summer. The objections to the ordinary type of greenhouse are, first, too much light for fishes and plants, producing an excessive growth of algæ (including green water) ; second, high cost of heating in cold weather and too much heat in the warm season; third, attendant risks due to glass breaking from various accidents, including, in some sections, large Summer hailstones. Where an all-glass greenhouse is used, different methods are employed to cut down the light in Summer. The principal one is to coat glass on the outside with a mixture of white lead and gasoline.

The chief objection to the long-narrow type house with opaque roof is that it is not compact and multiplies walking steps. A successful modification in nearly square form has been worked out, in which enough light is secured in the centre of the building by a series of skylights in the roof, comprising about one-quarter of the roof area.

When the windows or sashes are open they should be fitted with inside screens of ¼ inch mesh to keep out insect enemies but admit gnats and other forms of insects which, together with their larvæ, form an important item of fishfood.

The most satisfactory form of heating is with the hot-water system, this being much more flexible than steam, and cheaper to operate. Modern invention has produced automatic heat-control devices which can be installed at moderate cost. These are extremely vauable in guarding against the dangers of sudden cold spells at night, particularly where tropical fishes are kept or when young goldfishes have been hatched in the late winter or early spring months. Oil stoves are not to be recommended and should only be used in emergencies. The carbonic product of combustion while small in quantity is, nevertheless, injurious. Water absorbs most gases very freely.

The cement floors of fish houses should be provided with gutters next to the tanks, these all draining to a single point so that the floors can easily be flushed down.

A description of methods of building concrete ponds and tanks will be found on page 220.

**Commercial Breeding of Tropical Fishes.** The detailed descriptions of breeding habits described on pages 92 to 100 will give a practical working basis for anyone wishing to enter this field commercially. There are, however, a few generalizations which ought to be of value here. In Nature the fishes manage to reproduce themselves without the help of man. The three principal reasons are because they have water of the proper temperature, food of the right character and plenty of opportunity for the young to hide. All of the conditions can be produced artificially. The European breeders use tubs, introduce a thick growth of plants, place in one or more pairs of breeders as occasion demands, feed plenty of daphnia, mosquito larvæ, etc., and disturb the fishes as little as possible. In the absence of greenhouses the tubs are sunk in the ground, covered with wire netting in warm weather and with glass on cool nights or days. Quite large tanks are sometimes used, placing different species with the same breeding habits together, not attempting to sort out the various young until fall. In the livebearing groups there is no likelihood of hybridization if males and females of the same species are both present. Some fishes do not like plants and will tear them out (cichlide group, for instance), but as a rule the young very early appreciate their value and quickly hide among them. They also hunt sloping, shallow edges where the larger fishes cannot follow, particularly if Salvinia or other small floating plants are along the edge.

A continuous, warm temperature is imperative for some species and for these it is not worth while attempting to breed outdoors in a temperate climate.

In selecting a stock to breed from for commercial purposes it is inadvisable to choose the species which have already become common, even though they are easy to breed. It is much better to pay more for something out of the ordinary if there seems to be a reasonable chance of breeding it. The "fashions" change so rapidly in tropical fishes that we could not attempt here to advise what to breed, as our book would be likely to look old by the time it is off press.

*Chapter Six*

———

# Some Hardy Native Freshwater Aquarium Fishes

## NATIVE AQUARIUM FISHES

It seems to be human nature, especially in America, to assume that the best things come from distant lands—the more distant, the better. In this search for the rare and interesting we are apt to overlook excellent material close at hand. There are many handsome native fishes admirably adapted to aquarium purposes. They are easily managed, tenacious of life, varied in habits and easily tamed. Those who have made collections of our own fishes have found much pleasure in this form of the aquarium hobby.

## THE RED-BELLIED DACE

*Chrosomus erythrogaster*, not exceeding a length of three inches is one of the most satisfactory of hardy aquarium inhabitants. During the breeding season the belly, mouth and base of the dorsal fin of the males

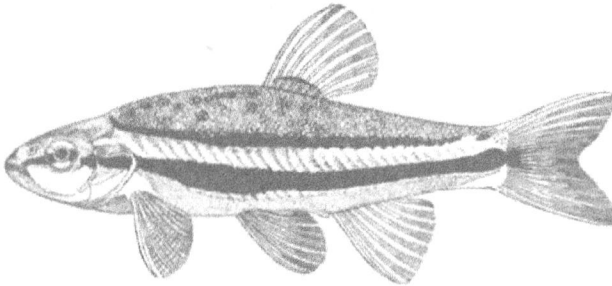

FIG. 51.   RED-BELLIED DACE (*Life size*)

are bright red. There are two black lateral lines on the sides, separated by a band of pale gold, so that even when not in breeding colors, the Red-Bellied Dace is an individual of attractive appearance. It is perfectly harmless, will eat any prepared food and is of active habits. Native to the small streams of the Middle West. They are believed to be community breeders requiring large space. The author placed six of them in a 3 x 5 foot tank in May and several months later took out 30 well developed young, but the breeding was not observed.

Owing to their extreme agility it is necessary to catch the wild stock in a minnow seine, operated by two persons.

## THE ROSY-SIDED DACE

### *Leuciscus vandoisulus*

One of the less known, but very attractive aquarium fishes is the Rosy-Sided Dace. The general color is silvery to green. A nearly black lateral line runs the length of the body, and below this on the males is a long patch of red, starting from the edge of the gills, as shown in illustration. This varies in intensity from day to day, and is brightest from February until September. As these fishes dart about the aquarium

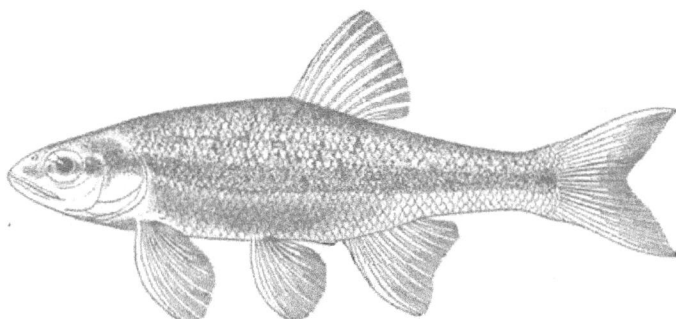

FIG. 52.  ROSY-SIDED DACE (*Life size*)

the flame-like appearance of the red patches is most striking. Even when not in color there is an interesting bronze-green effect to the scales at the lateral line. This is always visible by reflected light, and seems to show mostly at night. If the light is turned on them at night they show very little red color, but in a few minutes it is quite plain.

The Rosy-Sided Dace is a large minnow and takes kindly to the aquarium and is perfectly harmless, but unless plenty of room is provided it will slowly decline. Found in clear cool brooks, from the foothills of the Alleghenies to the Carolinas.

## THE BLACK-NOSED DACE

### *Rhinicthys atronasus*

The Black-Nosed Dace is one of the best of our native fishes for aquarium purposes. Found in abundance in small swift-running streams of the Delaware Valley, it is an extremely active swimmer and not easily caught unless cornered in a small pocket. From constant swimming against the current it has developed some specialized kind of balance, so that when introduced into the still water of the aquarium, the forward part of the body continually drops so a level position is only maintained by an effort. This condition disappears in a few weeks and a new equilibrium becomes established.

The Black-Nosed Dace is well rounded and full of body, the belly is clear white and the black band encircling the body is quite intense. It is perfectly harmless and will take almost any food. It is quite subject to a parasite which embeds itself deeply in the sides of the fish, pro-

FIG. 53.   BLACK-NOSED DACE (*Enlarged one-quarter*)

ducing an appearance that can best be described as looking like "fly-specks." This is common to many of the small wild fishes, and while it is not known to have any serious results it is unsightly. Specimens free from the parasite should be chosen where possible. The usual length is from two to three inches.

They have been known to survive in the aquarium for several years.

## THE STICKLEBACK

Froebel, the writer of kindergarten fame, in telling the children of the civilized world the life story of the stickleback, has given great promi-

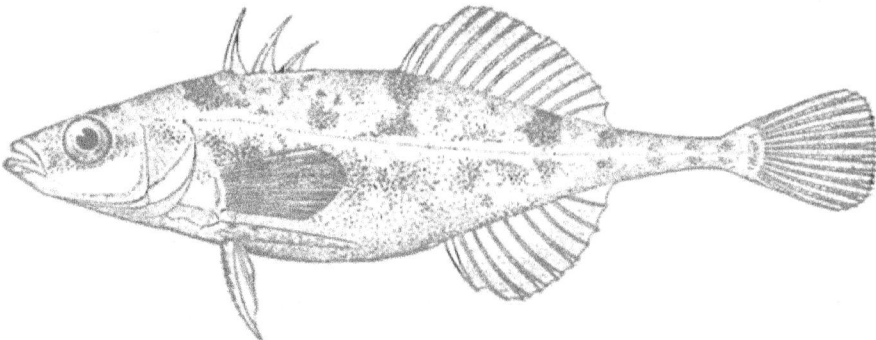

FIG. 54.   THE STICKLEBACK (*Enlarged twice*)

nence to this interesting little fish. The interest centres chiefly in the breeding habits. Sticklebacks are nest-builders. The male is architect, contractor and workman. He selects a suitable location, and by tireless efforts gathers together bits of plants, refuse, etc., and makes them into the form of a ring with a roof over it, leaving only an opening for the female to enter to deposit her eggs. The nest is glued together by a sticky substance exuded from the body of the male fish, who assumes a bright red color in parts of the fins at this period. After the female has deposited her eggs he drives her away, looking after the nest and young himself until they are about 10 days old. He is very pugnacious at this time and will attack any living thing that approaches. Different species probably vary somewhat in details of breeding habits. An English authority claims that in Nature the male persuades as many females as possible to deposit their eggs in his nest. The Stickleback is well known as an aquarium fish, but it should not be kept with other fishes. It prefers to eat daphnia or bits of small worms.

## THE CHAETODON

Chaetodons build their nests directly among plants off the bottom. These fish are less of fighters and depend more upon hiding their young

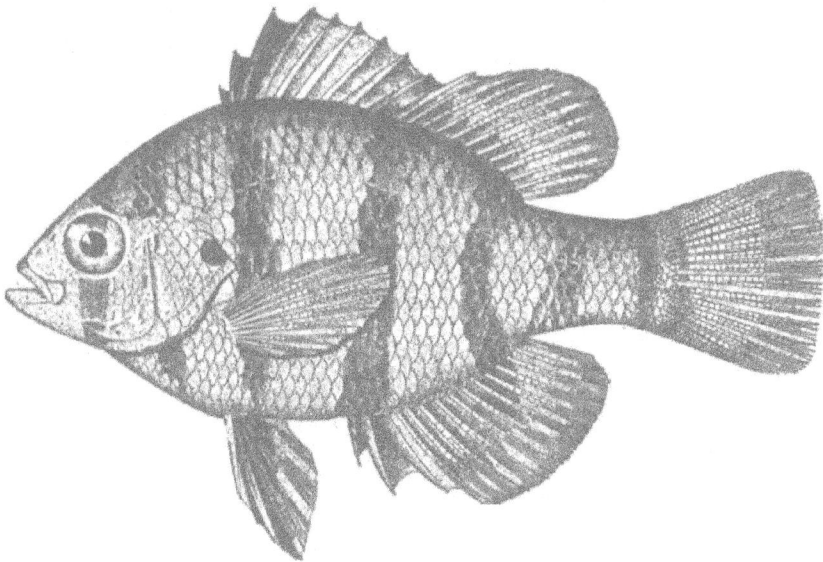

Fig. 55. The Chaetodon (*Enlarged one-quarter*)

than upon boldly protecting them. The Chadetodon is one of the most charming of all aquarium fishes. Many of them are exported to Europe, where they are highly esteemed and bring good prices. This fish has quite an individuality—its peculiar markings, precise movements and genteel manners setting it quite apart from most other fishes. It swims principally by use of the pectoral fins, which are so transparent as to be scarcely observable, giving the fish the appearance of moving about by will-power, without physical effort. Chaetodons greatly prefer live daphnia to all other foods. If fed upon them regularly it is difficult to get them to touch anything else, starvation under these circumstances not being uncommon. They do fairly well on dried shrimp once they take it.

## THE SUNFISH

The Sunfish is one of the most widely distributed and best known of our freshwater fishes, American boys being well acquainted with them. Most of us have seen the tidy, clean spots fanned out by a pair of sunfishes. This is the "nest" in which the eggs are deposited. Both parents protect the young, attacking all comers in a vicious manner. Excepting the Chaetodon, or black-banded sunfish, all of the several species are pugnacious, especially when large. They should not be kept with other fishes unable to protect themselves and it is inadvisable to have one much larger than its fellows, as it will "bully" the other inmates of the aqua-

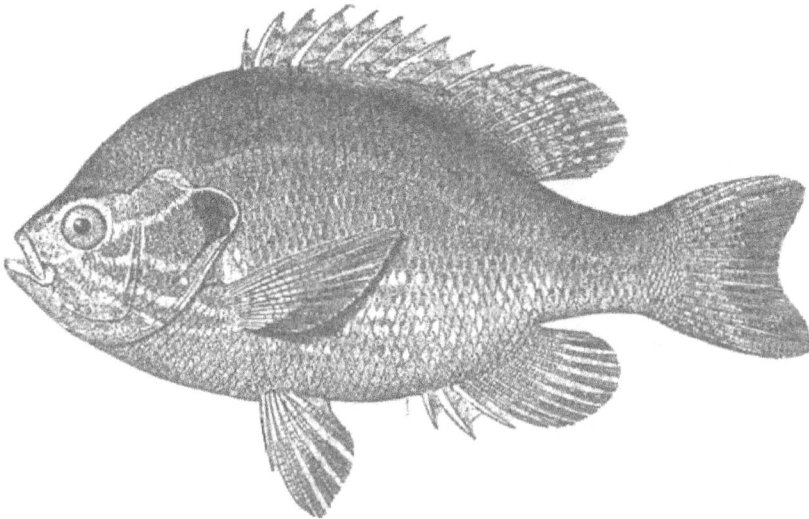

FIG. 56. THE COMMON SUNFISH

rium. Sunfishes have a decided carnivorous tendency, much preferring live worms or flies to prepared foods. In winter they will take shreds of raw liver. Of the dry foods, ground dried shrimp is the best for them. The coloring of the sunfish shows to excellent advantage in the aquarium, and it will be found a very tame and interesting pet. It can withstand severe temperature changes and will survive for years if suitably fed.

## THE SILVERFIN

Of all the native fishes tried in the aquarium by the writer the Silverfin (*Notropis analostanus*) stands out as one of the most satisfactory. For aquarium purposes the male fish should be selected. The ends of their fins are of a whitish, phosphorescent color from May till September. Darting around in the aquarium, their sleek bodies overcast with a pale steel-blue, and sides laced with black edgings of scales they make a most attractive appearance. Two of them will often indulge in what appears to be a game of tag, during which they will chase each other around a short circle, producing the effect of a pinwheel.

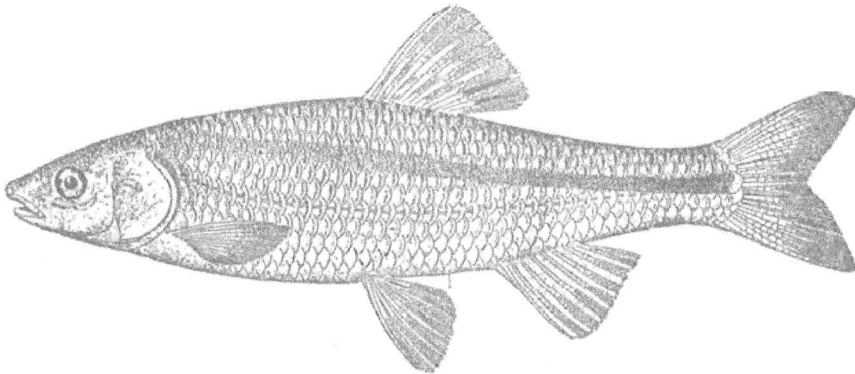

Fig. 57. The Silverfin or Satinfin (*Slightly enlarged*)

A 50-gallon aquarium, with plenty of open space, containing about fifteen adult male silverfins is most fascinating.

They are very hardy, tame, and will eat any prepared food. Harmless to other fishes.

They may be caught in the open reaches of the fresh tidal portion of the Delaware as well as its upland tributaries.

Silverfins have been kept in aquaria for several years, but care should be exercised to cover with a screen to prevent their leaping out.

### The Darter

The darters have no swimming bladders and are therefore considerably heavier than water. They move along the bottom in jerky motions somewhat like hopping. When in reach of their prey they make a short leap. Although this seems to be short of the object they always succeed in getting what they go after. One would imagine them to have a long tongue like a frog, moving with invisible rapidity. There is something quaint and droll about the darters. The majority of them cannot stand warm water.

THE RAINBOW DARTER *Esteoma coerulea* is probably the most brilliantly colored of our native fishes, being barred with red, blue, orange and green in most striking fashion. On account of its brilliant coloring it is

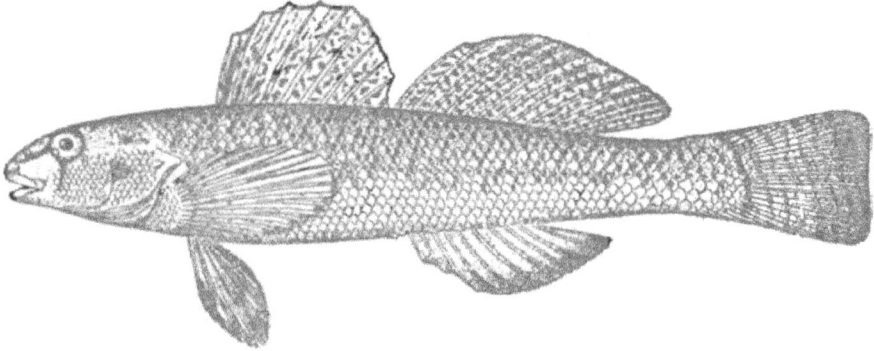

FIG. 58. THE DARTER *(Enlarged nearly twice)*

known as the Soldier Fish. It occurs in shallow streams of the Middle West. Extremely fond of daphnia or very small worms, but may become educated to taking shreds of raw meat. They can be kept successfully and are well worth the trouble.

## THE KILLIFISH

Killifish, both fresh and saltwater forms are among the most hardy of the smaller fishes. Used largely as bait-fish on account of their tenacity of life, they exhibit the same quality in the aquarium, standing

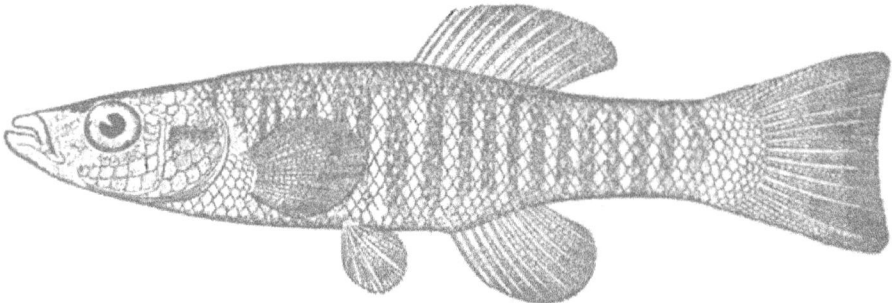

FIG. 59. THE KILLIFISH OR BULLHEAD MINNOW *(Enlarged one-half)*

very bad treatment before succumbing. The barred sides and fleeting irridescent colors are most attractive, particularly in the saltwater form of *Fundulus diaphanus*. They will eat anything and are harmless to other aquarium fishes. Boys usually know this fish in streams as the "bull-head" minnow, while the popular name on the New Jersey coast for the saltwater form is "Mummychug." Size 3 to 4 inches.

## THE GOLDEN ORFE OR IDE

Originally imported from Southern Germany, the Golden Orfe has become one of the best ornamental pond fishes. They do not stir up the mud as do goldfishes and are more active in avoiding their enemies.

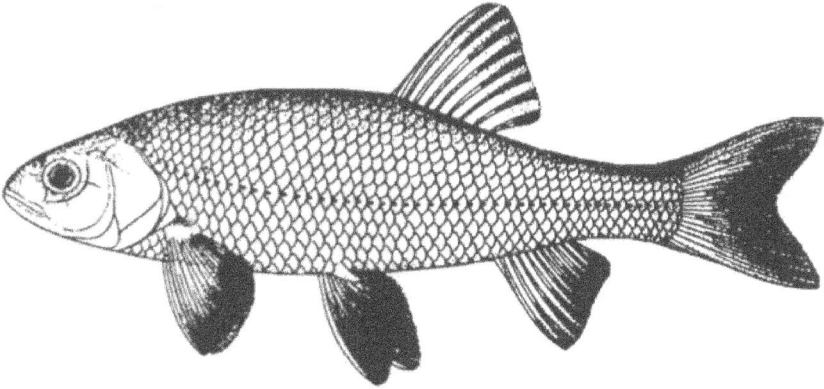

FIG. 60.  THE GOLDEN ORFE OR IDE (*Young*)

The color on the back is orange dotted with black, shading to lighter on the sides and white on the abdomen. The extreme length is two feet, requiring probably ten years of growth under favorable circumstances. The young are suitable for aquarium keeping, but the top must be screened to prevent their leaping out. They do best in spring or running water and have been successfully bred in the Government fish ponds at Washington.

## THE CATFISH

Any of the forms of Catfishes are well able to take care of themselves in an aquarium. If not large they will not touch other wild fishes,

FIG. 61.  STONE CATFISH

but should not be kept with goldfishes, as they are likely to nibble at their long fins. Catfishes like animal food best, but will take boiled cereals.

## THE GOLDEN TENCH

*Tinca aureus.*

As a showy fish of golden orange hue the Golden Tench is considered second only to the goldfish itself. Covered with exceedingly fine scales and dotted with black it presents by reflected light an irridescent

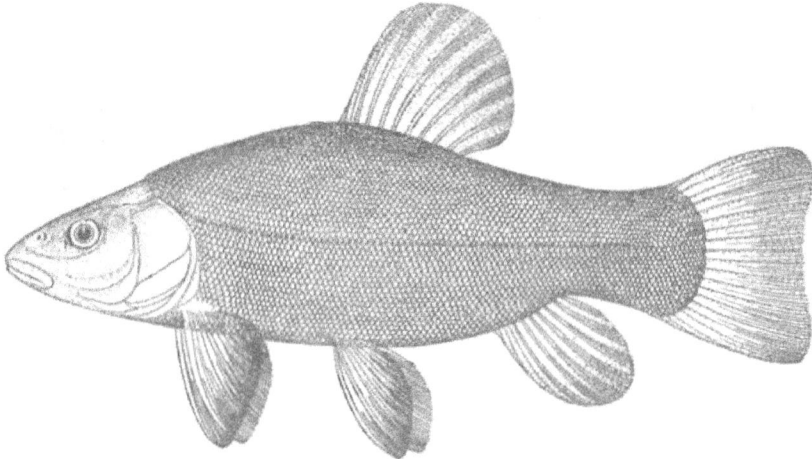

FIG. 62. THE TENCH (*Young*)

effect, comparable to that of an opal. By transmitted light they are sufficiently translucent to show the skeleton and internal organs. Although timid they become quite tame and will live on any kind of fish-food. Harmless to other fishes and otherwise thoroughly desirable. Tenches should be bred in open ponds with mud bottoms.

The Green Tench is the ancestor of the Golden Tench and differs principally in coloring, its color being of a bottle-green character. "Tench-green" is a popularly recognized shade of color in some parts of Europe. Tenches are liberally supplied with protective slime and it is believed by some that fishes injured by accident search out a tench to rub the injured part against. For this reason it has been known as the "Doctor Fish."

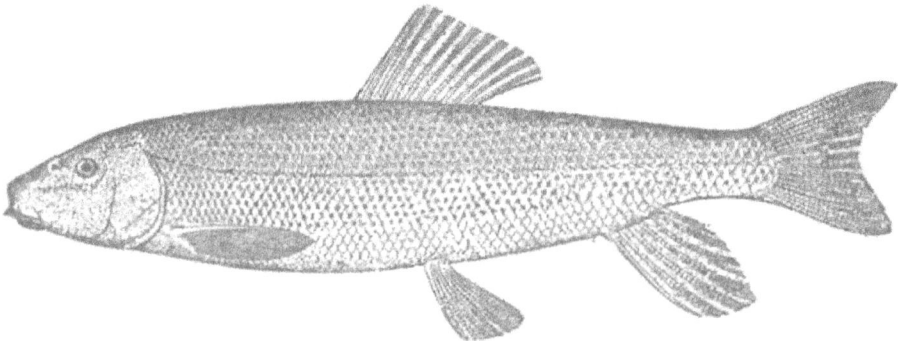

FIG. 63. THE SUCKER (*Young*)

## THE SUCKER

As a novelty the Sucker may be kept in an aquarium. It is by no means a handsome fish, appearing somewhat awkward and clumsy. Preferring vegetable foods, it will also take earthworms. In habits it is perfectly harmless.

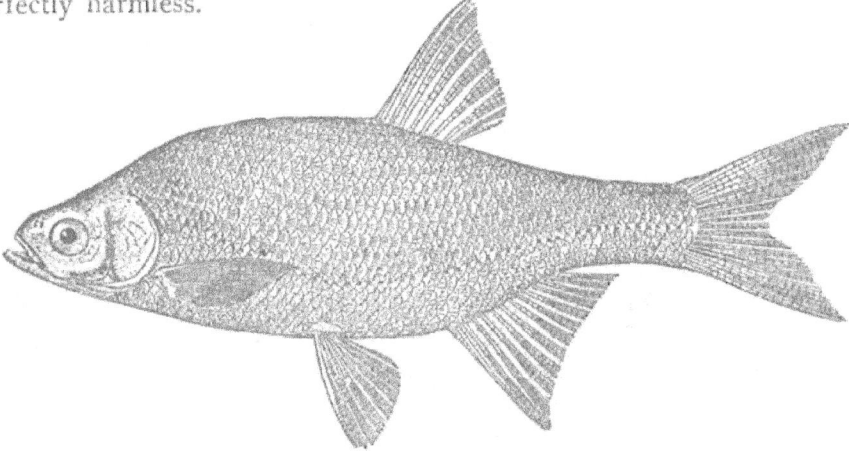

FIG. 64. THE SHINER

## THE ROACH, OR SHINER

Here we again have one of the very hardy small aquarium fishes. It is decidedly active, and if kept in a bright light shows its brilliant silvery sides to advantage. The Roach is seldom still and has a stimulating effect upon the more lethargic members of a general collection. It is of a gentle nature and is not at all particular as to what it is fed.

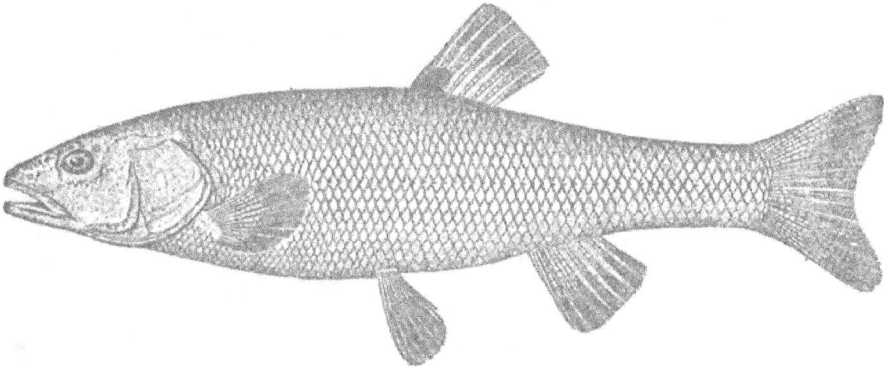

FIG. 65. THE CHUB (*Young*)

## THE CHUB

Not usually known as an aquarium fish the Chub, in the smaller sizes, does very well and may be kept with other fishes whether small or large. It is a nest-builder, but requires a much larger space than is to be thought of in an ordinary aquarium. The Horned Dace, or Creek-Chub, is the most lively, and is the best species for the aquarium. Chubs are vegetarians, thriving on boiled cereals or white wafer food.

## THE MULLET

Sometimes known as the Chubsucker, the Mullet in the smaller sizes makes a satisfactory aquarium fish, entirely harmless and of rather

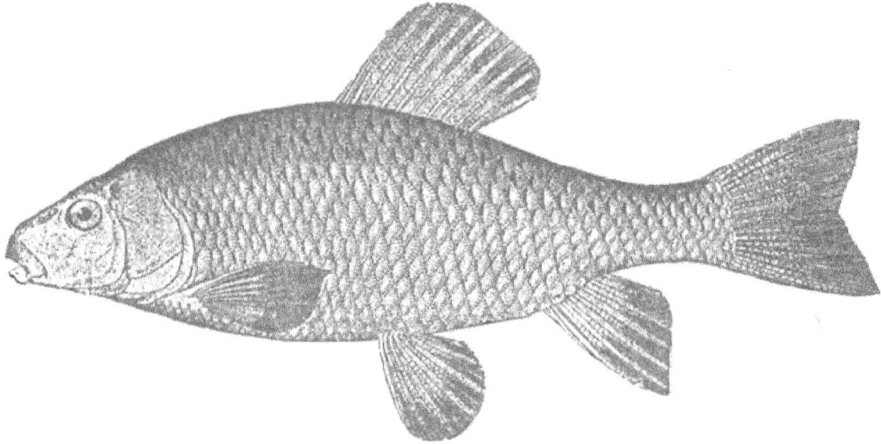

Fig. 66.   The Mullet (*Young*)

attractive appearance.  The back is green, sides are yellow and abdomen is white.  May be fed on ordinary fishfood but has pronounced vegetarian tendencies.

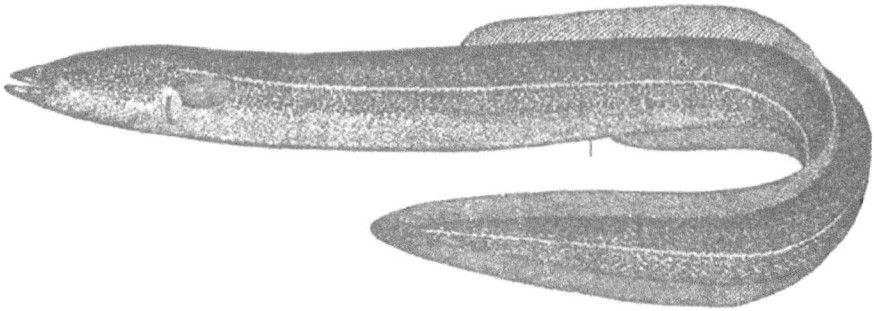

Fig. 67.   The Common Eel (*Young*)

## THE EEL

Small eels may be kept with a collection of wild fishes, but they look out of place with and are dangerous to goldfishes, having the same habit as the sunfish and catfish of nibbling at the long fins.  They are good scavengers, quickly eating any dead snails or other decomposing matter. Nothing is too bad (nor too good) for them to greedily eat.

## THE SOLE

### *Achirus fasciatus*

Among the interesting novelties in aquarium fishes is the Sole, often known as the Freshwater Flounder. Aquarists popularly call it the Aeroplane Fish on account of its easy, horizontal progress through the water, the swimming being accomplished mainly by an undulating motion of the fins at the edges of the body, as shown in the two upper figures of the accompanying illustration. The third figure indicates the under side of

FIG. 68. THE SOLE *(Young)*

the fish, while the lowest pictures the Sole as it lays half concealed in the mud. In the aquarium these fishes frequently fasten themselves flat to the sides of the glass by suction. They may be gathered from the muddy flats of tidewater streams of the Atlantic Coast. Chopped worms make a suitable diet for them. Sizes such as pictured are good aquarium inhabitants.

## THE CARP

The Carp is one of the most widely known of fishes. Its tenacity of life is extraordinary considering that it is not an air-breather or labyrinth fish. When sold as a food fish it is kept alive for a day or two when barely moistened with water. Common goldfishes well wrapped in wet Anacharis or Myriophyllum and packed in a tight tin box can safely be sent on a 12-hour journey or more.

A number of varieties of carp are kept as ornamental pond and large aquarium fishes. The principal ones are the Mirror, the Leather and the Golden Carp. There are in this country at the present time some extremely handsome fancy carp of Japanese breeding, having blue backs, red sides, white bellies, and with the large irregularly placed scales of the Mirror Carp. It is to be hoped these will be propogated here.

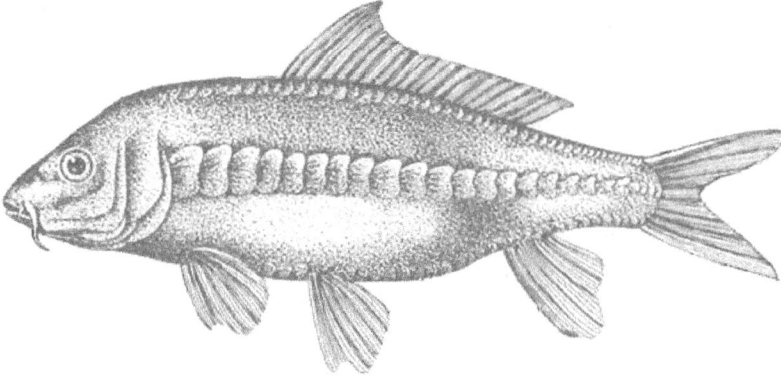

FIG. 69.   THE MIRROR CARP (*Young*)

## THE CARNIVOROUS FISHES

The Pike, Bass, Perch and other predaceous fishes are not suited to the household aquarium, although small ones are sometimes kept. If fed upon meat it is important that no uneaten particles be allowed to remain.

## COLLECTING IN STREAMS AND PONDS

There are pleasures connected with the stocking of a wild-fish aquarium which are unknown to those interested only in goldfishes. The actual contact with Nature, the study of the fishes in their native habitat, the ever-present possibility of finding something new, the companionship and health afforded on outings are some of the more important assets of the collector. For this work two kinds of nets should be provided.

These consist of a minnow seine and a large landing net of small mesh, fitted with a sectional rod. The seine should be operated by two persons. Poles are attached to the lower lines containing the sinkers, while the float line is pulled forward by the hand, slightly behind the lower line. They can be operated with great success in any shallow stream where the fish can be manœuvered into a corner for the final sweep. Care should be exercised to put back all fish not actually wanted, and also not to try to carry so many home that they all suffocate before arrival. The landing net is used mainly in streamlets. It is operated by a quick overhead swoop and the net pulled rapidly over the bottom towards the fisherman. The net should be of a depth of about 25 inches and had best be secured to the frame by brass rings of about ⅝ inch diameter, procurable in upholstery stores. These prevent the cutting of the net when dragging over stones. Very little success can be had by scooping upwards.

*Chapter Seven*

———

# Alphabetical List

of the

# Principal Aquarium Fishes

From Tropical and Temperate
Waters, followed by a Description of
their Requirements, Peculiarities
and Breeding Habits

NOTE.—A number of the foreign dealers in their
catalogues use obsolete scientific names of fishes.
As these books have heretofore been the only
source of information to many fanciers, we
include the old designations in this list, bracket-
ing them, as far as possible, with the correct
names.

# Alphabetical List of Aquarium Fishes

*For detailed description corresponding to key numbers in "Breeding" and "Nature" columns, see pages 93 to 100.*

| Scientific Name | Meaning or Popular Name | Home | Length (Inches) | Temperature Celsius | Temperature Fahr. | Breeding Habits | Food | Nature |
|---|---|---|---|---|---|---|---|---|
| Acanthophthalmus kuhlii | Kuhl's | E. India | 3" | 25 | 77 | B 13 | Omnivorous | N 1 |
| Acara bimaculata | Two-spotted | Brazil | M. 6"; F. 5" | 23 | 74 | B 5 | Carnivorous | N 6 |
| Acara coeruleopunctata | Blue-spotted | S. America | M. 4"; F. 3½" | 25 | 77 | B 5 | " | N 6 |
| Acara festiva | Decorated | Amazons | 3" | 23 | 74 | B 5 | " | N 6 |
| Acara nassa | Fish-trap mouth | Amazons | 3½" | 25 | 77 | B 5 | " | N 6 |
| Acara tetramerus | Divided in 4 | Amazons | 3" | 25-30 | 77-86 | B 5 | " | N 6 |
| Acara thayeri | Thayer's | Amazons | 3" | 24 | 75 | B 5 | " | N 6 |
| Achirus fasciatus | Sole | E. Coast Streams | 1½"-6" | 20 | 68 | B 1 | " | N 1 |
| Alestes chaperi | Chaper's | Nigeria | 2½" | 23 | 74 | B 4 | Omnivorous | N 3 |
| Alfaro amazonum | Of the Amazons | Amazon River | 2" | 23 | 74 | B 9 | Omnivorous | N 2 |
| Ambassis lala | Worthless | E. India | 1½" | 23 | 74 | B 1 | Live food | N 6 |
| Ambloplites rupestris | Rock-bass | N. America | 4" | 20 | 68 | B 2 | Carnivorous | N 6 |
| Amblyopsis spelaeus | Blind cave fish | Kentucky | 2" | 16 | 61 | B 9 | Omnivorous | N 1 |
| Ameirus nebulosus | Catfish | N. America | 24" | 20 | 68 | B 13 | " | N 6 |
| Anabas africanus | Climbing Perch | W. Africa | 4" | 18-25 | 64-77 | B 7A | " | N 4 |
| Anabas fasciolatus | Climbing Perch | W. Africa | 3½" | 18-25 | 64-77 | B 7A | " | N 4 |
| Anabas scandens | Climbing Perch | India | 5" | 18-25 | 64-77 | B 7A | " | N 4 |
| Apeltes quadracus | Stickleback | Atlantic States | M. 1¼"; F. 2" | 20 | 68 | B 14 | " | N 6 |
| Aphredoderus sayanus | Pirate Perch | N. America | 5" | 15 | 55 | B 2 | " | N 1 |
| Apomotis cyanellus | Blue-spotted Sunfish | N. America | 8" | 20 | 68 | B 2 | Omnivorous | N 6 |
| Badis badis | Chestnut brown | E. India | 2" | 24 | 75 | B 15 | Live food | N 6 |
| Barbus camptocanthus | Flexible spines | W. Africa | 3" | 26 | 79 | B 1a | Omnivorous | N 1 |
| Barbus chola | color of galls | E. India | 3" | 23 | 74 | B 1a | Live food | N 1 |
| Barbus conchonius } Barbus pyrrhopterus } | red-finned | E. India | 3" | 23 | 74 | B 1a | " | N 1 |
| Barbus fasciolatus | Banded | W. Africa | M. 2"; F. 3½" | 18-25 | 64-77 | B 1a | Omnivorous | N 1 |
| Barbus lateristriga | Side-striped | E. India | 3" | 20-24 | 68-75 | B 1a | " | N 1 |

| Scientific name | Common name | Origin | Size | 18-25 | 64-77 | B | Diet | N |
|---|---|---|---|---|---|---|---|---|
| Barbus maculatus | Spotted | E. India | 3" | 25 | 77 | B 1a | " | N 1 |
| Barbus pentazona | 5-belted | E. India | 2½"..... | 25 | 77 | B 1a | " | N 1 |
| Barbus phutunio | Glittering | E. India | 1½" | 25 | 77 | B 1a | " | N 1 |
| Barbus semi-fasciolatus | ½-banded | W. Africa | M. 2"; F. 3½" | 18-25 | 64-77 | B 1a | Omnivorous | N 1 |
| Barbus ticto | Native name | E. Asia | 2½" | 25 | 77 | B 1a | " | N 1 |
| Barbus vittatus | Striped | E. Asia | 2" | 25 | 77 | B 1a | " | N 1 |
| Barilius neglectus | Neglected | E. Asia | 3" | 23 | 74 | B 1a | " | N 1 |
| Belonesox belizanus | Viviparous Killifish | Central America | M. 3"; F. 3½" | 25 | 77 | B 9 | Live Fish, &c. | N 2 |
| Betta bellica | War-like | Sumatra | 4" | 25 | 77 | B 7 | Omnivorous | N 4 |
| Betta pugnax | Fighter | Singapore | 3½" | 22 | 72 | B 10 | " | N 4 |
| Betta rubra | Red | Siam | 2" | 25 | 77 | B 7 | " | N 4 |
| Betta splendens | Splendid | Siam | 2" | 25 | 77 | B 7 | " | N 4 |
| Boleophthalmus pectinirostris | Comb on nose | E. Asia | 3½" | 25 | 77 | B 6 | Live food | N 6 |
| Boleophthalmus viridis | Green | E. Asia | 3½" | 25 | 77 | B 6 | " | N 6 |
| Calamichthys calabaricus | Reed fish | W. Africa | 14" | 25 | 77 | B 13 | " | N 6 |
| Callichthys callichthys | Panther fish | E. S. America | 3" | 23 | 74 | B 13 | " | N 1 |
| Capoeta damascina | Danascus carpling | Asia Minor | 3" | 24 | 75 | B 3 | Omnivorous | N 1 |
| Carassius auratus, &c. | Goldfish | China & Japan | 12" | 15-25 | 59-77 | B 3 | " | N 1 |
| Carnegiella strigata | Striped | Brazil | 3" | 23 | 74 | B 4 | Carnivorous | N 3 |
| Centrarchus macropterus | Round Sunfish | Ill. and South | 5" | 22 | 72 | B 1a | " | N 3 |
| Chilodus punctatus | Dotted | S. America | 3" | 22 | 72 | B 4 | Omnivorous | N 3 |
| Chirodon arnoldi | Finger-teeth | Mexico | 3½" | 24 | 75 | B 8 | " | N 3 |
| Chirodon nattereri | Natterer's | S. America | 2" | 24 | 75 | B 8 | " | N 3 |
| Chrosomus oreas | Painted | S. E. U.S. | 3" | 18 | 64 | B 1 | " | N 1 |
| Chrosomus erythrogaster | Red-bellied Dace | Middle West | 3" | 20 | 68 | B 1 | " | N 1 |
| Cichlasoma aureum | Golden Cichlasoma | C. America | 3"-4½" | 23 | 74 | B 5 | Carnivorous | N 6 |
| Cichlasoma bimaculata | 2-Spotted Cichlasoma | C. America | 3"-4½" | 22 | 72 | B 5 | " | N 6 |
| Cichlasoma facetum | Banded Cichlasoma | C. America | 3"-4½" | 22 | 72 | B 5 | " | N 6 |
| Cichlasoma fenestratum | Window-marked | C. America | 3"-4½" | 22 | 72 | B 5 | " | N 6 |
| Cichlasoma mojarra | Mojarra Cichlasoma | Yucatan | 3"-5½" | 22 | 72 | B 5 | " | N 6 |
| Cichlasoma nigrofasciata | Black-banded Cichlide | C. A. & S. A. | 3"-4½" | 22 | 72 | B 5 | " | N 6 |
| Cichlasoma salvini | Salvini's Cichlasoma | Guatemala | 3"-4½" | 22 | 72 | B 5 | " | N 6 |
| Cichlasoma severum | Severe Cichlasoma | Brazil | 3"-6" | 22 | 72 | B 5 | " | N 6 |

| Scientific Name | Meaning or Popular Name | Home | Length (Inches) | Temperature Celsius | Temperature Fahr. | Breeding Habits | Food | Nature |
|---|---|---|---|---|---|---|---|---|
| Clarias angolensis | From Angola | W. Africa | 6" | 23 | 74 | B 13 | Carnivorous | N 6 |
| Clarias dumerilii | Dumeril's | W. Africa | 6" | 23 | 74 | B 13 | " | N 6 |
| Clarias magur | From Magur | E. India | 6" | 23 | 74 | B 13 | Omnivorous | N 6 |
| Cnesterodon decemmaculatus | Ten-Spotted | E. S. America | 1"–1½" | 23 | 74 | B 9 | " | N 1 |
| Cobitis fossilis | Weatherfish or Loach | Europe | 8" | 20 | 68 | B 13 | " | N 1 |
| Cobitis taenia | Loach | Europe | 4" | 20 | 68 | B 13 | " | N 1 |
| Copeina arnoldi | Arnold's | S. America | 2" | 23 | 74 | B 12 | " | N 3 |
| Copeina callolepsis (see Pyrrhulina nattereri) | With pretty scales | S. America | 2½" | 23 | 74 | B 4 | " | N 3 |
| Corydoras macropterus | big-finned | S. America | 4" | 23 | 74 | B 13 | " | N 3 |
| Corydoras paleatus | with neck-lobes | S. America | 3" | 23 | 74 | B 13 | " | N 3 |
| Corydoras undulatus | undulated | S. America | 3" | 23 | 74 | B 13 | " | N 3 |
| Cremicichla lepidota | Curved-toothed | Brazil | 3"–4½" | 26 | 79 | B 5 | " | N 6 |
| Cremicichla notopthalmus | With Eye on back | Brazil | 3"–4" | 26 | 79 | B 5 | " | N 6 |
| Ctenops vittatus | Croaking gurami | Further India | 1½"–2" | 26 | 79 | B 7 | " | N 6 |
| Cynolebias belotti | Dog Lebias | La Plata | 2½"–3" | 20 | 68 | B 8 | Live food | N 3 |
| Cyprinodon dispar | Dissimilar Cyprinodon | Asia Minor | 1½"–2" | 23 | 74 | B 8 | Omnivorous | N 3 |
| Cyprinodon variegatus | Variegated Cyprinodon | E. N. A. | 1¾"–2¼" | 20 | 68 | B 8 | " | N 3 |
| Cyprinus carpio | Carp | N. America | 4"–16" | 16 | 61 | B 3 | " | N 1 |
| Danio albolineatus | White-lined Danio | E. Indies | 1¼"–1½" | 25 | 77 | B 1 | " | N 1 |
| Danio anali-punctatus | With Spotted Anal Fin | E. Indies | 1"–1¼ | 25 | 77 | B 1 | " | N 1 |
| Danio malabaricus | Malabar Danio | E. Indies | 2"–3½" | 25 | 77 | B 1 | " | N 1 |
| Danio rerio | Zebra Danio | Ceylon | 1"–2" | 23 | 74 | B 1 | " | N 1 |
| Dormitator maculatus | Spotted Dormitator | Mexico and South | 2"–12" | 23 | 74 | B 6 | " | N 1 |
| Eleotris lebretonis | Robber | W. Africa | 2" | 24 | 75 | B 6 | " | N 3 |
| Eleotris marmoratus | Marblet | E. India | 4" | 25 | 71 | B 6 | Carnivorous | N 4 |
| Enneacanthus gloriosus | Spotted Sunfish | E. U. S. A. | 3" | 12-22 | 53-72 | B 2 | Omnivorous | N 6 |
| Enneacanthus obesus | Little Sunfish | E. U. S. A. | 3" | 12-22 | 53-72 | B 2 | " | N 6 |
| Epicyrtus microlepsis | Small-scaled | S. America | 2" | 23 | 74 | B 2 | " | N 3 |

| Species | Description | Region | Size | 24 | 75 | B 5 | Carnivorous | N 6 |
|---|---|---|---|---|---|---|---|---|
| Etroplus maculatus | Spotted | E. Indies | 3"–4" | 24 | 75 | B 5 | Carnivorous | N 6 |
| Eupomotis gibbosus | Sunfish | N. America | 4" | 10-20 | 50-68 | B 2 | " | N 6 |
| Fitzroya lineata | With lines | Argentine | 3" | 16-22 | 61-72 | B 9 | " | N 2 |
| Fundulus arnoldi | Arnold's | W. Africa | 2" | 26 | 79 | B 8 | " | N 3 |
| Fundulus bivittatus | 2-bands | W. Africa | 3" | 26 | 79 | B 8 | " | N 3 |
| Fundulus catenatus | Chain-marked | S. Central U. S. | 3" | 22 | 72 | B 8 | " | N 3 |
| Fundulus chrysotus | Gilded | S. N. America | 3" | 23 | 74 | B 8 | " | N 3 |
| Fundulus diaphanus | Translucent | E. N. America | 3" | 22 | 72 | B 8 | Omnivorous | N 3 |
| Fundulus dispar | Unequal | N. America | 3" | 22 | 72 | B 8 | Carnivorous | N 3 |
| Fundulus gularis | Big-throat | W. Africa | 3½" | 25 | 77 | B 8 | " | N 3 |
| Fundulus heteroclitus | Different | N. America | 3½" | 22 | 72 | B 8 | " | N 3 |
| Fundulus lönnbergi | Lönnberg's | W. Africa | 3" | 25 | 77 | B 8 | " | N 3 |
| Fundulus notatus | Spotted | Central U. S. | 3" | 25 | 77 | B 8 | " | N 3 |
| Fundulus nottii | Nott's | Florida | 2½" | 23 | 74 | B 8 | " | N 3 |
| Fundulus pallidus | Pale | N. America | 3" | 22 | 72 | B 8 | " | N 3 |
| Fundulus seminolis | Half-finned | Fla. to La. | 2" | 23 | 74 | B 8 | " | N 2 |
| Fundulus sjöstedti | Sjöstedt's | W. Africa | 3" | 25 | 77 | B 8 | " | N 3 |
| Gambusia affinis } Gambusia holbrooki } Gambusia patruelis | Top Minnow | S. U. S. A. | M.1½";F.2½"; | 23 | 74 | B 9 | " | N 2 |
| Gambusia bimaculata | 2-spotted | C. America | 2½" | 24 | 75 | B 9 | " | N 2 |
| Gambusia episcopi | Bishop's | C. America | 2" | 24 | 75 | B 9 | " | N 2 |
| Gambusia nicaraguensis | From Nicaragua | C. America | 2" | 24 | 75 | B 9 | " | N 2 |
| Gasteropelecus fasciatus | Banded Belly | Brazil | 1½" | 23 | 74 | B 4 | " | N 2 |
| Gasteropeleus stellatus | Axe-belly | Brazil | 2" | 23 | 74 | B 4 | Omnivorous | N 2 |
| Geophagus braziliensis | From Brazil | Brazil | 3½" | 24 | 75 | B 5 | Carnivorous | N 6 |
| Geophagus gymnogenis | Naked cheeks | Brazil | 4" | 23 | 74 | B 5 | " | N 6 |
| Geophagus jurupari | From Jurupari | Brazil | 3½" | 23 | 74 | B 5 | " | N 2 |
| Girardinus caudimaculatus | With spot on tail | Brazil | 1½" | 23 | 74 | B 9 | " | N 2 |
| Girardinus decemmaculatus | 10-spotted | Brazil | 1½" | 23 | 74 | B 9 | " | N 2 |
| Girardinus denticulatus | Toothed | C. A. & W. Indies | 1½" | 23 | 74 | B 9 | " | N 2 |

| Scientific Name | Meaning or Popular Name | Home | Length (Inches) | Temperature | | Breeding Habits | Food | Nature |
|---|---|---|---|---|---|---|---|---|
| | | | | Celsius | Fahr. | | | |
| Girardinus reticulatus } Phallopticus januarius } | Net-marked | Brazil | M. 1"; F. 1½" | 23 | 74 | B 9 | " | N 2 |
| Glaridodon latidens | Broad-toothed | C. America | 2" | 24 | 75 | B 9 | " | N 2 |
| Gobius pleurostigma | Bleeker | Sumatra | 2" | 22 | 72 | B 6 | " | N 4 |
| Gobius xanthozona | Goldband | Borneo | 1" | 23 | 74 | B 6 | Carnivorous | N 4 |
| Haplochilus cameronensis | From Cameroon | W. Africa | 2" | 24 | 75 | B 8 | " | N 3 |
| Haplochilus chaperi | Chaper's | W. Africa | 2" | 24 | 75 | B 8 | " | N 3 |
| Haplochilus calliurus | Pretty tail | W. Africa | 1½" | 24 | 75 | B 8 | " | N 3 |
| Haplochilus fasciolatus | Narrow banded | W. Africa | 3" | 23 | 74 | B 8 | " | N 3 |
| Haplochilus grahami | Graham's | Africa | 2" | 23 | 74 | B 8 | " | N 3 |
| Haplochilus latipes | Broad-fin (Medaka) | Japan | 1¼" | 20 | 68 | B 8 | " | N 3 |
| Haplochilus longiventralis | Long ventral fins | W. Africa | 2" | 24 | 75 | B 8 | " | N 3 |
| Haplochilus macrostigma | Big-spots | Congo | 2" | 24 | 75 | B 8 | " | N 3 |
| Haplochilus celebensis | From the Celebes | Celebes, Java, etc. | 1¼" | 25 | 77 | B 8 | " | N 3 |
| Haplochilus panchax | Worthy of praise | E. India | 2½" | 23 | 74 | B 8 | " | N 3 |
| Haplochilus rubrostigma | Red-spotted | E. India | 3" | 23 | 74 | B 8 | " | N 3 |
| Haplochilus schoelleri | Schoeller's | Nile region | 2" | 22 | 72 | B 8 | " | N 3 |
| Haplochilus senegalensis | From Senegal | W. Africa | 2" | 24 | 75 | B 8 | " | N 3 |
| Haplochilus sexfasciatus | Six-striped | W. Africa | 3" | 23 | 74 | B 8 | " | N 3 |
| Haplochilus spilauchen | Spotted throat | W. Africa | 2" | 24 | 75 | B 8 | " | N 3 |
| Haplochromis moffati | Moffat's | W. Africa | 3" | 24 | 75 | B 11 | " | N 6 |
| Haplochromis strigigena } Paratilapia multicolor } | Mouthbreeder | Africa | 2" | 23 | 74 | B 11 | " | N 3 |
| Hemichromis auritus | Golden | Africa | 3" | 20 | 68 | B 5 | " | N 6 |
| Hemichromis bimaculata | 2-spot | Africa | 3½" | 23 | 74 | B 5 | " | N 6 |
| Hemichromis fasciatus | Banded | W. Africa | 3" | 23 | 74 | B 5 | " | N 6 |
| Hemigrammus unilineatus | 1-lined | N. S. A. Trinidad | 2" | 23 | 74 | B 4 | Omnivorous | N 2 |
| Hemirhamphus fluviatilis | Lives in rivers | Sumatra | 2½" | 24 | 75 | B 9 | " | N 2 |
| Heros facetus | Chanchito | S. America | 3"-4½" | 18 | 65 | B 5 | Carnivorous | N 6 |
| Heros spurius | False Heros | S. America | 3"-4½" | 22 | 72 | B 5 | " | N 6 |

| Scientific name | Common name | Origin | Size | | | | Food | |
|---|---|---|---|---|---|---|---|---|
| Heterandria formosa / Girardinus formosus | Mosquito Fish | Florida and N. Carolina | M. ¾"; F. 1"; | 23 | 74 | B 9 | " | N 2 |
| Heterogramma agassizi | Agassiz's | S. America | 2½" | 24 | 75 | B 5 | " | N 6 |
| Heterogramma corumbae | From Corumba | S. America | 2½" | 24 | 75 | B 5 | " | N 6 |
| Heterogramma pleurotaenia | With side-stripes | La Plata | 2½" | 23 | 74 | B 5 | " | N 6 |
| Idus idus | Golden orfe | Germany | 2-8" | 16 | 61 | B 3 | Omnivorous | N 1 |
| Iguanodectes rachovii | Rachow's | Amazons | 2" | 25 | 77 | B 4 | " | N 2 |
| Jenynsia lineata | Lined | S. America | 2" | 23 | 74 | B 4 | " | N 2 |
| Letinas sophiae | Sophia's | Persia | 2" | 23 | 74 | B 8 | " | N 3 |
| Lebistes reticulatus / Acanthocephalus r. / Girardinus guppyi | Net-marked | N. S. America W. Indies | M. 1"; F. 1½"; | 23 | 74 | B 9 | Omnivorous | N 2 |
| Lepomis auritus | Long-eared Sunfish | U.S.A. | 4"-8" | 20 | 68 | B 2 | " | N 6 |
| Lepomis megalotus | Large-eared | U.S.A. | 4"-8" | 20 | 68 | B 2 | Carnivorous | N 6 |
| Leporinus melanopleura | Black-sides | S. America | 3" | 23 | 74 | B 4 | Omnivorous | N 2 |
| Leporinus nattereri | Natterer's | S. America | 3" | 23 | 74 | B 4 | " | N 2 |
| Loricaria parva | Small Loricaria | S. America | 4" | 22 | 73 | B 13 | " | N 1 |
| Macrones vittatus | With bands | India | 3" | 23 | 74 | B 13 | " | N 2 |
| Macropodus ctenopsoides | Comb-like | Hankow | 2½" | 23 | 74 | B 7 | " | N 4 |
| Macropodus cupanus (Polyacanthus) | From the Cupans | Farther India | 3" | 23 | 74 | B 7 | " | N 4 |
| Macropodus viridi-auratus | Paradise fish | China | 3" | 23 | 74 | B 7 | " | N 4 |
| Mastacembelus argus | Guenther | Siam | 4" | 23 | 74 | B 13 | " | N 1 |
| Mesogonistius chaetodon | Black-banded Sunfish | E. U.S.A. | 3" | 23 | 74 | B 2 | Live food | N 6 |
| Mesonauta insignis | Insignificant | S. America | 1½-3½" | 25 | 77 | B 5 | " | N 6 |
| Metynnis unimaculatus | 1-spot | S. America | 3" | 23 | 74 | B 4 | Omnivorous | N 6 |
| Mollienisia formosa | Green speckled | Mexico | 1½" | 23 | 74 | B 9 | " | N 2 |
| Mollienisia latipinna | Wide-fin | S. U.S.A. | 2½" | 23 | 74 | B 9 | " | N 2 |
| Mollienesia petenensis | From Lake Peten | Yucatan | 3" | 23 | 74 | B 9 | " | N 2 |
| Mollienisia velifera | Sail-bearer | S. U.S.A. | 3" | 20 | 68 | B 9 | " | N 2 |
| Monocirrhus polyacanthus | Many Spines | N. S. America | 3" | 23 | 74 | B 2 | " | N 6 |
| Myletes maculatus | Spotted | S. America | 3" | 23 | 74 | B 4 | " | N 6 |

| Scientific Name | Meaning or Popular Name | Home | Length (Inches) | Temperature Celsius | Temperature Fahr. | Breeding Habits | Food | Nature |
|---|---|---|---|---|---|---|---|---|
| Nannacara taenia | Striped | S. America | 2" | 23 | 74 | B 5 | Carnivorous | N 6 |
| Nandus marmoratus | Marbled | S. E. Asia | 3" | 23 | 74 | B 2 | Carnivorous | N 6 |
| Neetroplus carpintis | Carp-like | C. America | 3" | 23 | 74 | B 5 | Omnivorous | N 6 |
| Nanostomus eques | Horse-like | S. America | 2½" | 23 | 74 | B 4 | " | N 3 |
| Neolebias unifasciatus | 1-striped | W. Africa | 2" | 24 | 75 | B 8 | " | N 3 |
| Notropis bifrenatus | Bridled Minnow | Me. to Va. | 2½" | 20 | 68 | B 1 | " | N 1 |
| Notropis metallicus | metallic | S. U. S. A. | 3" | 20 | 68 | B 1 | " | N 1 |
| Nuria danrica | Flying Barb | E. Indies | 2¼" | 23 | 74 | B 1a | " | N 1 |
| Ophiocephalus marmoratus | Marbled | Singapore | 5" | 22 | 72 | B 7a | " | N 4 |
| Ophiocephalus punctatus | Dotted | E. Indies | 3" | 23 | 74 | B 7a | " | N 4 |
| Osphromenus cantoris | Cantor's | Singapore | 5" | 23 | 74 | B 7 | " | N 4 |
| Osphromenus trichopterus | Hair-fin | E. Indies | 3½" | 23 | 74 | B 7 | " | N 4 |
| Pantodon buchholzi | Buchholz's | W. Africa | 3½" | 23 | 74 | B 7a | Live food | N 1 |
| Paragoniates microlepsis | Small scaled | S. America | 2½" | 23 | 74 | B 4 | Omnivorous | N 3 |
| Parosphromenus deissneri | Deissner's | E. India | 2" | 23 | 74 | B 7 | " | N 4 |
| Pelmatochromis arnoldi | Arnold's | Africa | 3" | 26 | 79 | B 5 | Carnivorous | N 6 |
| Pelmatochromis subocellatus | Eye-spot below | Africa | 3" | 26 | 79 | B 5 | " | N 6 |
| Pelmatochromis taeniatus | Striped | W. & M. Africa | 3" | 26 | 79 | B 5 | " | N 6 |
| Periophthalmus barbarus | Mud Springer | Asia & Africa | 4" | 23 | 74 | B 6 | Live food | N 6 |
| Petersius spilopterus | Spotted fin | W. Africa | 3 | 23 | 74 | B 4 | " | N 3 |
| Platypoecilus maculatus | Spotted Moonfish | Mexico | M. 1½"; F. 2"; | 23 | 74 | B 9 | " | N 2 |
| Platypoecilus nigra | Black Moonfish | Mexico | M. 1½"; F. 2"; | 23 | 74 | B 9 | " | N 2 |
| Platypoecilus pulchra | Pretty Moonfish | Mexico | M. 1½"; F. 2"; | 23 | 74 | B 9 | " | N 2 |
| Platypoecilus rubra | Red Moonfish | Mexico | M. 1½"; F. 2"; | 23 | 74 | B 9 | " | N 2 |
| Plecostomus commersoni | Commerson's | S. America | 4"–20" | 23 | 74 | B 13 | " | N 6 |
| Poecilia amazonica | Amazonian | Amazons | 1¼" | 24 | 75 | B 9 | " | N 2 |
| Poecilia caucana | From Cauca | Columbia | 1¼" | 23 | 74 | B 9 | " | N 2 |
| Poecilia dominicensis | From Dominica | W. Indies | 1½" | 23 | 74 | B 9 | " | N 2 |
| Poecilia dovii | Dove's | W. Indies | 1½" | 23 | 74 | B 9 | " | N 2 |
| Poecilia heteristia | Changeable | Brazil | 1¼" | 23 | 74 | B 9 | " | N 2 |

| Scientific name | Common name | Origin | Size | | | B | Diet | N |
|---|---|---|---|---|---|---|---|---|
| Poecilia mexicana | Mexican | Mexico | 1½" | 23 | 74 | B 9 | " | N 2 |
| Poecilia poecilioides | Like poecilia | Barbadoes | 1¼" | 23 | 74 | B 9 | " | N 2 |
| Poecilia reticulata | Net-marked | Barbadoes | M. 1"; F. 1½"; | 23 | 74 | B 9 | " | N 2 |
| Poecilia sphenops | Wedge-shaped mouth | Mexico | 2½" | 23 | 74 | B 9 | " | N 2 |
| Poecilia unimaculata / Poecilia vivipara } | One-spotted | Brazil | 2" | 23 | 74 | B 9 | " | N 2 |
| Poecilichthys coerulea / Etheostoma coerulea } | Rainbow Darter | N. America | 2½" | 18 | 65 | B 6 | Carnivorous | N 4 |
| Poecilobrycon trifasciatus | 3-striped | S. America | 3" | 23 | 74 | B 4 | " | N 3 |
| Poecilobrycon unifasciatus | 1-stripe | S. America | 3" | 23 | 74 | B 4 | " | N 3 |
| Polyacanthus dayi | Day's | E. Indies | 2½" | 23 | 74 | B 7 | " | N 4 |
| Polycentropsis abbreviata | Shortened | W. Africa | 2" | 26 | 79 | B 7 | " | N 6 |
| Polycentrus schomburgki | Schomburgk's | S. America | 2" | 24 | 75 | B 15 | Live fish | N 6 |
| Prochilodus bimotatus | 2-spot | S. America | 2" | 23 | 74 | B 4 | Carnivorous | N 1 |
| Prochilodus insignis | Insignificant | Brazil | 13" | 26 | 79 | B 4 | Omnivorous | N 3 |
| Pseudocorynopoma | Doria's | Brazil | 2" | 23 | 74 | B 4 | " | N 3 |
| Pterophyllum scalare | Wing-fin | Amazon River | 5" | 23 | 74 | B 15 | " | N 6 |
| Pyrrhulina australis | Southern | Argentina | 2" | 23 | 74 | B 4 | " | N 3 |
| Pyrrhulina guttata | Spotted | Brazil | 2" | 23 | 74 | B 4 | " | N 3 |
| Pyrrhulina filamentosa / Pyrrhulina nattereri (see Copeina) | Thread-like | N. S. America | 2" | 23 | 74 | B 12 | " | N 1 |
| Rasbora cephalotaemia | Striped head | E. Indies | 3" | 23 | 74 | B 1a | " | N 1 |
| Rasbora daniconius | Daniconius's | E. Indies | 3" | 23 | 74 | B 1a | " | N 1 |
| Rasbora elegans | Elegant | India | 4" | 23 | 74 | B 4 | " | N 3 |
| Rasbora heteromorpha | Varied colors | Further India | 2" | 23 | 74 | B 1a | " | N 1 |
| Rasbora maculata | Spotted | Further India | | 23 | 74 | B 1a | " | N 1 |
| Rhinichthys atronasus | Black-nosed | F. N. America | 2½" | 18 | 65 | B 2 | " | N 1 |
| Rivulus flabellicauda | Fantail | Mexico | 3" | 23 | 74 | B 8 | " | N 3 |
| Rivulus harti | Hart's | Venezuela | | 23 | 74 | B 8 | " | N 3 |
| Rivulus ocellatus | Eyed | S. America | 3 | 23 | 74 | B 8 | " | N 3 |
| Rivulus poeyi var. rubra | Red | Brazil | 3" | 23 | 74 | B 8 | " | N 3 |
| Rivulus strigatus | Streaked | Brazil | 2" | 23 | 74 | B 8 | " | N 3 |
| Rivulus urophthalmus / Rivulus poeyi | Eye in tail | Brazil | 3" | 23 | 74 | B 8 | " | N 3 |

| Scientific Name | Meaning or Popular Name | Home | Length (Inches) | Temperature Celsius | Temperature Fahr. | Breeding Habits | Food | Nature |
|---|---|---|---|---|---|---|---|---|
| Saccobranchus fossilis | Bladder-gilled | India | 4"-24" | | | B 13 | " | N 6 |
| Scatophagus argus | Many eyed | E. India | | 23 | 74 | B 2 | Carnivorous | N 6 |
| Stegophilus maculatus | Spotted | S. America | 12" | 22 | 72 | B 13 | Omnivorous | N 6 |
| Tetragonopterus aeneus | Metallic | C. America | 2½" | 23 | 74 | B 4 | " | N 3 |
| Tetragonopterus ocellifer | Eye-bearing | Brazil | 3½" | 23 | 74 | B 4 | " | N 3 |
| Tetragonopterus rubropictus | Red-painted | N. S. America | 1½" | 23 | 74 | B 4 | " | N 2 |
| Tetragonopterus rutilus | Ruddy | Mexico and South | 1½" | 22 | 72 | B 4 | " | N 3 |
| Tetragonopterus ulreyi | Ulrey's | S. Brazil | 1½" | 23 | 74 | B 4 | " | N 3 |
| Tetragonopterus unilineatus | 1-lined | N. S. A. Trinidad | 1½" | 23 | 74 | B 4 | " | N 2 |
| Tetrodon cutcutia | 4-teeth | Further India | 3" | 23 | 74 | B 5 | Live snails | N 6 |
| Tetrodon fluviatilis | River dweller | Sumatra | 3" | 26 | 79 | B 8 | " | N 3 |
| Tilapia microcephala | Small head | W. Africa | 5" | 23 | 74 | B 5 | Carnivorous | N 6 |
| Tilapia nilotica | From the Nile | Egypt | 4" | 23 | 74 | B 5 | " | N 6 |
| Tilapia tholloni | Thollon's | Congo | 4" | 23 | 74 | B 5 | " | N 6 |
| Tilapia zilli | Zill's | Egypt | 4" | 23 | 74 | B 5 | " | N 6 |
| Tinca Aurata | Golden Tench | Europe | 12" | 18 | 60 | B 3 | Omnivorous | N 1 |
| Tinca viridis | Green Tench | Europe | 12" | 18 | 60 | B 3 | " | N 1 |
| Torpedo electricus  Malopterus electricus | Electric | W. Africa | 4"-12" | 23 | 74 | B 13 | " | N 6 |
| Trichogaster fasciatus | Striped | India | 4" | 23 | 74 | B 7 | " | N 4 |
| Trichogaster labiosus | Strong lipped | India | 2½" | 23 | 74 | B 7 | " | N 4 |
| Trichogaster lalius | Dwarf gurami | India | 2" | 23 | 74 | B 7 | " | N 4 |
| Trichopodus trichopterus | (See Osphromenus trichopterus). | | | | | | | |
| Umbra krameri | Kramer's | Hungary | 3" | 18 | 65 | B 8 | " | N 3 |
| Umbra limi | Mud minnow | N. America | 3" | 18 | 65 | B 8 | Omnivorous | N 3 |
| Umbra pygmaea | Mud minnow | N. America | 2½" | 14 | 55 | B 8 | Carnivorous | N 3 |
| Xiphophorus rachovii | Swordtail | Mexico | 2½" | 23 | 74 | B 9 | Omnivorous | N 2 |
| Xiphophorus strigatus  Xiphophorus helleri | Swordtail | Mexico | 3" | 23 | 74 | B 9 | " | N 2 |

For detailed explanation of "B" and "N" columns, see following pages.

## DESCRIPTIVE KEY

### To Foregoing List of Aquarium Fishes

For all practical purposes the breeding habits of known aquarium fishes may be classed under 18 headings. Instead of needless repetition, each of these is described but once. By matching the following key letters and figures with those in the preceding Alphabetical List, full information regarding any of the listed fishes may be had.

*EXPLANATION: The letter B stands for "Breeding" and the figure in alphabetical list specifies to which breeding group each fish belongs.*

*The letter N stands for "Nature" or disposition of the fish, particularly with reference to whether it may be kept with other fishes, and if so, under what conditions.*

### B1 GROUP

DANIO GROUP. All fishes of this group drop their eggs freely in the water, while actively swimming alongside their mates, frequently more than one male participating in the (external) fructification of the eggs as extruded. This group of fish have a tendency to devour their eggs as soon as dropped and under aquarium conditions this should be guarded against by providing shelter for the eggs to fall amongst, such as stones, densely-growing vegetation, etc. The eggs are non-adhesive and can be moved by the action of the water or otherwise at any period during development, which lasts only from 3 to 5 days, according to the temperature of the water, action of sunlight, etc. The young fish hang like "commas" against the glass sides of the aquarium in which they hatch (the parent fish having been carefully removed immediately after spawning was completed), and after a couple of days they adopt the position of normal adult fish in the water, swimming horizontally in search of food, such as infusoria, etc., and later small daphnia and cyclops. Young fishes of this group take kindly to finely powdered dry fish foods and do well on it. As they grow, the larger specimens should be separated from the smaller ones or the latter will be starved. Temperature of the water should be maintained at the MAXIMUM given under temperature herein or slightly higher and so kept until at least two months later before allowing it to drop at all.

### B1a GROUP

BARBEL GROUP. Same as the preceding, except that the eggs are adhesive to the plants, stones or glass aquarium sides.

## B2 GROUP

THE BASS OR THE SUNFISH GROUP. Eggs are fertilized externally of the parent fish, deposited in a hollow excavated in a sandy bottom by the adults for this purpose and carefully guarded by the male until they hatch a few days later and also after the young fish first emerge and are defenceless against their enemies. Microscopic live food in the form of Infusoria must be abundantly provided for the young fish, who, even later, do not take kindly if at all to prepared dry foods.

## B3 GROUP

THE CARP FAMILY, including all the varieties of the Goldfish. Spawning habits same as Group B1a, differing only in respect to the fact that the fish under B3 deposit their eggs all over the plants, mainly at the surface. Fish of Group B1a usually deposit their spawn near the bottom. See page 48.

## B4 GROUP

THE CHARACIN FAMILY, mostly distinguishable by the small adipose or fat rayless fin situated on the back between the dorsal fin and tail. Spawn like Group B1a.

## B5 GROUP

THE CICHLID GROUP. Fish of this family deposit adhesive eggs on stones or, in the aquarium, on the convex side of a large flower-pot, laid on its side. Eggs hatch in 3 or 4 days, during which period the parents take turns in swimming over the eggs and fanning fresh water over them all the time. When the young hatch out, the parents carry them in their mouths and deposit them in a depression previously made in the sand at the bottom, where they jealously guard them against all comers—human or aquatic—frequently removing dirt, etc., from the "nest" and transferring the baby fish to new nests three or four times a day. For the first ten days after hatching the young fish eat nothing but live in a swarm at the bottom, while they absorb the contents of the um-bilical sac or bag of yolk-of-egg-like fluid beneath the abdomen. At the end of this period they begin to look like fish and then they all get up off the bottom and swim around their parents who continue to guard them closely. From this time on they require "baby" fishfood—small cyclops, daphnia, etc., though they will eat dried fish food if finely powdered. Ten days after they begin to feed, the *parents* should be removed, each to a *separate* aquarium. The Cichlids dislike and destroy plants, so none should be provided but they require *clean, pure water,* so some should be changed (siphoning all dirt from the bottom)—daily, replacing it with hydrant water, blended hot and cold to same temperature as that in the aquarium, which should be of an uniform summer heat. Keep no other fish with Cichlids.

## B6 GROUP

THE GOBY FAMILY (Gobiidæ). These include *bottom* fish from all over the world, occurring in shallow streams or shallow shore-waters— marine, brackish and fresh. Little is known of their spawning habits, beyond the fact that some spawn among—and on—the stones on the bottom. Others—small species—will spawn on the *inside—i. e., concave* side—of a piece of drain pipe laid on its side in the aquarium and others spawn among the weeds (roots) on the sand or mud. Some protect their spawn. Others do so but little if at all. As to rearing the young, aquarists must experiment and persevere, as very few have had much success with them and those who have reared any have been European aquarists with abundant time and patience.

## B7 GROUP

LABYRINTH FISH (possessed of an air-cavity or cell beneath each gill-cover, in which a supply of air is stored for breathing). These fish are all air-breathers, coming frequently to the surface to replenish the air in the "storage chamber." Most of the Labyrinth fish build "bubble nests", i. e., secrete a "glue" in their mouths, and blow air-bubbles coated with this glue, which float in a mass and in which the male places the eggs, immediately after fertilization, which takes place in mid-water, the parent fish intertwining their bodies immediately under the nest of bubbles at frequent intervals, extruding a few eggs at a time. Then as the fish relax their embrace, the male catches the eggs in his mouth and blows them—each one separately—into the air-bubble nest.

As soon as all the eggs have been extruded from the female and fertilized in the external embrace of the parent fish, the male having gathered all eggs into the floating nest, he then drives the female to as distant a corner of the aquarium as possible (as he knows that she will eat the eggs if she gets a chance) and for about 36 hours the male fish guards the nest and eggs and re-arranges the eggs and adds more bubbles where required. Towards the end of the hatching process, the male spreads the nest out as much as possible, to give the hatching young as guards the nest and eggs, re-arranges and adds more bubbles where required. Towards the end of the hatching process, the male spreads the nest out as much as possible, to give the hatching young as much air surface as he can and indeed it is difficult for the newly hatched young to escape from the air-bubbles, as they are held there by the attraction of cohesion. Within the next three days they become independent and scatter from the nest, whereupon the male fish must at once be removed. The female should be removed as soon as she is observed to have finished spawning and has been driven away from the nest by the male. The temperature must be kept high—mid-summer temperature as in a hot-house—for at least two or three months after the young hatch out. The young fish being microscopic must be well supplied with Infusoria—the microscopic dust-like form of living creatures native to most old, standing water, which in turn must be cultivated. See page 57. Do not disturb the young fish. They must remain in the aquarium in which they hatch at all events until they are *plainly recognizable as fish of their own species* and at least a quarter of an inch long. As soon as they seem to have assumed *solidity*, i. e., dark, round bodies, which they should have at ⅛-inch long—they must be fed with finely-strained young cyclops and daphnia and from that time on the growth is rapid. All young fish —of whatever kind—which outgrow their fellows, must be separated into other aquaria or compartments, as otherwise they starve or eat the smaller ones.

## B7a GROUP

LABYRINTH FISH WHICH BUILD *NO NESTS* but deposit their spawn loose and floating in or on the water. This class includes the Snake-heads (Ophiocephalidæ) and the Climbing Perch (Anabantidæ). Hardy fish, generally accustomed to living in cooler water than the Nest-building Labyrinth Fishes—though at the breeding season the temperature should be raised to at least 80 degrees Fahrenheit and kept high for the first two or three months of the existence of the young fish. Parent fish both to be removed as soon as eggs appear—if they *do* appear—for it is difficult to get these fish to spawn. Care of young fish same as that indicated for the young of Nest-building Labyrinth Fishes.

## B8 GROUP

KILLIFISHES (Oviparous or Egg-laying Group)—These include the Haplochilus, the Fundulus or "Top-Minnows" native to our American streams, Cyprinodon, Lebias, Cynolebias and Rivulus. Haplochilus mostly spawns at or near the surface on floating bushy plants. So do Rivulus, and most varieties of the Fundulus. Lebias and Cynolebias bury their eggs separately in the bottom and they take *seven to eight weeks* to hatch, so not much success can be expected from them. Others again spawn nearer to the bottom and like Haplochilus and Rivulus eggs adhere to plants separately.

The general rule with Haplochilus and Rivulus is to keep sexes separated and then put the pairs together for three or four days in warm, sunny aquaria with dense plant growth, such as Riccia, the small, light green Utricularia, Anacharis, bushy Thread-Algæ or Willow Moss (Fontinalis).   Then remove parent fish, keep separate again ten days and repeat—each time using a separate aquarium and plants for receiving spawn.   Eggs take about ten days to hatch at summer temperature with Rivulus and Haplochilus and individual young fish must be fished out with a teaspoon and kept in *the same aquarium water at same temperature at which they hatch* and fed first with Infusoria and later with small Cyclops and Daphnia.

## B9 GROUP

LIVE-BEARING KILLIFISHES.   All the fishes belonging to this class are natives of America—the Southern States of the United States, Central America and South America (Northern).   They are generally easy to keep and breed in the aquarium, require mostly uniform summer temperature and clean water, and if well fed and kept in well-planted, spacious aquaria, reward their keeper abundantly with frequent large families. When the females are seen to be "heavy" with young (indicated by a dark patch in the abdomen and great fullness of that part) and when they act restlessly, seeking to avoid their mates and getting into the thickest vegetation in the aquarium, then these females may be considered as about to give birth to their young.   They must then be placed preferably in large straight-sided glass jars (8 inch), in about 3 inches of water, with thick floating vegetation occupying at least 2/3 of the jar and that placed toward the light in a sunny place and covered over with a piece of glass or a plate.   When the young are born, they instinctively seek shelter from their cannibalistic parent and swim toward the light.   If the vegetation is toward the light, most of the young ones will be safe from the mother until discovered, when the mother fish can be returned to the aquarium, most of the plants removed from the jar and the young fed on powdered fishfood.   The breeding jars shown on page 230 do away with the necessity for plants or other shelter for the young.

## B10 GROUP

MISCELLANEOUS FISHES.   Some species do not come under these classifications and are unknown in respect to their breeding habits.

## B11 GROUP

MOUTHBREEDERS.   The fish should be provided with a moderate sized aquarium with about two inches of clean sand in the bottom. The fish prepare a shallow nest in the sand, where the eggs are first laid and fertilized.  In most varieties the eggs are then taken in the mouth of the female, who, by a chewing movement of the jaws, keeps a constant flow of water among the eggs.  The parent not carrying the eggs should be removed.  So large is the volume of eggs that the head of the fish has a noticeably distended appearance.  The hatching takes from fifteen to twenty days.  After the young are hatched it may be several days before one may see them, for the mother at first only allows them to swim out in search of infusorian food at night.  At the first sign of alarm they rush back into her mouth.  When about a week to ten days old they are able to look after themselves and the mother should be removed and the young fed on microscopic food, daphnia, etc.  The best breeding temperature is about 75° Fahrenheit.  From the time of spawning until separated from the young the female should be offered no food.  As this is a drain on the health of the fish, they should not be bred oftener than twice a year.

### B12

PYRRHULINA FILAMENTOSA AND COPEINA ARNOLDI are the only fish listed in this work having the peculiar breeding habits here described.  Both fish leap out of the water and adhere for several seconds to the sides or cover of the aquarium, which should be somewhat rough.  Ground glass or slate will do.  Fifteen or twenty eggs are deposited at a time until from 100 to 200 are laid.  When spawning is completed the female should be removed.  The male, by swift movements of the head and tail, splashes water on the eggs at short intervals.  The eggs hatch in from two to four days, after which the male parent should be removed.  Feed young on infusoria and later on small daphnia.

### B13

EGGS ADHERE ON GLASS sides of aquariums or stones or plants, remaining there until hatched in a few days.  The young swim in a shoal around the old ones as in B5 Group.  Feed in similar manner.

### B14

STICKLEBACK male builds nests from bits of plants, glued together.  After female deposits eggs he drives her away and assumes entire parental responsibilities.  See also page 72.

### B15

POLYCENTRUS SCHOMBURGKI spawns on upper concave side of small flower-pot, laid on its side.  Newly hatched young hang from leaves by means of a hook on the top of their heads.  Eggs and young protected by male, as female is apt to eat them, and should be removed.

Badis badis spawns on the inside of a small, upright flower-pot, sunk half way in the sand.  Remove both parents when young are first observed.

### B16

PTEROPHYLLUM SCALARE spawn like B5 Group, except that eggs are deposited on glass sides or broad-leaved plants, and they do not bury the young, but stick them in different parts of the aquarium for several days.  Eggs hatch in 2½ days.  Parents should be removed in eight days.  To breed these fish requires a well-planted aquarium and plenty of seclusion.  Breeders should be well fed up on mosquito larvæ, young tropical fishes or freshwater shrimps.  They also eat Waterboatmen.  Breeding temperature, from 75° to 80°.

## INDEX TO NATURE OR TEMPERAMENT OF FISHES

*Different persons will have varying experiences with the same kinds of fishes under apparently identical conditions.  In fact one's own observations will sometimes change from year to year.  The writer, for instance, has heretofore always found that Mexican Swordtail fishes kill Coral Snails, yet this year they are living together in perfect accord.  Therefore we bespeak the indulgence of those whose observations do not agree in all details with the statements here published.  The data has been gathered from the most experienced experts the world over, and while some minor points may, from time to time, be open to question, the main facts stated are authentic and should form a practical guide for the handling of nearly all known varieties of aquarium fishes.*

### N1 GROUP

Indicates that fish so marked are of a generally peaceful disposition, not disposed to hunt trouble nor to persecute or devour other species kept with them.  This data applies mainly to the Barbus group among tropical fishes and the Cyprinoid minnows in the temperate division.  However, large fish of any kind take advantage of their size and tyrannize over their associates more or less and also monopolize the food.  So even if a fish is indicated "N. 1." it is as well to keep only such fish as are of approximately the same size together—just as large young fish should be separated from smaller ones of the same species.

### N2 GROUP

Fish of this class are generally amiable and peaceable and are mainly of the live-bearing Tooth-Carp group.  Some of these, again, such as Gambusia affinis and varieties, Pseudoxiphophorus bimaculata, Phalloceros caudimaculata and Belonesox belizanus—(this last not a Tooth-Carp)—should only be kept with their own species.  Males which "rule the roost" will fight with their rivals as roosters in a barnyard. Dense vegetation and sufficient space are the best protection for weaker fish, and females which have just had young should be isolated for several days before being placed with their males, or they may be persecuted to death. With the exceptions of the species herein specified, most live-bearers will live together in harmony in a large aquarium. It is not good policy to keep Live-bearers, Egg-droppers (Barbus), Egg-layers (Oviparous Tooth-Carp) and Labyrinth fish all together. Such things *can* be done in very large aquaria but the weaker will soon show signs of persecution.

## N3 GROUP

Members of this group are mostly the egg-laying Tooth-Carp, such as Haplochilus, Fundulus and Rivulus. These can be kept in large numbers together, if of same size, but otherwise are best kept in pairs. The larger species such as H. sexfasciatus, Rubrostigma, &c., are best kept only with their own species as their tendency is generally warlike. They eat their own and other smaller species and individuals. Dense vegetation and space are the best remedy.

## N4 GROUP

Fish of this classification are more or less inclined to hunt trouble, but when kept in numbers together, each fish is afraid of a rear-attack from his fellows and consequently harmony prevails. This refers to the Labyrinth fish or Bubble-nest builders and is noticeably manifest among Paradise fish, Polyacanthus cupanus and dayi, Osphromenus, &c. The Dwarf gourami is remarkable for his peaceable and amiable nature but he is not entitled to undue credit on that account as it is more than likely that his shyness has much to do with his decent behavior. At breeding time he will attack his mate should she approach the nest containing eggs or young—but then she should be taken out anyhow and that rule applies to all Labyrinth fish.

## N5 GROUP

Very large Goldfish and other members of the Carp family sometimes eat their smaller brethren, but in the main they are peaceable and devoid of the combative element. Except for a scavenger fish or two it is better to keep highly developed goldfishes by themselves.

## N6 GROUP

This group includes the most voracious species, such as the Cichlids, &c., which should be kept separately, even from their mates, except at breeding time and then large flower pots should be provided for shelter and no plants kept with fish. Large, shallow aquaria and abundant clear water are requisite.

*Chapter Eight*

———

# Tropical Aquaria

## TROPICAL AQUARIA

**General Conditions.**  Where one has limited space and wishes for a variety of fishes, it will be found that many of the tropical varieties now available will do admirably.  Most of them stand close quarters, thriving in aquaria which are nothing more than quart jars.  Some of the fishes are of such belligerent disposition that they must be kept alone, and in these cases it is well that they will stand cramped quarters.  Larger aquaria with divisions for separating the different species are a convenience, especially if artificial heating has to be resorted to.

The question of space, however, is not the chief point in favor of tropical fishes.  It is the endless variety of habit, structure and coloring, opening as it continually does new avenues for personal study and observation.  Some idea of the variation in breeding habits alone is contained on pages 92 to 98.

**Feeding.**  The majority of tropical fishes are not heavy feeders like goldfishes and there is not great danger of overfeeding.  Care should of course be taken to leave no unconsumed food in the water.  When they are warm and comfortable they may be fed twice daily, although this is not essential.

The proper types of food are shown on pages 84 to 91.  Those indicated as "omniverous" may be fed the same as goldfishes, see page 128.  An exclusive diet of dried shrimp agrees with most tropical fishes, but some variation is better.  In summer they should have some daphnia, and in winter, enchytrae, see page 136.

**Heating.**  The majority of tropical species thrive in temperatures ranging from 65° to 80° F.  Nearly all will do well at 70°.  For short periods they will stand temperatures below that at which they will thrive, and it is very probable that after a few generations in our climate they become accustomed to cooler water.  When fishes are new and rare it is emphatically a mistake to experiment on seeing how low a temperature they will stand.  That should be left for a later period after breeding has been accomplished and a stock secured.  Tight-fitting glass covers should be provided for all tropical aquaria.  This helps keep the temperature up and prevents the fish from leaping out.  Forgetfulness of replacing covers has caused the loss of many prized fishes.  They will not suffocate if glass is down close.

Fig. 69-a. *Mollienesia petenensis.*
(LIFE SIZE)

There are two other forms of Mollienesia used largely in the aquarium, *M. latipinna* and *M. velifera*, the principal external differences being in the size of the dorsal fin. The above shows the handsomest and rarest variety. The male has the extraordinary dorsal development, but the fin is only held fully erect in moments of excitement, at which time he is strikingly beautiful. The young are born alive. Those shown in illustration are about twelve weeks old. Mollienesias are naturally salt or brackish water fishes, but appear to become thoroughly acclimated to fresh water. See pages 97 (B 9) and 99 (N 2).

Fig. 69-b. *Periophthalmus barbarus.*
(Incorrectly listed in dealers' catalogs as *P. koelreuteri.*)
(Popular names, "Mud Springer" and "Stone Skipper.")
(TWO-THIRDS SIZE)

This is one of the most remarkable of fishes and seems to form a connecting link between aquatic and amphibious animals. As the tide recedes, these little fellows make no effort to follow it, but instead come out on the mud flats, stones and even climb small bushes in search of insect prey, which they are adepts at catching "on the wing." The pectoral fins, nearly developed into legs, are used in vigorously leaping. The eyes roll independently and have a wide field of vision. Although these "Stone Skippers" are extremely abundant where they occur, and are most tenacious of life, they are difficult to import, and bring high prices. It is probably difficult to feed them on the necessarily long voyages. See pages 95 (B 6) and 100 (N 6).

Fig. 69-c. *Rasbora heteramorpha.*
(SLIGHTLY ENLARGED)

Of a light reddish color, with a vivid black triangle of black on the sides, this fish is most striking in appearance, particularly in a small aquarium. It lives for years if kept at a warm temperature, but is difficult to breed, nobody in the United States having yet succeeded in propagating them. Here is an opportunity for a clever aquarist to accomplish something well worth while. See pages 93 (B 1a) and 99 (N 1).

*Fig. 69-d. Mollienesia formosa.*
(LIFE SIZE)

These fish well illustrate the pronounced color differences shown between the sexes of some species. To the uninitiated the difference is sometimes so great that a pair would not be recognized as belonging to the same family. *Mollienesia formosa* is one of the handsomest of the live-bearers. See pages 97 (B 9) and 99 (N 2).

*Fig. 69-e. Hemichromis bimaculata.*
(THREE-FOURTHS SIZE)

Of the savage Cichlids, *hemichromis bimaculata* is the fiercest we know. Even small specimens cannot be safely kept together. If the fancier is fortunate enough to get a pair safely mated, he will be rewarded by seeing the male develop the most gorgeous colors. Even when not in full breeding colors, these fish are of attractive appearance and become perfectly tame, as fear is something they do not know. See pages 94 (B 5) and 100 (N 6).

*Fig. 69-f. Fundulus bivittatus.*
(SLIGHTLY REDUCED)

One of the most graceful of the Killifishes, known as "top minnows." The general color of this variety is reddish brown, flaked and dotted on body and fins with carmine. As with many other fishes, the male has the brighter coloring, and longer, more pointed fins. See pages 96 (B 8) and 100 (N 3).

*Fig. 69-g. Cichlosoma nigrofasciatum.*
(TWO-THIRDS SIZE)

This is one of many tropical fishes whose vivid coloring cannot be done justice in an illustration, particularly in black-and-white. The white dots represent a glistening metallic blue, almost fiery in its brightness. The upper and lower fins are edged with vermilion. The Cichlid group are all fighters, and, unless maintained in large aquaria, should be kept alone except at breeding season. Even at this time they must be watched in the first part of mating. The sexes are equally savage and cannot always be told by color markings. As a rule, the male has slightly more-pointed ends to the dorsal and anal fins. See pages 94 (B 5) and 100 (N 6).

*Fig. 69-i. Danio rerio.*
(LIFE SIZE)

A moderate-sized aquarium, containing a number of *Danio rerios*, placed in a good light, gives us a beautiful picture. Their steel-blue stripes, alternating with white and carried through the fins, make a brilliant effect as the fish play through the water, never still a moment. The males have a slight yellowish cast in the lighter portion of the fins during the breeding season. Easily bred. See pages 93 (B1) and 99 (N1).

*Fig. 69-j. Lebistes reticulatus.*
(Incorrectly known as *Girardinus guppyi.*)
(LIFE SIZE)

The extraordinary variation in the coloring of the males makes this species a never-ending source of fascination. No matter how large the collection, it is practically impossible to find two just alike. The black and red dots are encircled by rings of iridescent rainbow colors, while the rest of the body resembles the fleeting tints of mother-of-pearl. They are popularly and appropriately called the "Rainbow Fish." The female is much larger than the male, and of a dull, olive hue. She frequently presents her owner with numerous young, born alive. They are easily reared. See pages 97 (B9) and 99 (N2).

*Fig. 69-k.   Haplochilus chaperi.*
(SLIGHTLY REDUCED)

One of the best-known and easily bred of the tropical fishes.  Not as large as some of the other Haplochilus division, it is also less likely to be cannibalistic, while in beauty it takes a high place.  See pages 96 (B 8) and 100 (N 3).

*Fig. 69-l.   Scatophagus argus.*
(SLIGHTLY REDUCED)

In its native habitat, *Scatophagus argus* is a scavenger fish, living on sewer offal.  In the aquarium it will take any food, and its quaint appearance adds a note of novelty to a collection.  See pages 94 (B 2) and 100 (N 6).

*Fig. 69-m. Cynolebias bellotti.*
(NATURAL SIZE)

The majority of imported aquarium fishes, especially the more handsome ones, come from tropical climates and naturally require fairly warm water. *Cynolebias bellotti* is one of the exceptions. It prospers at a temperature of 68° or lower, and is beautifully marked, especially the male, which is distinguished by clear white, pearl-like dots. The prevailing color is blue. See pages 96 (B 8) and 100 (N 3).

Fig. 69-n. *Barbus semifasciolatus.*
(SLIGHTLY REDUCED)

The small Barbels are excellent aquarium fish. They are usually of a lustrous silver color, marked with black bars or dots. Very gentle in disposition and thoroughly hardy in moderate temperatures. See pages 93 (B 1a) and 99 (N 1).

Fig. 69-o. *Torpedo electricus* (ELECTRIC CATFISH).

This most curious aquarium fish, when taken in the hand, gives an electric shock which may be clearly felt as high as the elbow. How this is accomplished is not clearly understood, as it is supposed to be necessary to touch two electric poles to receive a current. If the head and tail of the fish were the poles, the current would only pass from one part of the hand to the other, instead of up the arm. The fish is able to cause a shock either in or out of the water. This is doubtless a means of self-defense, as the current is scarcely strong enough to kill a victim intended for food. See pages 98 (B 13) and 100 (N 6).

Fig. 69-p.  *Belonesox belizanus* or *Viviparous Killifish.*
(SLIGHTLY REDUCED)

These little fish are quite as bloodthirsty as their expression would appear to indicate.  After they attain adult size they prefer being fed on small living fish, although worms are taken under protest.  The males in live-bearing or viviparous fishes can be distinguished by the prominent organ of intromission just behind the ventral fins.  In this instance the male also has a clear black spot on the tail.

They are live-bearers and show their own young no more consideration than though they were strangers.  See pages 97 (B 9) and 99 (N 2).

*Fig. 69-q. Danio malabaricus.*
(LIFE SIZE)

In life the colors are not so strikingly apparent as shown in the illustration. The light metallic blue body has a beautiful, delicate, opalescent color, which should be observed by reflected light. The fins are shaded with reddish brown. Being of good size, great activity and gentle nature, *Danio malabaricus* is a favorite wherever kept. The males are distinguished by the black line running horizontally through the tail, while in the female it broadens out and turns slightly upward. See pages 93 (B 1) and 99 (N 1).

FIG. 70. *Sphenops vittatus* (Croaking Gourami)

This picture illustrates one phase of the breeding habits of the bubble-nest builders. The males takes entire charge of the nest and young.

Fig. 71. The Chanchito (*Heros facetus*)

Fig. 72. *Polyacanthus dayi*

Upper Fish, ♂ (Male)
Lower Fish, ♀ (Female)

If one is not blessed with a heated greenhouse or a room of warm, even temperature, artificial heating becomes necessary. There are several devices which accomplish this purpose, but only a few are satisfactory. In general those are to be avoided which concentrate the heat on a small portion of the aquarium water. This action drives out oxygen and other life-giving qualities and also produces uneven temperature for the fish to

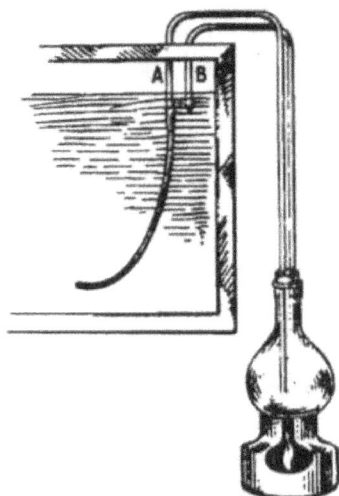

FIG. 74. INDIRECT EXTERNAL HEATER

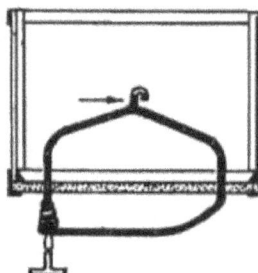

FIG. 73. DIRECT EXTERNAL HEATER

FIG. 75. INDIRECT SYSTEM THROUGH BASE, SHOWING IMPROVED VAPOR EXPANSION HOOK UNDER WATER

pass through. Such an arrangement is shown in Fig. 73. Aquarium water is directly heated in the small outside reservoir and circulated back again. With this device the water intake may easily become clogged, which soon causes the water to boil. This heating method is frequently used, but it is bad in theory and in practise. A better arrangement is shown in Fig. 74, which is a complete hot water system not using the aquarium water. The tubing is of copper, 1/4 inch inside diameter, and of thin walls. Before bending any such work to shape it should be packed quite hard with dry sand and the ends corked up. This prevents buckling at the sharp curves. At the very top of the loop rising from the heating coil should be bored a 1/4-inch hole and a small funnel soldered around this. All hot water systems create some vapor. If this were allowed to collect in the pipe there could be no circulation and boiling would soon take place. The two open ends need not be soldered together. They can be satisfactorily joined by rubber tubing, but this should be arranged to occur in the rising side of pipe in the water. This whole arrangement can be hooked over the edge of any aquarium and has the advantage that the aquarium does not have to be raised to heat from underneath. The first filling of the system is not always easy. Water is poured in the funnel until it will take no more. Then the hand is placed over the funnel and the pipe turned upside down. Turn upright again and put in more water. Hold at different angles. When it will take no more water, try heat under the coil. If the water in funnel moves up and down there is still air in the tube. Sometimes it can be removed by actively filling and discharging a fountain pen filler in the opening. When it works smoothly and the heat travels past the funnel, it is all right to use. The funnel must always contain water, or boiling will soon occur. If a filled bottle with small neck is inverted, stood in funnel and secured in some manner, it will last a long time without refilling. The copper tubing should be heavily nickled after bending into shape, as copper is fatal in the aquarium.

Fig. 75 shows a modification of the same idea with the pipe carried through aquarium base. The little hook at top of the hot water system was devised by the writer to avoid the necessity of filling the funnel, and to have the heater more concealed. The tubes within the water are of glass, connected by rubber, the end hook also being a separate piece. By removing this the system is easily filled. When it is on, the vapor collects in top of hook, and when enough has collected to force a bubble out, a drop of water is automatically sucked back to take its place. The air space in hook also prevents any circulation between hot water system and aquarium water proper. This system also gives a higher percentage of heating efficiency than the outside hook-on form.

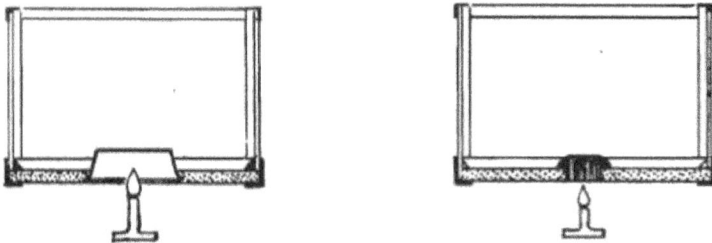

FIGS. 76 AND 77. DIRECT HEATING THROUGH PAN AND THROUGH METAL DISC

For the highest efficiency and greatest all-round satisfaction, note should be taken of Fig. No. 76. This is a 4-inch agate pan set in the cement base described on page 216. When making the aquarium it is no extra labor to set this in. For aquaria already constructed it is somewhat of an undertaking to cut a sufficiently large hole, but it can be done and the pan cemented on top. Fig. 77 shows a simple and fairly effective expedient. After hole is cut in slate, pour in lead or tin. When the metal is poured, use a form made of putty so that the surface of metal will come as high as the sand. The object in using the inverted pan is to have the heating surface come just above the sand. Then the heat is the most efficient as well as fairly diffused and does not interfere with the roots of plants. The objections to this type are that the aquarium has to be raised and that there is an occasional drip of condensed water caused by combustion. The best flame to use is a small gas Bunsen burner. They may be had of some scientific apparatus concerns or dealers in German aquarium supplies. These dealers also handle a rather good all-glass aquarium for heating by lamp, and which does not need to be raised. There is, however, the eternal liability of cracking. All-glass aquaria at best are liable to crack, and particularly when unevenly heated. In the German catalogs and aquarium publications will be found numberless heating devices, but after trying many of them and inventing some defective ones himself, the author finds those described here the most practical. Smells are caused by chilling the flame before combustion is complete. No more than the tip of flame should be allowed to touch the heating surface. Even this is not necessary in system shown in Fig. 76.

**Heat Control.** In a room where there are violent changes of temperature, particularly when these dip to the cold side, it is desirable to have some means of heat control. To start in the simplest way first, an aquarium may be kept noticeably warmer over night by covering with a thick blanket, quilt or any warm fabric. If near a window the curtain should be pulled completely down. Another help for any aquarium near a window is to have a sheet of glass standing on the base and leaning against the top of the aquarium. This sheds much of the cold air which constantly falls from a window in cold weather.

Tropical aquaria may be kept at a satisfactory temperature standing on a hot-water radiator, the heating result not being so extreme as might be supposed.

The most satisfactory means of controlling temperature is to heat by gas and use a gas thermostat to control gas flow. See Fig. 78. This is placed either in the water or tightly against the outside of the aquarium and insulated from the influence of surrounding air by plenty of wool or cotton batting. It contains a large body of mercury over which the gas passes through a small space. As the water rises in temperature, the mercury expands and so reduces the gas supply, and *vice versa*. It is a very ingenious and effective device and may be obtained from makers of scientific glassware at small cost. Those selling them are glad to give instructions regarding regulation, etc. The Arthur H. Thomas Company, of Philadelphia, are specialists in this line. With this equipment in operation one never need worry about aquarium temperature as long as the wind cannot blow out the small pilot light.

For devices to heat aquaria electrically we recommend the Simplex Electric Co., Cambridge, Mass. They are experts and sell their apparatus at moderate prices.

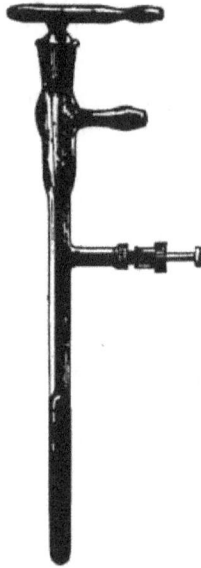

FIG. 78. GAS THERMOSTAT

*Chapter Nine*

———

# Marine Aquaria

## MARINE AQUARIA

The maintenance of a marine aquarium is really much simpler than is generally supposed. If aquarium lovers realized the great charm and the unlimited possibilities of a marine tank, there can be no doubt many more would interest themselves in this particular form of the hobby. It is safe to say that not a score of persons in America at this time have saltwater aquaria, although when once established they are as easily kept as the freshwater kinds. Then, too, there is the fascination of collecting from a field of inexhaustible variety, giving the student always something new to work on, with the ever-present possibility of discovering some fact of value to science or to his fellow aquarist. To those living within easy journey to the shore is the added attraction of the trip to the seaside, the pleasures of which are doubled by the pursuit of such a delightful and absorbing study. .

**Aeration.** There are just a few points of radical difference between the fresh and saltwater aquaria. We have carefully pointed out the oxygenating value of aquatic plants, and shown how their work is necessary to a "balanced," or reciprocating aquarium. This factor must be left out of consideration in the saltwater aquarium, for marine plants perform this function to so small a degree as to become unimportant. The Ulva, or Sea Lettuce is the most satisfactory of the easily obtained plants. It has been known to do well for quite long periods. A few bits of cork placed beneath will cause it to float to the top, where it looks and does best, at the same time shading the water. The beautiful Actiniæ, or Sea Anemonies, which are flower-formed animals, present a bewildering array of form and color far surpassing any freshwater plants. These were once supposed to form a connecting link between the animal and vegetable worlds, but this is an error, the beautiful creatures belonging purely to the animal kingdom. Other attached animals also make up for the lack of vegetable life as far as appearance is concerned.

For the lack of oxygen from plants we have either to depend upon mechanical processes, or to substantially reduce our number of aquarium inmates. The surface of the water takes up enough oxygen to maintain a few animals, but if our ideas are more ambitious it will be best to install an air pump such as described on page 10. This will more than compensate for any plant deficiency, especially if the air is liberated in very small bubbles. In the case of large maine aquaria where the water is constantly pumped out, filtered and returned, the oxygenating is accomplished by a very simple, and at the same time, clever device. The water is discharged with some force from a small pipe into the open end of another pipe just enough larger that the water discharge pipe will fit loosely in it. The second pipe is the liberator, and is carried to the bottom of the aquarium, where it is bent to a right-angle so as to shoot the air somewhat horizontally across the aquarium. If the aquarium is very deep (3 to 5 feet), the liberator pipe should extend about 8 inches above the surface of the aquarium. Otherwise the air in the column of water in the liberator pipe would make it so light that it would back up instead of discharging in the bottom of the aquarium. In shallower aquaria the liberator pipe will not need to stand so high above water-level. By this method the air bubbles are mostly very minute, producing the effect, from a little distance, of smoke. The heavy specific gravity of marine water enables us to break up the air finer than in fresh water.

**Marine Aquaria.** While it may not always be possible to entirely avoid having metal come into contact with the water of the marine aquarium, this risk should be reduced to a minimum. Copper, brass and zinc are particularly dangerous. The metal now coming into use, Monel metal, is not entirely free from copper, but, on the whole, is very satisfactory, and has the advantage of great strength as well as a pleasing light color. Marine bronze is also good and not so expensive as Monel. Iron pipes and valves lined with lead are now made, especially for resisting chemicals. These are very fine for carrying marine water to and from the aquarium. Something less expensive, but quite satisfactory for large work, is wooden pipe. Quantities of this piping are used in the marine division at the Philadelphia Public Aquarium, with perfectly satisfactory results. For the aquarian, working on a comparatively small scale, lead pipe is best.

With the all-glass aquarium we have no metal problem to contend with. Aquaria of the smaller sizes are satisfactory for marine purposes if not overstocked. In the executive offices of the Battery Park Aquarium in New York City, they have in successful operation a number of bell-jar aquaria, one of them having continued without interruption, except for change of animals, since 1900. This should give reassurance to those who hesitate to establish marine aquaria.

In using metal-framed aquaria a narrow strip of glass should be placed over the cement in the corners. A recent improvement is a glass rod of suitable diameter, say about one-quarter inch. This can be pressed in all the way to the glass and the surplus cement wiped away, making a substantial, quick and neat result. The disadvantage of glass strips is that no thin glass is straight, the bend always making an unsatisfactory job.

**Lighting.** Another radical difference from the freshwater aquarium is that the marine aquarium requires considerably less light. When we see such intense light at the shore, it is difficult to realize that only a few feet down the light is so absorbed as to produce a very subdued effect; yet such is the case. If a moderately strong light is kept on marine water it will quickly turn green. To clear it will take several weeks of standing in the dark. Requiring only a weak light should, in many instances, prove a strong recommendation for the keeping of a marine aquarium where one has insufficient light for the successful development of freshwater plants. Mussels will usually clear green freshwater. The author tried a liberal quantity of marine mussels to clear marine water, but three hours of direct sun and five hours of strong diffused light multiplied the green vegetal organisms faster than the mussels could keep pace with. The same aquarium in the same light, when used as a regular goldfish container, never became green.

**Strength of Marine Water.** For some reason not understood, pure ocean water is not as successful in the aquarium as that which has been somewhat diluted. The reason may be that while the fishes can stand the change successfully, many of their microscopic enemies are unable to do so—exactly the reverse of the theory of treating freshwater fishes with a saltwater solution. Be the theory what it may, experienced marine aquarists have obtained better results with diluted water in still aquaria. Naturally, if new seawater can be continuously pumped in, nothing could be better, particularly as this contains the desirable small food otherwise difficult or impossible to supply.

A hydrometer for testing the strength of salt in the aquarium water should be provided. Natural seawater has a strength of 1.023 to 1.031. If this is reduced to about 1.020, the animals will do better than at full strength. It should not go below 1.017, nor above 1.022.

Having established a certain water-level at a proper hydrometer strength, it ought to be maintained at that point by the addition of pure, freshwater, never using marine water to make up for evaporation. The salts do not evaporate, and soon the aquarium would be in the lifeless condition of the Dead Sea or Salt Lake. A glass cover will prevent some evaporation, but if an air pump is used, some evaporation will be inevitable. No trouble will be experienced if the water is kept to a level, as suggested, by the addition of freshwater.

**Shipping Seawater.** If seawater must be shipped, careful consideration should be given to the kind of carriers used. The action of saltwater on zinc, copper, brass and iron is rapid, the resultant chemical action charging the water with poisonous metallic salts. Of the metals mentioned, iron is the least injurious and zinc the most, on account of the rapidity of chemical action of salt on this metal. Therefore, galvanized iron is to be particularly avoided, as it is zinc-plated. The author on one occasion could only secure a galvanized pail in which to bring a collection home. As the trip was only three hours and the pail was a well-seasoned one he thought the chances of success were reasonably good. When the can was opened the water showed a slight milkiness and the fishes were nearly dead, although they had not been crowded. On being placed in the aquarium they soon revived. The best metal in which to ship is tin. This, or any other metal, should first receive a coating of asphaltum varnish. Even galvanized iron when asphaltum-coated is safe for journeys of moderate length, but the asphaltum will eventually chip off and the pail or can should be carefully looked over each time before using. It might be well to say here that the life of tin pails for freshwater will last much longer if coated with asphaltum varnish. A thin coat spread evenly lasts better than a thick one.

The very best water-shipping medium is a protected glass bottle or carboy. Arrangements can usually be made to rent or borrow a few of these from drinking-water concerns. If possible the water should be taken from several miles out at sea and not near the mouth of any large river. Clear seawater may be stored indefinitely in carboys in a subdued light, although it would be better to first filter it to remove the larger microscopic life.

**Artificial Seawater.** Experience varies regarding the use of artificial seawater. This may be due to difference in the degree of purity of chemicals used or care in their mixing. The author has not been particularly successful with artificial marine water, although some writers claim it to be better than ocean water because of its freedom from impurities and marine bacteria. The following is a correct working formula for artificial seawater. There are other elements in the ocean, but in such small quantities as to be negligible for our purposes:

```
Sodium chloride (Tablesalt)..2 lb. 8ʒ. 2ƺ.      18 gr.
Magnesium chloride ........         3ʒ. 5ƺ.      13 gr.
Magnesium sulphate ........      2ʒ. 3ƺ. 1ɔ   8 gr.
Potassium sulphate .........           5ƺ. 2ɔ  10 gr.
and sufficient wellwater to bring the whole to ten gallons.
```

These proportions of salts, expressed in the Metric system, would be:
```
Sodium chloride ......................663 grams.
Magnesium chloride .................... 75   "
Magnesium sulphate ................... 50   "
Potassium sulphate ................... 15   "
        Added to 25 litres of wellwater.
```

For chemical reasons the salts should each be dissolved separately and enough water finally added to make ten gallons. Any good drinking water will do to mix with, although distilled water is not to be recommended because of its total lack of mineral content. Turk's Island salt is evaporated seawater and has been successfully used by the Government at Washington. In mixing this or in preparing the foregoing artificial water, the final test for strength should be by hydrometer as previously directed. As chemicals vary in strength and in weight owing to different degrees of moisture, the hydrometer used in solutions of about 60° Fahrenheit furnishes the only accurate gauge.

Newly made artificial marine water ought not be used for several days, but be given a little time to ripen. An occasional stirring helps the process.

**Cleaning Marine Water.** It is desirable to keep the marine aquarium crystal-clear, both for the benefit of the inmates and the pleasure of the observer. To this end several factors must be borne in mind. Start with clear water. Do not overcrowd nor overfeed. Use only subdued light. Quickly remove decaying plants, dead mussels, anemones, etc. Occasionally siphon off the bottom (see page 229) and after setting, pour back the clear water or return through filter. Very little loss of water is occasioned if the dregs are thrown away after water has settled, particularly if a tall jar is used. The filter arrangement described on page 233 is very desirable for the marine aquarium. The more pretentious establishments run the water off into deep filter-beds of fine sand, squirting it back into the aquarium under pressure to increase oxygenation. This, next to running seawater, is the ideal arrangement, but is out of reach of the ordinary mortal.

**Temperature.** This matter depends very largely upon the climate from which the aquarium inhabitants come. For this reason it is not well to mix animals of tropical and temperate zones. Many of the tropical fishes come north in summer and can successfully withstand a temperature of 62° F., but in the confines of an aquarium they will not prosper in the lower temperatures required by the fishes of our own climate. Tropical fishes are happy in a temperature ranging from 68° to 75°. Some of them can succeed when it is even warmer, but it becomes difficult to satisfactorily oxygenate the water.

Fishes and other marine animals of the temperate zone prefer a range from 55° to 68°. It will be noted that the tropicals and temperates meet at 68°, so if the attempt is made to mix them, this is the temperature that should be closely adhered to.

**Collecting Specimens.** The best places for collecting a miscellaneous assortment of marine animals are the back bays, pools, pockets, marshes and small streams where the ocean overflows at high tide and recedes from at low. Rocky coasts furnish particularly fertile fields for the aquatic hunter, and those of New England offer rich attractions in varied and wonderfully beautiful vegetation. Wood's Hole is a particularly famed point for all sorts of marine naturalists and collectors. However, anybody can go to the beach nearest home and gather material that will well repay for the effort. Two persons in bathing suits operating a seine 4 by 14 feet (see page 82) will be surprisingly successful right in the surf anywhere. As before stated, the little sheltered places, pools around breakwaters, piers and rocks should be thoroughly investigated by hand and net. As with freshwater, let the collector not be too ambitious for numbers. It is better to get a few good specimens home alive and well than have a bucketfull of dead and dying. Unfortunately for those inland there is nobody at the present time in America making a commercial business of marine collections for the household aquarium. We have reason to believe this could soon be developed into a profitable business, such as has been done by many in Europe. Germany, with no seacoast of her own, has thousands of successful marine aquaria stocked mostly by dealers.

Tropical marine fishes are of dazzling beauty, a fact enthusiastically attested by those visiting any of our large American public aquaria, or by those so fortunate as to travel in Bermuda. Most of our tropical specimens are collected at Bermuda and at Key West, Florida. The various kinds of kelp and coral fishes make quarium specimens of such bewitching beauty that any attempted word-description of them would appear extravagant. Anyone wishing to make a collection of them should employ a local fisherman at the collecting point who knows the haunts and ways of the fishes, and who understands the danger of sudden tropical storms. Such collections should be shipped in a liberal quantity of water and artificially aerated by pump or pouring whenever the train is still for more than fifteen minutes. On shipboard, new water of the proper temperature should be frequently given.

**Stocking the Aquarium.** Perhaps we can repeat to advantage that it is better to under- than to over-stock the aquarium. This is particularly true of the marine aquarium, first, because if we spoil the water by dead animals it is some trouble to obtain more, and second, because the creatures are used to more oxygen in the vast ocean than can be had in a crowded aquarium.

Particular vigilance needs to be exercised when the animals are first introduced, as some of them may not survive the change.

It is best to start with some of the more hardy fishes, such as the marine killifish, to see whether the aquarium conditions are in proper working order. It will be time enough to branch out more elaborately after this is proven. The author some years ago received this same advice from a leading expert and, although loath to follow it, decided that advice worth asking for was worth following. This proved to be of value, for the killifish were all dead in a few days, and the same would have been true of more valuable specimens.

Anemones and other creatures attached to rocks should, if possible, be placed in the aquarium without detaching. Low forms do better if handled with a dipper or spoon. Whether or not mussels are alive can be determined by tapping lightly on the shell with a small stick. In health the shell will promptly close. Gentle disturbances of the water will show whether anemones and other low forms are living, as they will respond by slight movements. Care on this point is of vital importance, as decomposition is very rapid.

**Sea Horses.** Owing to the vastness of the field we cannot here go into a detailed list of marine aquarium inhabitants, but we cannot pass the subject without special mention of those quaint fishes, Sea Horses (*Hippocampus*). Although appearing like some mythological animal in miniature, they are true fish. They make a very striking appearance in the aquarium, always attracting great attention. Their tails are prehensile and are used much the same as a monkey's, fastening themselves to twigs, bits of grass or any small object, ready too let go in a moment, swim a short distance and fasten somewhere else or perchance socially link tails with another. Their movements through the water might be described as being very sedate. Locomotion is produced mainly by a propellor-like movement of the dorsal fin, the body being tipped forward at a slight angle. Although the movement through the water is not rapid, it has the appearance of being accomplished entirely without effort. The breeding habits of the Sea Horse are also most peculiar. The female develops an intromittent organ as the breeding season approaches, while the brood-pouch on the belly of the male becomes thickened and vascular. The fishes face each other, the female advances, places one or more eggs in the pouch of the male, retreats and repeats until the spawning is finished. When the eggs have hatched, the pouch splits slightly and he works the young out of it by gently rubbing against a firm surface. The young are as perfectly formed as the parents.

Sea horses feed upon small marine crustacea about equal in size to daphnia. Some European aquarians claim to have gotten them to eat dried shrimp, but, so far as we are able to learn, nobody in America has been successful in this. Although different attempts have been made to induce them to eat daphnia, it has seldom been accomplished. The author was fortunate enough to induce Sea Horses to modify their ideas on diet, the process taking considerable patience. Daphnia can only live about 5 minutes in seawater, so at first they all die while the Sea Horses are apparently thinking the matter over. By repeated trials the smaller fishes finally started to eat and the larger ones took the hint from the smaller. Shrimp will eat the dead daphnia, but if much is left over it should be quickly siphoned out or otherwise removed. Sea Horses can, no doubt, be brought to living in saltwater of a hydrometer strength of 1,017, which would probably increase the length of life of daphnia in the marine aquarium to 10 minutes or more. As the Sea Horses usually eat by reaching out for food while attached by their tails to a piece of sea-weed, it is necessary to gently circulate the daphnia through the aquarium by the aeration system or other means.

FIG. 79. THE SEA HORSE (*Life size*)
*Hippocampus hudsonius*

These strange fishes are of worldwide distribution. On the Atlantic Coast they are more plentiful in September than at any other time, when they are often brought up clinging to fishermen's nets. Only one species occurs on the Atlantic Coast. This is the one shown in Fig. 79.

**Feeding in Marine Aquaria.** Practically all marine animals are carnivorous. Chopped oysters, clams, fish, worms, crab meat, scraped lean beef and shrimp form the principal articles of diet. Uncooked shrimp, shelled and put through the finest meat chopper is excellent and is particularly valuable, as it can be had all winter in the better fish stores. Anemones should have small bits of food offered them with forceps (shown on page 229), lightly touching their tentacles with the offering. Three times a week is often enough to feed these lower forms.

The fishes may be fed every day or two, according to temperature, always remembering that animal food not quickly eaten soon fouls the water.

**Diseased Marine Fishes.** Very little is known about treating the ailments of marine fishes. As salt is the general cure-all for freshwater fishes, it has been discovered that less salt is the best general treatment for marine fishes that are out of condition. Short trials at hydrometer test 1.010 are beneficial, this, of course, being brought about gradually. Otherwise we see no reason why animal parasites, injuries, etc., should not be treated the same as for freshwater fishes.

*Chapter Ten*

———

# Terraria and Aqua-Terraria

## TERRARIA

The terrarium has not as yet aroused any marked degree of interest in America, but as we have followed Europe in the cultivation of exotic fishes, it is not unlikely that we shall follow their study of exotic amphibians and other inhabitants of the terrarium and aqua-terrarium. Certainly the subject can be made one of absorbing interest, offering special attractions to those fond of making their own collections. Unfortunately, even in Europe the terrarium itself has not been developed into a thing of beauty. Most of the numerous designs shown for sale are stiff and clumsy-looking, but this may be largely overcome by artistic planting. Undoubtedly there is still plenty of room for individuality of treatment which would give one more the feeling of a bit of Nature brought to the home rather than into a miniature prison.

The variety of animals which may be kept is extremely large and many of them are of distinctly attractive appearance, even to the novice or outsider. Those of us who have learned to admire the Telescope Goldfish should suspend judgment on some of the apparently less attractive specimens in the terrarium, for it may be that both standards operate on the same general principle, that is, the *more hideous, the more admired.*

Aside from the matter of beauty there is a wonderful range for observation, study and original research in the terrarium. In looking over the European catalogs one is struck with the large number of lizards, frogs, newts, turtles, reptiles, etc., which are exported from North America. It will be seen therefore that we do not have to leave our own shore to obtain good collections.

Terraria are divided into four natural divisions, according to the needs of their occupants: dry-temperate, dry-tropical, moist-temperate, and moist-tropical. The differences in these will readily suggest themselves to the mind, being matters mainly of ventilation and artificial heat. The sides are usually of glass, one of them, as well as the top, being removable in order to work inside or to introduce or take out specimens.

The dry-temperate terrarium is naturally the simplest in construction, the principal requirements being open ventilation and a small drinking pool with cement edge and mirror bottom. This seems to be necessary to some of the creatures, as they are accustomed to seeing the sky reflected in water and without this they do not at first recognize it as water.

The moist-temperate form is only slightly ventilated and is supplied with a larger water pool, as the animals are usually amphibians. It is well to be able to drain this off without removal.

FIG. 80. THE RED TRITON (*Sperlerpes ruber*)

FIG. 81. ENCLOSED AQUA-TERRARIUM, AWARDED FIRST PRIZE BY THE TRITON SOCIETY

Tropical terraria, whether moist or dry, are heated artificially from below, the heating device being concealed in a false bottom. The heat may be applied either to a pan of sand or water or used in the form of a miniature hot-water heating system as indicated in figure 75 for heating tropical aquaria. The pipes are not carried over the top, but through or around the bottom.

The forms of terraria are quite diverse, according to requirements or fancy. Quite a number are divided into two halves, one side containing a shallow pool with tall bog plants, the other side being for dry terrestrial plants, the two sometimes being connected by a sloping ladder over the division, so that the animals may cross at will. The same arrangement is further developed into the aqua-terrarium by having the moist side in regular aquarium form and filling about two-thirds deep with water. Where tree frogs or other climbing animals are kept there should be a ladder or other arrangement to enable them to seek varying levels at different times, as this desire seems to be an important part of their nature. Tree frogs in some parts of the world are better known as "weather frogs." They are kept where they may either remain in water or climb to different levels at will, and are regarded as good barometers to foretell approaching weather conditions. Undoubtedly the state of the atmosphere has something to do with their movements in this respect.

Terraria for moths and insects usually have three sides of screen and one side of glass for clear observation.

**Aqua-terraria** may be considered a higher development of terraria, since their possibilities are so much enhanced on account of accommodating both terrestrial and aquatic animals and plants. One of the most interesting kinds is devoted to the observation of aquatic insects. These only contain a few inches of water, in which is planted bog plants, so that the leaves stand well out of water. Very few of the aquatic insects spend their entire lives in the water and some such provision is needed for them. It is important that stones or other creeping-out places be provided for turtles, frogs, newts and other amphibians, for it is a great cruelty to oblige them to remain constantly in the water.

Quite artistic effects can be obtained in the arrangement and planting of the terrarium and the aqua-terrarium. Natural bridges, lakes, waterfalls, archways, ledges, hollows, cliffs, caves, and other details may be used to good purpose, but care should be exercised not to combine the incongruous nor introduce objects out of keeping with the general scheme. Stones cemented together are capable of good pictorial effects. For moist terraria, pumice or other porous stone will be found useful, as it retains so much moisture and makes a good foothold for ferns and creeping plants.

An aqua-terrarium constructed for pictorial effect is made in the form of an ordinary aquarium with terrestrial plants arranged in the rear corners, thus giving the effect of a complete bit of landscape. The great possibilities of this treatment are shown in the illustration on page 122. This has the earth in slate containers reaching all the way to the bottom, but in a form devised later the soil is in cement pans 6 inches deep which are hung by hooks on the top edge of the aquarium proper, thus giving more light at the bottom of the aquarium.

Swamp aquaria have received little attention, although they can be made very picturesque, as will be seen in Fig. 82.

**Plants.** Most of the plants flourishing in greenhouses will prosper in the moist terrarium, so that the selection is very large. The dry terrarium is much more limited in this respect, the possibilities being confined practically to cacti, agaves, aloes, houseleeks and certain hardy ferns which have come from dry situations.

**Planting.** The main point in planting the terrarium is to procure proper drainage by the use of pebbles. Plants can be set either directly in soil above the pebbles or in pots. Fertilizer may be used in the lower part of soil but very sparingly in moist terraria. In planting it is well to keep in mind the natural surroundings of the animals and to provide, so far as possible, those conditions which are agreeable to their natures. For instance, the reptiles like to sun themselves in open, dry spots and in planting for them this can easily be arranged. Amphibious animals like to secrete themselves and hide from the light at times in thick vegetation, a provision easily made in the moist terrarium. These same considerations will present themselves when it comes to selecting a place for the terrarium. The snakes delight to sun themselves for hours, so in planting it is well to use only such plants that will stand plenty of direct sunlight. Terraria have one important advantage over aquaria in that at least the smaller sizes may be shifted from one place to another with very little effort, so that light conditions may be changed at will and hours of sunshine increased as opportunity offers.

**Occupants for Terraria.** The large majority of cold-blooded animals of suitable sizes may be introduced. In the moist terrarium the principal animals used are young alligators, newts, salamanders, tadpoles, frogs, water snakes, turtles, aquatic insects and their larvæ. For the dry terrarium we have tree toads, hop toads, horned toads, beetles, spiders, lizards, chameleons, tortoises, snakes, butterflies, moths and other insects.

**Feeding in the Terrarium.** The different occupants of the terrarium naturally require a varying range of foods. Those containing chameleons, frogs, toads, tree toads, do well on flies. It is a good plan to have a fly trap which can be emptied into the terrarium. It is quite an amusing thing to see the animals waiting for the flys to emerge after they have learned that they are fed in this manner. The dexterity with which they are caught and eaten is a never-ending marvel. While these animals can live on little, they ought to be well fed in warm weather, giving them

FIG. 82 SWAMP AQUARIUM

once daily all the flies they can consume which will be found to be a considerable number. In winter when flies are scarce they may be fed on meal worms and meal bugs, which are easily cultivated in bran flour, once a small stock is started. Particular care should be taken not to allow any of the meal breeding stock to escape into the house, as it is liable to become a pest in the kitchen.

Newts and salamanders are fed on bits of meat, fish, oysters, fish eggs and worms.

Snakes and lizards require large and small insects, worms, small live fish and animals.

Alligators and carnivorous turtles want live fish, tadpoles, crayfish, small animals. In the absence of living food they can sometimes be induced to take chopped oysters, fish, etc.

Box tortoises and land turtles are largely vegetarians and should be supplied with berries, garden vegetables, mushrooms, cooked cereals, snails and worms.

As with the aquarium, particular care should be exercised not to allow any excess of food which is liable to decay, all such surplus being removed immediately after the feeding hour.

*Chapter Eleven*

———

# Fishfoods

## PREPARED FISHFOODS

Nearly all aquarium fishes naturally desire a variety of foods, and the nearer we can approximate Nature in this matter, the better will be our results. Whatever foods we employ we should always keep in mind the necessary balance of vegetable, animal and mineral content required. One of the poorest fishfoods obtainable is the white wafer usually sold in pet shops and drug stores. Of recent years many better foods have been placed on the market, most pet stores keeping at least one of them. They are granular in form, usually of a dark color and are composed of a mixture of dried insects, meat, fish roe, flour, codfish and other ingredients. Unless one needs a large quantity of fishfood it is better to purchase a prepared article of the sort described.

An extremely good fishfood is puppy biscuit broken up and ground in a coffee mill to small sizes. This is cheaper than regular fishfood and is very satisfactory. It is used as a base by some manufacturers to add a few ingredients to and then place it on the market under their own label.

A food used with considerable success is oatmeal prepared exactly as it comes to the breakfast table, containing the same amount of salt. This is especially recommended for feeding young fish when daphnia have become scarce. The shape of a fish is permanently influenced by its body development in the first few months, and different methods of feeding produce, to a certain extent, different shapes. The effect of oatmeal, fed plentifully, is to build the short, round body so generally desired. For fish under ten weeks old the oatmeal should be squeezed through cheesecloth to take out the kernels. Let the young fish have as much as they can eat all day, but let none remain over night. This does not apply to fish in their second year or over, although oatmeal in much smaller quantity is good for them also. Large fish may be allowed to eat uncooked rolled oats.

An improvement on boiled oatmeal is secured by adding a moderate portion of powdered shrimp, dried fish roe or powdered shredded codfish. For preparation of these ingredients see page 129.

A cereal known as Cream of Barley when cooked is a good fishfood and may be used in conjunction with oatmeal.

Dried bread crumbs make good food for goldfishes, especially if Graham or whole wheat bread is used.

In feeding any kind of dried granular food it is best to use small sizes. Water causes the grains to swell considerably. This sometimes produces indigestion when the food swells after being swallowed. Many fanciers in Germany scald food just before feeding, which is no doubt a good practise.

For those wishing to make a general fishfood suitable for all except strictly carnivorous fishes, the following recipe will be found to be very good:

> Quarter tumbler powdered cod
> Half tumbler powdered liver
> Three-quarters tumbler powdered shrimp
> Three tumblers flour
> One teaspoonful Epsom salts
> Three teaspoonfuls baking powder
> Three teaspoonfuls powdered chalk

Add two raw eggs and sufficient water to make the mixture into the usual consistency of bread dough. Place in pan and bake in oven. When properly baked allow to cool and cut into thin slices. After thoroughly drying grind in coffee mill and sift into desired sizes. *Keep all dry fishfoods well secured in bottles or other actually tight receptacles.* Moths and other insects gain a foothold and soon turn the food into a mass of worms and refuse.

In above recipe the cod is prepared by purchasing a package of shredded cod, drying over slow fire and grinding fine in coffee mill. The liver should be parboiled, cut into thin strips, dried and ground. Dried shrimp may be had at Chinese grocery stores. It needs to be broken in pieces, put through a coarse setting of the mill, then well dried for a few days and lastly ground fine.

Whole wheat flour is preferable to white flour.

Powdered cuttlebone or eggshell may be used instead of chalk.

Those desiring to experiment on a food according to their own ideas of ingredients and proportions may safely use any of the following items, in addition to those already mentioned: Pea flour, rice flour, rye flour, vermicelli, boiled fish, boiled yellow of egg, fine corn meal, ant eggs, chopped earthworms, water crackers, dried bread, chopped meal worms, dried and powdered lettuce leaves, dried fish roe and dried daphnia. In preparing the latter two ingredients they should be parboiled with a moderate amount of salt, then placed in cheesecloth; water squeezed out, spread out thin on tin plates and dried quickly in the sun or slow oven. The drying must be thorough and quick. In drying it will be found that the shrinkage in volume will be very great. It should, therefore, be remembered that these ingredients are highly concentrated and be used accordingly.

When fish have been without fresh or living food for some time it is well to occasionally give them a small quantity of scraped raw beef (scraped crosswise to grain) or the dark, soft part of oysters, chopped and slightly rinsed. Fresh shrimp, obtainable in most fish markets in Winter, if passed through a fine meat chopper, makes an excellent change of diet.

## LIVING FISHFOODS

Living fishfoods are divided mainly into larvæ and crustacea, the latter on the whole being the more important and the more generally

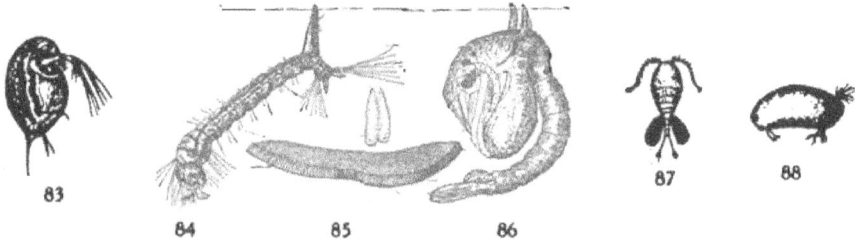

FIG. 83. DAPHNIA (*Greatly enlarged*)
FIG. 84. MOSQUITO LARVA (*Greatly enlarged*)
FIG. 85. EGG RAFT AND INDIVIDUAL EGGS (*Greatly enlarged*)
FIG. 86. PUPA BEFORE TRANSFORMING TO MOSQUITO (*Greatly enlarged*)
FIG. 87. CYCLOPS (*Greatly enlarged*)
FIG. 88. CYPRIS (*Greatly enlarged*)

obtainable. Those which are of practical value to the breeder of fancy aquarium fishes are few in number. Like the insect enemies of fishes, four is the number of really important kinds.

**Daphnia.** Undoubtedly the best food for aquarium fishes is living daphnia and this should be used at all times in preference to prepared foods if obtainable. The fish will consume great quantities of these crustaceans without suffering the usual effects of being overfed. A certain degree of care must be exercised not to place so much daphnia into the aquarium as to suffocate the fish. Daphnia breathe the free oxygen in water the same as do fish and therefore too many will soon exhaust oxygen from water. The fish will die of suffocation sooner than the daphnia. Many fanciers have lost fish in this way. A good practise is to give the fish all they can eat in about a quarter of an hour and still leave some few daphnia swimming about.

A popular name for daphnia is "ditch fleas." This will give a key to their appearance, as they are approximately the size and shape of a flea, except that they have two rather long, branched swimming arms which are always in motion and which gives the animal a sort of hopping motion through the water. Without this perpetual swimming the daphnia would sink to the bottom, as they are heavier than water and have no air bladder. A greatly magnified illustration is shown in Fig. 83.

Daphnia (incorrectly pronounced "daffney") are known among fish breeders as "insects," but they are really not such, being perfect fresh-water crustaceans as much as a crayfish. The shell though soft contains mineral elements which are very desirable, while the flesh itself is easily digested and nutritious. This little creature is found nearly all over the world, principally in still pools where there are no fish. For the practical purpose of catching daphnia in sufficient quantities to feed fish the collector should hunt pools in which there is considerable animal or vege-table decomposition in process. This decomposition favors the growth of infusoria, small members of the animal kingdom on which daphnia feed. Such conditions are found to perfection in the pools on the grounds where city refuse is dumped. When the conditions are favor-able the daphnia rise to the surface in such quantities as to color the water, the usual color being a rusty red. The color varies from this to olive and gray. Fish breeders like to see the daphnia as bright a red as possible, although it is an open question as to whether the red ones are better food. The same individuals will alternate in color, probably due to a difference in food. Usually these crustaceans are not so plentiful as to color the water and we have to use our eyes more closely to locate them. The collector should provide himself with a cheesecloth net about 12 inches in diameter and 15 inches deep, fastened on a pole or jointed handle not less than 6 feet long. If an examination of the water does not at first reveal any daphnia, the net should be tried anyhow, using a gentle stirring motion back and forth, to stir up the bottom water. Daphnia have very peculiar habits and one can never tell from day to day just how they are to be found, so that the collector will always have to depend somewhat on his own resources. If an examination of the net after dipping for a few minutes shows nothing, try elsewhere. If a colony has been located do not take too many into the net at one time, as the weight of the top ones crushes those beneath. A mass that would bulk about equivalent to an orange should not be exceeded. Reverse the net into carrying pail and repeat until the water is thick with daphnia. In cool weather the pail may be carried in this crowded condition for about an hour. If the day is hot, a piece of ice should be added to the water—enough to keep temperature down until home is reached. News-paper wrapped about the can helps the ice melt more slowly. As soon as home is reached, add fresh water to the pail and transfer the daphnia to tubs or tanks kept for the purpose. Like fish, the water they are in should have as much air surface as possible. Do not try to keep too many in stock, as overcrowding suffocates a number and these in turn decomposing kill the living ones. The cooler they are kept, the longer they will last. In hot weather they can be kept about three days and in October about two weeks.

**A method of carrying live food** which is growing in favor is to crate them (without water) in layers in a box. Frames about 10 x 12 inches, made of ⅞-inch square wood, are covered on one side with cheesecloth. These are floated in the water, the daphnia dropped in, spread out evenly and placed in carrying box which, of course, needs to be airtight. The number of layers are only limited by the depth of the box. Daphnia may be spread to a depth of about ¼ inch, but mosquito larvæ may be piled to ½ inch without injury.

In transferring from carrying pails to stock tanks it is well to first pour in small portions to a white enamel basin which enables one to carefully go over the catch and remove any insect enemies. (See page 156.) If the daphnia are too thick to be readily examined, some water should be added. A little care in keeping out the enemies at the start is energy well invested. Most of the enemies and the dirt may be sifted out (under water) by using a screen just large enough for the daphnia to pass through.

A beginner will do well to make the acquaintance of an experienced daphnia collector and go along with him on a trip. There are now aquarium societies in many of the large cities, part of their activities being the dissemination of such knowledge. All those interested in aquaria should have either active or corresponding membership in one of these organizations. If return stamps are enclosed the publishers of this work will always be glad to put the beginner in touch with the nearest society.

All beginners seem to have the idea that sufficient daphnia can be raised in a tub or trough to feed with. This has been tried many times but never with any degree of success. If the daphnia pools are too far distant to make collecting practicable it is best to try to inoculate some suitable pond nearby, but there should be no fish in the pond. Daphnia if not crowded may be shipped quite a distance. There are several Philadelphia collectors constantly making shipments in season.

The practical way to raise daphnia for food purposes is described in the chapter on Wholesale Breeding (page 62).

**Cyclops.** Wherever Daphnia are found, Cyclops is pretty sure to be, and also in a great many places where the former does not exist. They are crustacea of about the same size and color as Daphnia, but under close examination are of entirely different structure and also of different action, going rapidly through the water in straight lines with a jumping movement. Like Daphnia they are divided into many species and are practically worldwide in distribution. The two tabs seen near the lower portion of the illustration are the egg-pouches of the female. These develop in warm weather every two days, become detached and fall to the bottom with 16 to 32 eggs which arrive at maturity in 30 days. They are called Cyclops because, like the giant of mythology, they have but one eye.

**Mosquito Larvæ.** These are often known as wrigglers and are familiar to those who have looked in rain barrels. Their bodies are straight and about a quarter of an inch long. They rest at an angle to the surface of the water as shown in Fig. 84, with head down, and are always ready to "wriggle" to the bottom at the first sign of danger. From midsummer on they may be found in still water where there are no fish. They are taken in the same manner as daphnia, except that one has to get them with a quick sweep before they can get down into the water. They can usually be seen floating together in black masses. The city entomologist anywhere will give information as to where they may be obtained and will be glad to have his burdens lightened by the fish breeder.

Mosquito Larvæ may be termed a special food. It can only be had in large quantities towards the middle and end of Summer, and is only suited to the fish large enough to easily swallow it. As a food for putting growth on fish an inch long or over it has no equal. The main drawback to these larvæ is that those not eaten quickly by the fish are liable to turn to mosquitoes. This difficulty can be discounted by proper management. Keep the stock of larvæ in a tank covered by a sheet of glass, leaving about two inches at one end not covered. Over this open space place a piece of mosquito netting, drawing it up several inches over the opening into a sort of inverted bag. Then draw a string around top edge of tank to fasten netting down. As the mosquitoes hatch they will fly upward into the netting bag, where they may be killed before lifting the lid to get larvæ for the fish. The larvæ should be kept out of the sun and as cool as possible so as to retard hatching. They will stand great crowding, their only requirement being that there is room for them all to get to the surface at one time, for they breathe air. This is one advantage in placing larvæ with fish, for, unlike daphnia, they extract no oxygen from the water. By feeding them to the fish we not only do well for the fish, but serve the interests of humanity by cutting down the mosquito pest. In open pools goldfishes are one of the best agents in keeping the neighborhood free of mosquitoes. Unfortunately the mosquito larvæ can live and hatch in temporary pools and in water too foul for any fish to survive in.

**Cypris.** Incorrectly known as "hardshell daphnia," Cypris forms an important article of fish diet. These crustacea inhabit stagnant pools, particularly those well stocked with decomposing vegetal matter. Although capable of swimming freely they are more apt to remain close to the bottom, but more especially to decaying wood. They are of a dull, purplish black color about twice the size of an ordinary pin-head. Inexperienced observers frequently mistake them for Daphnia. Fishes do not appear to be quite so fond of them as of Daphnia but they are a good second choice. They are extremely hardy and will withstand dense overcrowding in the foulest of water. Under favorable conditions Cypris multiplies with astounding rapidity. They have been known to attack newly hatched fishes.

**Blood Worms.** In freshwater pools nearly everywhere can be found deep-red, jointed worms about half an inch long. See figure 89. They usually stay at the bottom, living chiefly on decomposing vegetal matter. Often they will writhe their way awkwardly through the water in

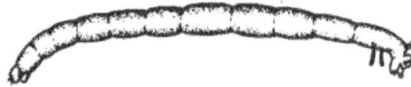

Fig. 89. Bloodworm (*Larva of Chironomus*) (*Enlarged four times*)

a series of figure eights. They are the larvæ of midges and form an important article of diet for our native fishes. They are often found in large numbers in daphnia pools and should always be taken when possible. If too large for the young fish, they make choice morsels for the older ones.

**Tubifex Worms.** These are small thread-like worms living in mud and sand. They form a tube or case below the surface, extending the upper ends of their bodies from this in search of small organic food, causing a circulation of water about themselves by a constant weaving

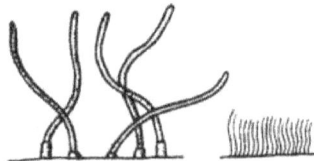

Fig. 90. Tubifex Worms Magnified and as the Ends Appear Above the Bottom

motion. When alarmed they draw back into the case. They are extensively cultivated in Europe as a food for tropical fishes. A similar variety is often introduced into goldfish aquaria when feeding daphnia, where they become an unsightly nuisance, for goldfishes do not eat them. To get rid of them it is necessary to boil or renew the sand or else keep other fishes in the aquarium for a long time. The worms have to be eaten off many times before the stock dies. Germicides strong enough to kill them will also destroy the plants, as they can withdraw into the sand. Along the edges of ditches they are often so numerous as to make a solid rusty red color. If they are scraped up together with the dirt and then washed free they are greatly enjoyed by small tropical fishes.

**Fairy Shrimp** (*Gammarus*). While freshwater shrimp is not plentiful enough anywhere to feed in large quantities, it is a delicate morsel for grown fishes and should be taken as opportunity offers. They are found principally in small streams, under stones and around decaying wood. Placed in a large aquarium or tank with plenty of vegetation they will multiply rapidly.

FIG. 91. FAIRY SHRIMP (*Enlarged 3 times*)
FIG. 92. WATER-ASEL (*Enlarged 3 times*)

**Water-Asel** (*Asellopus*) is found in still or slowly moving water, usually in the mud or clinging to vegetation. It cannot move rapidly like Fairy Shrimp, but both are enemies of very small fry and both are greedily taken as food by larger aquarium fishes, although the shrimp move so rapidly that highly developed fishes have trouble in catching them.

FIG. 93
*Asplanchnopus myrmelco*

FIG. 94
*Pterodina patina*

FIG. 95
*Noteus quadracornis*

THREE TYPICAL ROTIFERS (*Greatly magnified*)

**Infusoria and Rotifera.** Of prime importance as food for very small fishes are the Infusoria and other microscopic creatures of still water. Some idea of their minuteness may be had when it is pointed out that they are the natural food of Daphnia, Cyclops and other small crustaceans. All except the very largest of the infusorians will pass through ordinary cheesecloth nets, but silk bolting-cloth of fine texture will hold those which are large enough to be of real use. Further information on this point is contained on page 140. Other infusoria are shown in Fig. 96.

**Enchytrae.** These are thread-like small white worms usually bred in winter as a substitute for daphnia for feeding to tropical fishes. Goldfishes are also very fond of them, but it is a difficult matter to cultivate a sufficiently large quantity to satisfy the appetite of several goldfish. For some of the smaller fishes requiring living food they are almost indispensable in winter.

The culture of these worms is quite easy and requires very little attention after the start is made. Many of the dealers and fanciers in New York and vicinity have a stock of enchytrae, from whom a stock can be procured. These are placed in ordinary garden soil from which all worms and larvae have been carefully removed. Wooden or earthenware boxes about 15 inches long, 7 inches wide and six inches deep may be filled with the earth to a depth of 4 inches. A cover glass must be provided, this setting directly on the soil. Proper feeding is the principal keynote to success. They like milk, white bread, boiled potato, cheese rinds, etc. In a box of this size, four or five small holes are dug out with a spoon, the food placed therein and the earth replaced. This is done as often as the food is consumed and in three or four weeks the harvest of worms will be ready. Care should be taken not to overfeed, as this will sour the soil. The soil should be removed from the box about every two weeks, broken up, loosened and returned. This is considerably facilitated if about half the soil is composed of leaf mold. The breeding box does best in an average temperature of about 60 degrees Fahrenheit.

The worms are separated from the earth in a number of ways. If but a few are desired the simplest way is to remove two or three spoons full of soil and place same in water just deep enough to cover. In a very short time the worms will come out of the soil and entangle themselves in a bunch near the surface of the water, when they may easily be collected.

Another much quicker method is to take a piece of cardboard (the cover of a shoe-box answers nicely) spreading a quantity of soil thereon and holding over a heat; this soon causes the worms to crawl to the top of the earth, from which they are removed. However, great care must be exercised that they are not injured by the heat, which would destroy them, for the fish prefer the live worms at all times. As soon as they appear and bunch on the surface of the earth, the heat should be removed.

Another method of separating the worms from soil is to place a portion of the earth in an enameled dish, pouring sufficient water over same to cover and placing thereupon a sheet of glass, which should rest above and free from the moist earth. Because this will prevent sufficient oxygen from penetrating the dirt or water, the Enchytrae will promptly leave the soil, crawl up the sides of the dish and on the underside of the glass cover, clinging to same in a variety of entanglements. The cover can then be removed and the worms washed or scraped off and fed to the fish. This of course is a slow process, but by preparing an hour or so before it is desired to obtain same, an ample supply may be procured.

It is not advisable to feed all of the worms thus obtained as when a considerable number are placed in a tank at a single time, some are bound to escape from the bunch and, burying themselves in the gravel or sand, die and pollute the water. It is said that they can exist under water for about forty-eight hours and it has been noted that the larger specimens are usually the first to succumb.

Still another way to remove them from the soil is to take a section of blotting paper, placing the earth on it, and in a short time it will be noticed that they will have gathered in a ring around the outer edge of the soil, free from the dirt.

*Chapter Twelve*

———

# The Microscope
# In Aquarium Work

## THE MICROSCOPE IN AQUARIUM WORK

Aquarium work in general and fish breeding in particular can be made both more interesting and more successful by the use of a microscope. For most purposes a very cheap instrument is satisfactory. In fact, a low power lens is preferable to a high in examining water for infusorian food.

All aquaria contain various beautiful and highly interesting forms of microscopic life, some harmful, some negative, but mostly beneficial to fishes. The constant changing of varieties and quantities presents a vast field for new study, but we are here mostly concerned with the practical points of raising young fish. On page 135 we refer to the use of infusoria as food for young fish. To determine the presence of this food, touch the tip of the finger lightly to the surface of the water, preferably to the side nearest the source of light. This is because they are mostly at the surface and they seek the light. Place this drop on a glass slide and observe under a good magnifying glass or a low power microscope. The latter is rather preferable, as the focus can be changed as required, and it is fitted with a mirror to facilitate observation. In the absence of a microscope the small pocket folding lens known as a "thread counter" will do. This costs about twenty-five cents. In using this the frame of the counter should be laid directly on the glass containing the drop of water, and the whole placed over a mirror held at the proper angle to reflect light upwards, but too strong a light should not be used. A little experimenting will soon show the best light to work by.

The creatures which are of value as food to newly hatched fishes are generally of a size just too small to be detected by the naked eye, or at most they look like specks of dust. At the same time they are plainly observable under a good magnifying glass or low-power microscope. There is a great deal of life in the water of a smaller size than will be shown in this way and which probably has no food value to fishes. The high-power microscope would show many of these organisms and thus be apt to deceive the observer as to the actual food value contained in the water. Also with high magnification the field of vision and the area of sharp focus are smaller, while movements are apparently much more rapid, making observation difficult.

The majority of the valuable organisms are rotifers. These move in a steady, revolving or rotating manner. On page 57 will be found instructions for propagating these organisms for purposes of feeding young fish. Most rotifers can be readily identified as such because they swim through the water by means of circlets of hairs or cilia arising from the front of their heads, by the vibratile action of which they swim and disport themselves through the water. In fact, rotifers derive their name from the wheel-like appearance produced by the motion of the circlets of cilia while feeding and swimming. For culture water to have practical food value a single drop should contain at least half a dozen living objects that can be seen in the manner suggested. Water rich in life will show rotifers so thickly that they almost touch one another—probably two hundred in a small drop. In taking water from the culture tank to feed the fish it should be skimmed from the surface,

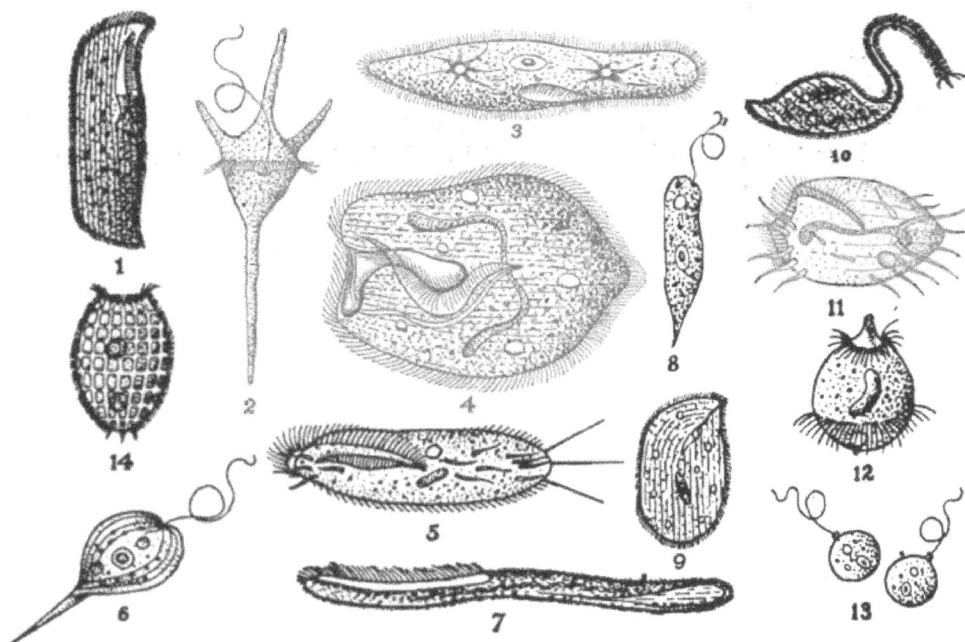

FIG. 96.  COMMON FORMS OF MICROSCOPIC ANIMAL LIFE IN FRESHWATER
(Greatly magnified)

1.  LOXODES, a very common form.
2.  CERATIUM, a very common form, especially in ponds and lakes.
3.  PARAMAECIUM, a very common form, the slipper animalcule.
4.  BURSARIA, a very common form, one of the largest.
5.  STYLONYCHA, a very common form, found everywhere.
6.  PHACUS, not so common as the above numbers.
7.  SPIROSTOMUM, common everywhere.
8.  EUGLENA, common everywhere.
9.  CHILODON, common everywhere.
10.  TRACHELOCERCA, common everywhere, the swan animalcule.
11.  EUPOLOTES, not an aquarium in America without examples.
12.  DIDINIUM, predacous, feeds on paramaecium and others.
13.  TRACHELOCERCA, small but plentiful.
14.  COLEPS, the barrel animalcule, common.

or the animals extracted from the water by a plankton net, which is nothing more than a small net of the finest bolting cloth.

Besides the examination of water for living food there are many other interesting possibilities for the microscope in aquarium work. Diseases, the development of eggs, plant structure, algae, the structure of daphnia, cyclops and other crustacean foods are a few of the subjects which may be taken up with profitable interest.

A study of the microscopic world within the aquarium will prove a most fascinating pursuit. Good microscopes for the purpose can be purchased very cheaply now compared with former prices. An instrument equipped with a 24 m. m. (1 inch) objective and a times 5 or 6 eyepiece will show everything needed, giving a magnification of 60 diameters.

Those wishing to explore this field a little further will find the following works to be helpful: "Aquatic Microscopy for Beginners," by Stokes; "Marvels of Pond Life," by Slack; "Evenings at the Microscope," by Gosse.

---

# Chapter Thirteen

# Diseases of Aquarium Fishes
# and Their Treatment

## DISEASES AND AILMENTS OF AQUARIUM FISHES AND THEIR TREATMENT

Even in a state of Nature fishes are sometimes attacked by disease and parasitic enemies. It is little wonder, then, that aquarium fishes, weakened by inbreeding and kept under artificial conditions should be subject to a number of maladies. The wonder is that the majority of the diseases can be so successfully treated, under the circumstances.

Half the battle is won by taking the trouble in time. The aquarist should always be on the alert to detect when his pets are a little out of condition. As elsewhere stated, this is shown by listless movements, loss of appetite, drooping dorsal fin (when the fish is in the habit of holding it erect), congested or frayed fins, white slime on body and bubbles in excrement. When a fish is even suspected of being in doubtful condition it should be observed carefully for a day or two, and, if improvement is not noted, given the required treatment—*promptly.*

Affected fishes should be immediately removed from their fellows. There is always the possibility that they are suffering from a contagious disease which may quickly spread. Great care should be exercised not to use the same nets in handling sick and well fishes unless they are sterilized after exposure to disease germs.

**Salt Treatment.** In Nature the sick fish seeks brackish water or saline earths, and we cannot do better than to follow this hint. Most of the disease-producing bacteria of fresh water are unable to live in moderate salt solutions. The point, then, is to find the strength of solution that will kill the bacteria without injuring he fish. As the salt treatment is the main one for curable diseases, we shall go into this at some length.

Kind of Salt. Ordinary table salt is likely to contain chemicals to prevent caking in damp weather. These are injurious to fishes. However, if no other salt is obtainable, this can be made to do. The very best medicine is real sea water, properly diluted. The next best is Turk's Island salt, which is the residue from evaporated sea water. Where the fish shows a tendency to constipation, one-quarter of the salt content may be Epsom salts. Some writers recommend this addition in all cases.

**Strength of Salt Solution.** Common practice among the uninformed is to throw a sick fish into a strong brine solution, leaving it there a few minutes until it shows signs of expiring. This treatment is usually better than none at all, but is unnecessarily severe and is not so successful as milder solutions. In fact, the strong salt takes the protective slime off the fish and leaves it in a condition where it is liable to be quickly again infected, and in a weakened condition where treatment is not likely to again be effectual. The usual practice of the author is to make a solution in which salt is just easily discernable to the taste. As the sense of taste varies in individuals, this is not a very accurate rule to give others. A suitable proportion is one ounce of salt (approximately two heaping teaspoonfuls) to each gallon of water.

**Methods of Treatment.** Nearly all sick fishes do best in shallow water and out of bright light. An enamel tray four inches deep by twenty inches square is very good, or a well-seasoned tub filled to a few inches is suitable. In placing the patient in the medicated water, see that there is no considerable change in temperature. In warm weather a change to very slightly cooler water is stimulating and probably does no harm. Except for the air-breathing species (Paradise fish, etc.) a change to several degrees warmer water is liable to produce suffocation, warm water holding less free oxygen than cool. Aquarium fishes can live indefinitely in the solution described, but in two days a salt solution begins to smell stale and needs to be changed. A daily change is better. Should the patient not show signs of improvement in four days, gradually increase the strength of salt solution for two or three days until it is up to two ounces (four heaping teaspoonfuls) to each gallon of water. After remaining in this for two days the salt proportion is slowly weakened down again to the first formula.

**Ammonia Treatment.** A popular treatment among European fish culturists for fungoid diseases is the ammonia method. This has not been generally accepted in the United States, but has been tried with remarkable success in some instances where other treatments have failed. We feel, however, that it should only be tried as a last resort. To one gallon of clean water add ten drops of ordinary household ammonia. (Unfortunately, this varies somewhat in strength.) Place the fish in this for five minutes, but take out sooner, should it turn over. Remove to plain water and then back to its tank. The treatment may be repeated at intervals of three days if necessary.

**Special Attention.** All fish should, if possible, be placed, after any chemical treatment, in a healthy tank containing green water. Sometimes this is, indeed, the only treatment required.

Another very good after-treatment which may be used in summer is to place the hospital tank under a small stream or drip. In making the final change from salt back to fresh water, this is a very good way to accomplish it. Dripping water may do all that is necessary, especially if a fish is only on the doubtful line, which is more often the case than not.

Summer offers one more treatment when all others fail—place the affected fish in a shallow mud-bottom tank or pool. This is especially beneficial to goldfishes.

In winter when a skilled aquarist finds a fish a little out of condition, but with apparently nothing radically wrong, his first treatment is to remove the fish to another tank if he has one available. This often has the stimulating effect of a change of climate and usually wards off more serious trouble that might be developing. *As with ourselves and all animals, it is much better to cure an ailment, if possible, by improved conditions, rather than by recourse to drugs or chemicals.*

In treating sick goldfishes it is important to give some attention to temperature, especially in winter. Best results can be had at about 68°, which is a little warmer than fishes are usually kept in the cool season.

Another point to bear in mind for those having air-pumps, is that in the majority of ailments a cure is accelerated by a gentle flow of air liberated in the hospital tank, but not agitating the water enough to worry the fish. If no pump is at hand an occasional spraying is of value.

The foregoing is general in character but will be found useful in most of the diseases that can be cured. We will now deal specifically with the diseases and ailments.

**Fin Congestion.** This is the commonest of all fish troubles, and is especially liable to attack the highly developed fins of fancy goldfishes. Their long fins are no doubt deficient in circulation, causing low powers of resistance. As soon as the fish is slightly indisposed through over-feeding, sudden chill, protracted low temperature or other causes, fin congestion is usually the first symptom. The fins of fancy goldfishes may be considered very good barometers of the condition of the fish. The appearance produced is well indicated by the name. The fins are more or less red and streaked with veins. In advanced cases the fins commence to split and fray, particularly the tails.

TREATMENT. Fin congestion, as well as being the commonest of gold-fish diseases, is also the most easily cured. The salt-water treatment described on page 144 is without a superior. When the trouble is confined to the tail, it may be dipped in a 10-per cent. solution of peroxide of hydrogen. Another method is to paint the fish with coal oil, keeping the head and gills wrapped in a moist cloth. Usually lighter feeding and plenty of room in fresh water will be all that is necessary if taken in time. Two grains of permanganate of potash to the gallon of water is a successful treatment. It is best to use this in an enamel or a glass receptacle. Organic substances, such as wood or floating particles of dirt, quickly decompose the chemical. The fish may be given the treatment several hours at a time, but a fresh solution should be made daily.

An entirely different kind of fin congestion is sometimes prevalent in the Fall, especially when the fishes are first taken in, young fishes being more liable to attacks. The base of the tail and other fins becomes suddenly blood-red, the color sometimes extending to the body immediately adjoining. If allowed to continue.this form of the disease is rapidly disastrous. Fortunately, it yields with surprising quickness to either salt water or permanganate of potash treatment. When alternatives to salt-water treatment are suggested, the fancier will certainly be on the safe side by giving the salt the first trial, particularly if carefully followed out as we have directed.

**White Fungus.** This is next to the most common disease among goldfishes, and is responsible for the majority of deaths, except among very young fry. It begins on the tail and other fins, extending over the body and into the gills. When it reaches this stage it is usually fatal.

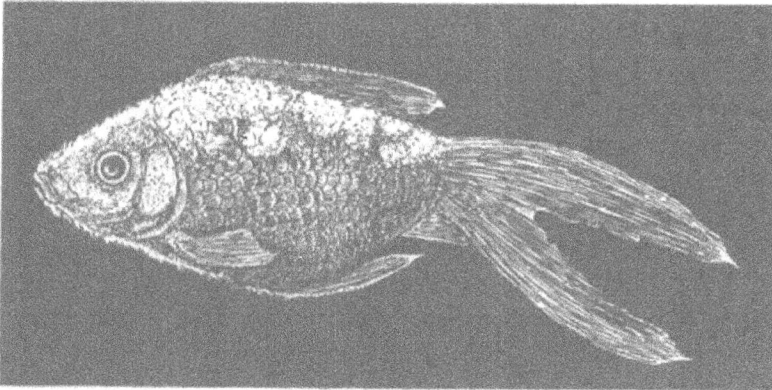

FIG. 97. FISH AFFECTED WITH WHITE FUNGUS
This illustration is characteristic of sick fishes in general. The fins are folded and drawn together and the general appearance is one of listlessness.

The progress of the disease is marked by the development of a white scum which destroys the fins, prevents the natural functions of the skin, and when the parasite enters the gills causes death by suffocation. The latter stage is not always reached, the fish often becoming so emaciated as to die in the second stage of the malady. The bacteria causing this disease are present in virtually all water, but can make no inroads on a fish in good condition. A weakened fish once infected will breed so many bacteria that they can successfully attack the remaining well fish. White fungus, there-fore, is contagious, and the sufferer should be removed from its fellows at once. This disease is caused by overcrowding, overfeeding, lack of proper plant life, transferring to water of different temperature and by bruises in shipment.

TREATMENT. Fishes suffering from white fungus should be treated exactly the same as those having fin congestion. If the fins have become very much frayed and it is necessary to trim them, this can best be done by a sharp knife, using a board to cut on. Scissors make a very poor result. It is well to treat the new cut edges with a permanganate solution of one grain to a glass of water. By grain we of course always mean a certain quantity of weight, and not simply a small particle.

Sometimes raw spots are left after the fungus has been removed. These or similar spots from other causes can be greatly helped by the fol-lowing method: Wrap the head and gills of the fish in a moist rag, dry the affected spot and apply some Turlington's Balsam with a small piece of absorbent cotton. Allow to dry for three or four minutes. This will not endanger the life of the fish so long as the gills are kept moist.

**Black Fungus.** Many have supposed this disease to be invariably fatal, but this is not the case. If taken in time, the majority of cases can be cured. The great trouble is that the fish is in a run-down condition before contracting the disease and has little power to withstand the necessarily severe treatment. This disease manifests itself more on the body than the fins, at first presenting a dark gray appearance, later turning black and peeling off, leaving raw spots. A common place for the first appearance is the center of the gill plates, and also on the sides of the fish where they would be most likely to rub, for the parasites are conveyed principally by contact. The Protozoans causing this serious complaint are animal parasites which soon lodge themselves so deeply in the skin of the fish as to make treatment difficult. If they get into the gills the case is considered hopeless.

TREATMENT. Start at once on the increasing salt method described on page 144, only carrying it further. Over a period of from three to four days the strength of solution should be carried to two and one-half ounces to the gallon. Goldfishes can stand a great deal of salt if brought to it gradually. As before noted, the strength should be slowly reduced before returning to normal water. (The same is true of most other aquarium fishes.) After the maximum strength of solution is reached the fish should be pencilled on the affected spots with a 50 per cent. solution of peroxide of hydrogen for a few moments (being careful not to slop over on the healthy parts). The next day the spots may be treated with

Turlington's Balsam as described for White Fungus. Feed on good nutritious substances, such as daphnia or chopped earthworms. If the fish seems to be standing it satisfactorily, keep in the strong salt for about one week, changing the water daily and relying on accurate measurements for salt quantities. A progressive permanganate of potassium treatment may also be used, but should not be continued as long, five days being about the maximum for a fish in poor condition. Start at one grain to the gallon and go up to three. With this chemical there is no need of gradually reducing the strength, but a new solution should be mixed daily, and twice daily is better, always remembering not to change temperature of water. Happily Black Fungus is not as prevalent as formerly, owing probably to the fact that we now have many more American wholesale breeders, thus doing away with the necessity of purchasing so many fishes that are in a thoroughly bad condition from hard trips across the Pacific Ocean, and shorter but equally hard travels across the American Continent.

Itch. The itch is one of the more common complaints in the aquarium. The fishes are observed to quickly rub their sides against the firmer objects in the aquarium, often against pebbles on the bottom. The affection is caused by different fish parasites.

TREATMENT. Although this trouble is caused by different organisms, they all yield to the progressive salt treatment (page 144). The aquarium should be cleaned out before fish are returned, and care exercised to keep it in a cleaner condition, paying particular attention to seeing that no uneaten particles of food are left lying about. The introduction of more snails and a small Weatherfish or two (see page 13) will help to avoid a recurrence. It is not improbable that mussels consume a large number of suspended parasites and bacteria of various kinds.

Constipation. Among the highly-bred, short-bodied fishes, constipation, as well as other mechanical disorders, is naturally common. The much shortened bodies throw the internal organs out of position, give rise to swimming bladder troubles and tie up the muscles which must discharge eggs and also the excrement of the fishes. Lack of proper exercise in the cramped confines of the aquarium and too highly concentrated foods are other causes leading to constipation. The excrement should be of a brown color and free from bubbles or any slimy appearance. In health it usually is seen in long sections.

TREATMENT. An equal mixture of sea salt and Epsom salts, made to a strength of one ounce of salts to the gallon, will usually prove beneficial. It is better not to feed the fish during the period of treatment—about two days. The trouble may be due to overfeeding, and in any case a short fast will probably do good.

Goldfishes readily eat Epsom salts. A pinch dropped in the aquarium once weekly is beneficial to the fishes, and at the same time replaces some of the mineral content of the water depleted by the plants and fishes drawing constantly upon it for the chemicals necessary to sustain life. This practice has a tendency to prevent constipation.

Chopped earthworms will be found a mild laxative. In severe cases some fanciers place a drop of castor oil well down the throat of the fish by means of a dropper. The author has never been convinced that the fish swallows any medication administered in this way, but it does no harm to try, and may do good.

**Tailrot.** This disease first affects the end of the tail and other fins; the appearance is one of being frayed and split. If allowed to continue until the base of the tail is affected, the fish will die. Taken in time the trouble is easily corrected. It must not be supposed that every case of split and ragged tails is one of tailrot. This is often a manifestation of a generally run-down condition, and in addition to the regular treatment for tailrot, also requires a general building-up under improved environment.

TREATMENT. The same treatment as that for white fungus is indicated. Dipping the tail in a 10% solution of peroxide of hydrogen is beneficial. Should the ends be hopelessly frayed, they may be eaten off by a 50% peroxide solution. On returning to the water the treated parts will be full of bubbles and will slough off in a few days, leaving a less sharp line than when cut with a knife.

**Consumption.** It is doubtful whether this is a real form of tuberculosis, but the wasted appearance of the suffering fish is such as to suggest it. The body becomes thin and so shrunken that the head appears to stand out from the body. Listlessness and loss of appetite are accompanying symptoms.

TREATMENT. This trouble seems to be deeply seated and is difficult to treat successfully. Unless the fish is a particularly valued one, it had best be destroyed. Place fish in an ample supply of green water or fresh water containing ½ ounce of sea salt to the gallon. Feed well on daphnia, chopped earthworms and soft bits of oyster. Unless living daphnia can be secured, a cure is scarcely worth attempting. Placing fish in a shallow muddy pond or tank may be beneficial.

**Dropsy.** The cause for this distressing complaint is not known, but it is considered to be due to a disordered liver. It is more apt to attack fancy fishes, and does so without apparent reference to the general health of the individual or the conditions under which it is kept. The manifestations are a swelling of the body and the scales standing out at an angle, producing a ruffled appearance.

TREATMENT. No cure is known for dropsy in fishes. They have been known to improve in an outdoor pool in summer, but on the approach of cool weather the symptoms returned with increased severity, death following as usual. There is a current belief that a few drops of digitalis in the water sometimes effects a cure. The author has never been able to verify a single such case. If the fish is valuable, its life may be prolonged by "tapping" it. This is done by inserting a fine needle beneath the skin, holding needle nearly flat to the body so that it again emerges in about a quarter inch. After repeating this at a number of points, enough liquid can be drawn off to relieve the fish, whose health and spirits do not seem to be particularly affected until shortly before death. The operation can be repeated when necessary.

**Swimming Bladder Trouble.** As before stated, highly bred, short bodied fishes are the more susceptible to this not uncommon disorder. Sometimes the victims are unable to rise from the bottom except by a violent effort, or again they may lie at the top of water at an angle, or even upside down. Scaleless varieties are the more susceptible, particularly the light colors. Reduced temperatures, even when brought about slowly, are responsible for most cases.

TREATMENT. No cure for swimming bladder trouble is known, but it is sometimes relieved by placing in very shallow, slightly salt warm water. If the fish is benefited it will always have to be kept in temperate water, preferably shallow.

It should be borne in mind that not all cases of loss of equilibrium are due to bladder trouble, but may be caused by accumulated gases resulting from indigestion. Treatment for constipation will relieve these cases, but such fishes will have to always be watched carefully thereafter.

**Gill Congestion.** There are two forms of gill congestion. The most important, generally known as "gill fever," is that attacking fry from two to five weeks old, and is easily responsible for more losses among goldfishes than all other causes combined. The gills become inflamed and swollen, presenting a distended appearance. Owing to the minuteness of the fish at this period a further observation is difficult except with a magnifying glass, which shows white threads like bristles sticking from the gill plates and openings. The disease is highly contagious, so that if one affected fish is found in a thousand, it is very difficult to save any of them, even though the sick fish be removed at once.

The other form affects mainly young fishes about 2 inches long. The gills swell rapidly, the infection spreading to the throat and producing a gray or whitish appearance. Without treatment, death is sure to come quickly. This was formerly a common disease among fancy fishes, but for some unknown reason has largely subsided, we hope permanently.

TREATMENT IN FRY. Innumerable experiments have been tried to cure this devastating disease, but without consistent results. So fatal is it considered by many expert fanciers that when they find a few affected fishes they destroy them, together with perhaps thousands of their fellows in the same tank without attempting a cure, throwing out bad and apparently good alike. The tank is then disinfected with strong salt water or more powerful germicides. The great trouble is that any chemical which will kill the vegetal parasites is also very apt to kill the delicate fry. However, it is almost certain a cure can be found, and it is a great pity to neglect an opportunity for experimenting. Cases have been cured, but exact data is lacking. Nevertheless we have two experimental points to start from. The first and more likely is with permanganate of potash. A well-known and thoroughly reliable breeder claims to have cured over one thousand fry by making the water a "pale purple" with this chemical, leaving the fish in it. To gauge a permanganate solution by color is most difficult. If one looks through 12 inches of water, the color will be 12 times as deep as through 1 inch. We would suggest trying ½ grain by weight to the gallon. This just flavors the water. (Tasting without swallowing will do no harm.) If fishes not yet affected are removed from their diseased companions and placed in such a solution for half a day, it is reasonably sure that many if not all could be saved, taking care, of course, not to return to an infected tank. Here it might be repeated to advantage that small fry should be lifted with a spoon and transferred carefully, avoiding pouring or any violent movements.

The other basis for experiment is with sulphate of copper in extremely diluted form—about 1 to 10,000 or weaker. Copper is fatal to all forms of life and therefore the treatment should only be temporary. We would suggest finding a strength that would kill the fry in an hour, then use that strength for 15-minute treatments for remaining fishes. Reports of cures by copper are current, but details are entirely lacking.

TREATMENT LARGER FISHES. This form of gill congestion has also been considered necessarily fatal, but such is not the case. The fish should be placed in strong salt water (3½ ounces to the gallon) until it rolls over from exhaustion. It is then transferred to a tank of gently running water which overflows. It appears as though the salt loosens the disease-germs and the running water carries them off while they are weakened. If this is a correct theory the cure could no doubt be hastened by pouring fresh water in the under side of the gills after the salt treatment, thus also helping to revive the fish. Treatment is repeated daily until improvement is noticed.

**Eye Inflammation.** The protruding eyes of telescope fishes are quite subject to injury, especially against the sides of cans in travel. Painstaking treatment can go far to relieve this condition and ward off permanent blindness.

TREATMENT. Make a saturated solution of boracic acid in tepid water. This is gently applied daily to the affected parts by a bit of absorbent cotton. The fish should be placed, if possible, in a large tank free from obstructions, that the injured eyes may not be further irritated.

**Ichthyopthirius.** This parasitic disease causes small whitish dots all over the fish. It is more apt to affect tropical fishes and has killed many fine specimens. Until recently it has been considered incurable, but two cures are now positively known. The fish should be placed in a plain glass jar and have the water changed (keeping temperature even) every eight hours, *disinfecting jar each time*. This takes a few days. It is claimed that plain water is as good as salt for this treatment, but the writer has had better success with brackish water, gradually increasing the strength and then as gradually reducing.

The second method of treatment is only suited to goldfishes. This consists of treatment in water in which two grains to the gallon of permanganate of potash have been dissolved. In a few days the old mucous coating of the fish peels off and leaves a new, healthy surface.

**Animal Parasites.** There are only three of these of sufficient importance to keepers of aquarium fishes to require mention. Food fishes and all wild species are more or less subject to numerous parasites, many of them serious or fatal. No doubt aquarium conditions are not favorable to their propagation; otherwise we would have more trouble in this direction on account of the large numbers of wild fishes being imported for aquarium purposes from all temperate and tropical parts of the earth.

**Leeches.** There is a small white leech about ¼ inch long occasionally introduced with living food (daphnia), more particularly in the spring. This attacks the bodies and gills, and if the fish is only a few weeks old the results are fatal. In an aquarium it is easily possible to see them on the glass and the breeder should be on the lookout for them. If any are discovered the fishes should be carefully removed to an aquarium where they can be kept under observation. The affected aquarium should be disinfected and the plant destroyed. These and larger leeches can be removed from the gills of larger fishes by the injection of strong salt water, or by the progressive salt water treatment previously described (page 144).

**Fish Lice.** While not very common, and seldom fatal, this crustacean parasite is very annoying. It is about ⅛ inch in diameter, very flat, of a nearly rounded outline and is quite translucent, but distinctly showing handsome iridescent colors under a good magnifying glass. They are free swimmers and are able to hold most tenaciously to their hosts. So tight is their hold that even after death by poisoning they still adhere where fastened. Owing to their translucent quality they are difficult to see. The fishes will scratch themselves much the same as in cases of the

"Itch," but one can notice small irritated spots, particularly on the tail and fins. The body, however, is not free from attack. The only treatment is to take the fish out of the water and scrape off the pests, for no chemical has been discovered that will cause them to let go, and no doubt if it would it would also kill the fish.

FIG. 98. FISH LOUSE (*Enlarged four diameters*)

**Flukes.** The detection of flukes is not easy without the aid of a miscroscope, the cause being a small parasite worm (*Gyrodactylus elegans*), chiefly infesting the gills. The fish breathes unnaturally fast, frequently coming to the surface of the water for air. The fins twitch and occasionally the fish will dash wildly and aimlessly about the tank, coming to a rest after exhaustion. Before death the body becomes thin and emaciated.

If the fish is not too far gone it will stand the formaldehyde treatment, which will usually effect a cure. Place the fish in a solution of 5 drops of formaldehyde to the quart of water. Add one drop per minute (per quart) until there are ten drops to each quart. Allow the fish to remain in this for ten minutes unless it shows signs of exhaustion sooner. Return to a thoroughly disinfected tank and repeat the operation next day. Two or three treatments will usually be sufficient. As a rule, all the fishes in a tank are affected, so if this parasite is positively identified, it will be well to treat every fish that has been exposed.

We can see no reason why the formaldehyde treatment should not be applied to any of the parasitic ailments. If carefully used it will at least cause no trouble.

**Diseases of Tropical Fishes.** Tropical fishes cannot stand the different chemicals and treatments recommended for goldfishes. The principal cause for their lack of condition is too low a temperature. If placed in a uniform warmer temperature, with one ounce of sea salt to each gallon of water, and fed up on daphnia or white worms (described on page 136) they will usually improve rapidly.

The most common disease among them is Ichthyopthirius, caused by an infusorian parasite burrowing into the skin, producing numberless white raised spots. This requires special and prompt treatment, carried out to the letter as described on page 153. The treatment is worthless unless the changes of water are made on time. Aside from chill this epidemic kills more tropical fishes than any other cause. It has long been considered incurable, but recent careful study by European scientists of the life history of the parasite has evolved the very simple treatment described, and there is no reason for further serious losses in this direction. This has been proven by the author and other American experimenters.

*Chapter Fourteen*

———

# Enemies of Aquarium Fishes

## INSECT ENEMIES OF FISHES

Among the troubles that beset the fish culturists, not the least are caused by insects and their larvæ. This applies both to the propagators of food fishes and those interested in fancy aquarium pets. We use the term "insect" here in its popular sense and not according to exact scientific definition.

Some of these enemies are much more readily detected than others, but most of them may enter the rearing tanks when so small that detection is practically impossible. Wire screen or netting will keep out those that fly, or a large enemy in the water can be separated from daphnia or other living food by passing the "catch" through a fine wire gauze under water, but despite these precautions it is essential in the summer season to be ever on the lookout for any of the pests which may have gotten by our keenest observation. Fortunately for the aquarist there are not many kinds of insect enemies with which he is actively concerned. There are only four, three of these being larvæ. While the others are none the less savage or fatal they are not so often met with, or else are so easily detected that they are not such serious factors with which to reckon. With the aid of illustrations made from specimens, mostly living, we will proceed to give descriptions of the four arch-enemies in the order of their destructiveness, and follow on with the others, adhering to the same plan as far as possible.

**Water Tiger.** This is the larva of the Predaceous Diving Beetle (*Dytiscus*), itself also a very powerful but easily detected enemy. The Water Tiger is easily the most rapacious, savage and insatiable enemy of

FIG. 99. WATER TIGER (*Life size*)

young fishes. It does not wait for its prey to pass nearby, but adopts business-like methods of going after its unwary victims. The flat head is furnished with a strong pair of hollow mandibles, through which it sucks enough blood to kill its victim and then wantonly goes after another. In this way a single individual may kill an entire hatching of fish over night. This larva can usually be recognized by its spindle-shaped body, flat, strong head, pale translucent brown color and a steady progress through the water, coming to the surface frequently to breath a moment through the rear end. Although growing to a length of 2½ inches, at which time it attacks larger fishes and any small aquatic animals, it is the smaller sizes with which we are principally concerned. From a length of ¼ to 1 inch they are not so easily seen but are capable of doing great mischief.

**Spearmouth.** While not quite so common as the Water Tiger its habits are similar and it grows to an even larger size, reaching 3 inches.

FIG. 100.  SPEARMOUTH (*Life size*)

The body is thicker and the mandibles are shorter. From the aquarist's standpoint both these larvæ could be classed as one. The Spearmouth is the larva of the large Water Scavenger Beetle (*Hydrophilus*).

**Dragon-Fly Larvæ.** Almost everyone who raises fish outdoors is familiar with these unpleasant individuals. There are two reasons why they are difficult to altogether avoid. When newly hatched they are very small and will go through the same strainer as daphnia; furthermore the

FIGS. 101 AND 102.  NYMPH OF DRAGON FLY AND LARVA CATCHING YOUNG FISH
(*Life size*)

mother Dragon Fly (*Odonata*) is an excellent flier and may deposit her eggs in any body of water that provides proper facilities for her needs. These larvæ live more by their cunning than by any agility as swimmers. Waiting on a dirty pond-bottom or attached to sticks, aquatic grass or other object they mark time until a victim comes within close reach. Then they quickly pounce forward, extending a vicious, pincer-like organ called the "mask," rarely missing the object of attack. The method of propulsion through the water is peculiar, being brought about by a series of expulsions of water from the hinder end. This enables them to make a very sudden leap towards a victim. The "mask" shown in Figure 102 when not in use is folded before and under the head. Dragon Fly larvæ are strictly carnivorous at all periods and will attack any pond creature reasonably near its own size. If given enough time a single individual will destroy an entire hatching of fishes, growing by what it feeds upon so as to be able to devour the remaining fishes which are also becoming larger.

**Water Boatmen and Back Swimmers** (*Corixidæ* and *Notonectidæ*) are found everywhere in still or slow-moving water. They are especially plentiful in ponds containing vegetal decomposition and filth, not because

FIG. 103.   WATER BOATMAN (*Slightly enlarged*)

they like these, but because such conditions are favorable to the growth of other creatures making good food for themselves. In daphnia pools from midsummer until the end of the season Water Boatmen are frequently found. Care should be exercised in picking them out of a net, as their bite is very severe, the sensation being described as akin to the sting of a hornet. Young fishes fall easy prey to these predatory insects. They are usually easy to see on account of their jerky, jumping movements, which are produced by use of their oar-like swimming legs. They are obliged to occasionally come to the surface of the water to take air, which gives an opportunity of seeing them. Both Water Boatmen and Back Swimmers fly clumsily at night, and are often attracted to electric lights. In some Southern climates they occur in enormous numbers. They are gathered by the natives, dried and sold as fishfood under the name of "African Flies."

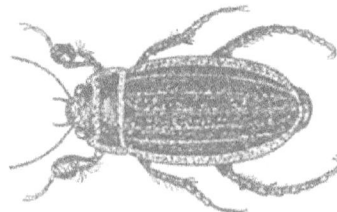

FIG. 104.   PREDACEOUS DIVING BEETLE (*Life size*)

**Predaceous Diving Beetle** (*Dytiscus*). Fortunately this beetle is of such size that it can scarcely escape notice, especially as it is obliged to come to the surface for air, which it takes at the end of the abdomen.

It is rapacious in extreme degree and is a good swimmer. A large specimen was once placed in an aquarium for observation. It so quickly attacked a goldfish that the scales fell in a small shower and the fish died before it could be rescued. The males may be distinguished by the ball-like development on the forelegs. They are usually of such a dark brown as to appear black, but are sometimes marked or bordered with yellow.

**Water Scavenger Beetle** (*Hydrophilidæ*). We mention this beetle here because of its resemblance to the large predaceous diving beetle. It swims differently, using its legs alternately, while the diving beetle moves opposite pairs together. The Scavenger Beetle is also different in that

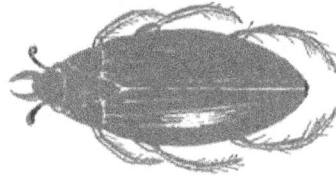

FIG. 105. WATER SCAVENGER BEETLE (*Life size*)

it breathes at the surface from the mouth. Instead of long antennæ they have palpi looking like club-shaped antennæ. This beetle lives chiefly on decomposing vegetal and animal matter, although taking soft living plants such as Nitella. It has been claimed to be predaceous but there is doubt about their attacking fishes. They have been kept in aquaria with them without doing damage. On general principles, however, it is best to exclude all beetles, large or small.

**Giant Water Bug** (*Belostomatidæ*) also known as the Electric Light Bug is one of our common bugs both on land and in water. Flying clumsily but strongly before electric lights, or patiently awaiting a victim at the bottom of a pond, the bug is one and the same. They are fiercely

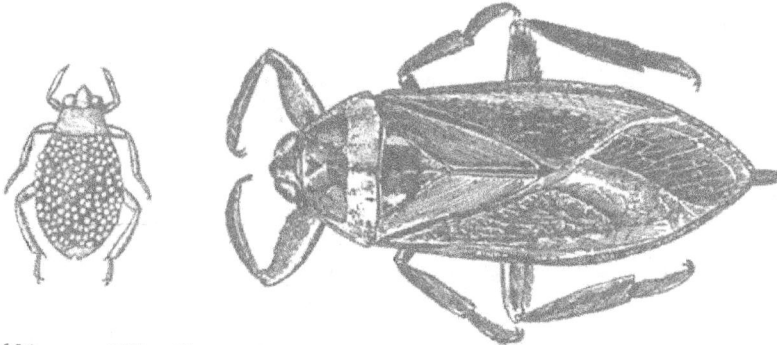

FIGS. 106 AND 107. GIANT WATER BUGS (*B. serphus and B. americana*) THE SMALLER A MALE WITH EGGS ON BACK (*Life size*)

predaceous and very powerful. The smaller sizes are the more to be feared, as they are not so easily seen. While this is a vicious enemy, it is not one that frequently gets into the fish tank except by flight and as only the adults fly they are easily detected by their size. In large outdoor rearing pools or lakes they are a very practical menace. The colors range from clear, dark reddish brown to dull olive. With some of the smaller genera, *Serphus* and *Zaitha* it was supposed that females lay the eggs on their own backs. Some writers have accepted this popular misconception without investigation. It has been fully established that the female fastens her eggs on the back of an unwilling male, who only submits to the indignity after a struggle.

**Water Scorpion** (*Nepidæ*). We have here another of the insects spending most of its time in aquatic dirt and rubbish awaiting innocent passers-by who, for their unwariness, will pay with their lives. Water

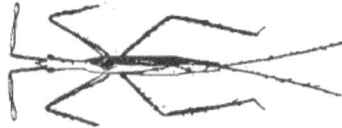

FIG. 108. WATER SCORPION (*Life size*)

scorpions depend upon their obscurity to get near their prey, which they quickly seize with their modified forelegs. While this insect is common enough to the naturalist, it is not one with which the fish-culturist need be seriously concerned.

**Whirligig Beetle** (*Gyrinidæ*). This well-known beetle is common to nearly all slow-flowing streams and pools, keeping up a perpetual movement on the surface of the water, on which they glide apparently without effort. On account of its size and shape it is often called the

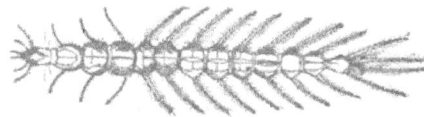

FIGS. 109 AND 110. WHIRLIGIG BEETLE AND LARVA (*Enlarged three diameters*)

coffee bug. The breeder of fishes is not harrassed by this insect but occasionally an aquarist will be tempted to introduce one in a fish-tank. This is a mistake. They are predaceous and can inflict a severe bite. The larva, which is not so well known, is also predaceous.

**Water Strider** (*Hydrometridæ*). Another of the predaceous aquatic insects is the Water Strider. Quite as well known as the Whirligig Beetle, it adopts somewhat the same methods of securing its prey, darting

FIG. 111. WATER STRIDER (*Life size*)

over the surface of the water, waiting for the stream to bring down some helpless insect victim that has fallen overboard. They are capable of catching young fishes which come to the surface.

**Mites** (*Hydrachna*). These odd-looking little balls of intense red are sometimes placed in small tropical aquaria with fishes. This is in-

FIG. 112. WATER MITE (*Enlarged about four diameters*)

advisable, as they are parasitic. It is doubtful whether they actually kill their host. They are common in the still water of lily ponds.

**Hydra.** Although Hydra is not an insect we include it here as an important enemy of young fishes. *Hydra* is a polyp which attaches itself to plants, stones or the sides of the aquarium. Being thread-like in appearance it is apt to be overlooked, especially by the inexperienced. It

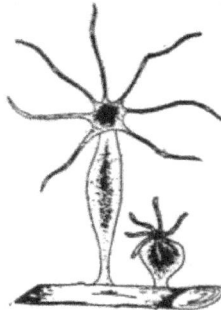

FIG. 113. HYDRA (*Greatly enlarged*)

is usually introduced with living food caught from pools. The spores are so small as to be unrecognizable, and therefore they cannot be avoided. The animal itself has a cylindrical body with from 5 to 12 tentacles surrounding a mouth. The shape varies so amazingly that an accurate description is impossible. The two figures shown in Figure 113 are of the same individual. When alarmed the tentacles are entirely withdrawn, making recognition still more difficult.

They rapidly deplete an aquarium of daphnia and newly hatched fishes. When a school of fry under 5-16 inch long is disappearing without apparent cause, it will be well to take a sharp look for some harmless looking hydra.

Hydra possess a poison which quickly stupifies their prey, and to fish large enough to eat the hydra this poison doubtless has an unpleasant taste. There is no fish known which will eat them. To get rid of this pest, remove all fish, snails, etc., from the tank and place in it a solution of permanganate of potassium of a strength of 3 grains to the gallon of aquarium water. Allow this to stand for two days, change water and replace fish. This treatment will not kill plants.

If no small living food be placed in the aquarium, hydra will in a few weeks be starved.

One experimenter has claimed that by raising the water temperature to 110° Fahrenheit for a few minutes the hydra will all be killed, while the plants will not be affected.

## LARGER ENEMIES OF FISHES

It should not be understood that the foregoing are the only serious enemies of pet fishes. In the greenhouse, outdoor pool, or even the library, misfortune is liable to descend in various guises. Chief among these are the cat, rat, muskrat, snake, heron, kingfisher and small boy. Fishes are also taken by the large frog, sandpiper, horned owl, crayfish, and blackbird. The latter specializes on picking out the eyes of telescope fishes if the water is near enough to the edge of tank for him to reach them.

*Chapter Fifteen*

———

# Aquatic Plants for the Aquarium, Tank and Pond

## AQUARIUM PLANTS

Whether aquaria are kept for scientific study or for the enjoyment of the beautiful, aquatic plants will always be found a useful—if not indispensable—adjunct. The fact that plants give off oxygen under the influence of light has been mentioned at several other places in this volume, but the principle is so important that it would be difficult to over-emphasize it. Aquaria containing good plant growth may be tightly covered and if placed in a good light they will support a fair number of fishes, the life-giving oxygen being supplied exclusively by the plants.

That the roots of healthy aquatic plants absorb the products of decomposition in the bottom of the aquarium is an established fact. When an aquarium has been established for some time, the sand has become a little dirty and the plants have spread so that the roots of some are against the glass, a close observation will show a condition similar to that pictured in figure 114. The sand near the roots is distinctly whiter than that beyond their reach.

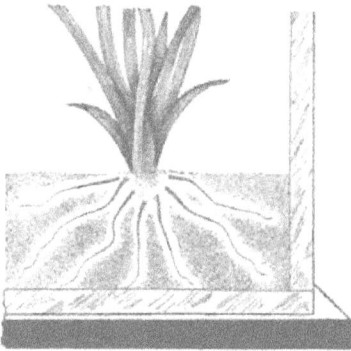

Fig. 114.  Absorption by Plant Roots

No arguments need be put forward to establish the esthetic value of plant life in the household aquarium or the pool in summer. Without them no one could attempt to reproduce the effects of Nature. So well understood is the value of aquatic plants that aquarists are constantly on the lookout for anything new which might enhance the beautiful results already achieved. Occasionally something of real merit is found. We are pleased to be able to list several of these newer species here, together with all the better-known favorites. Only those plants having been proven satisfactory are described, but naturally in such a large range it will be found that the same conditions are not suited to all.

It is a good general rule to select young plants. They transplant better and sooner adapt themselves to new conditions. If old plants are used the dying leaves should be removed.

Much discussion has been brought out as to the best methods of planting, principally as to whether to use soil, sand or pebbles, or whether, in some cases, planting is necessary at all. Success has been attained in

FIG. 115. SAGITTARIA NATANS (*Reduced one-third*)

many ways. The author believes in the use of coarse sand, either with or without a mixture of pebbles, this latter being a matter of taste only. The disadvantage of pebbles is that they are likely to get into a siphon and clog it. Pebbles without sand collect dirt which cannot be removed. There are no experienced advocates of fine sand. It packs too hard for the roots to penetrate. If soil is to be used in pots or otherwise, an inverted piece of turf is excellent. It is compact, comparatively clean and is not likely to turn sour. In all cases soil is covered with sand or gravel to prevent washing out. As to other points in reference to planting, the use of fertilizer, etc., the reader is referred to page 14.

## SAGITTARIA

This plant in the three described species comprises the most important group of aquarium plants. It has not the commercial importance of Cabomba, because the latter is convenient to use in small bunches in the "fish globes" seen everywhere; but to those who plant in real aquaria, Sagittaria receives first consideration.

It is a plant with bright green slender leaves of grass-like form, so that it is popularly referred to by aquarists as "grass." It takes its name from the arrow-shaped summer-leaves which stand above the water, Sagittarius being the sign of the archer in the Zodiac. The white flowers are the shape of miniature cups, with yellow centres, standing above the water. Although seeds are formed, the principal means of reproduction is by runners. Small tubers or corms are also formed among the roots, particularly in crowded situations. These produce plants.

A number of species are distributed throughout the United States, many of them quite large, frequently with leaves extending well above the water. These are only useful as bog plants and even for this purpose they are difficult to transplant successfully. The majority of wild Sagittarias are not suited to the aquarium.

There has been much discussion as to the classification of Sagittaria into a number of doubtful species. Environment makes such radical changes in its appearance that there is a tendency to claim new species when there is in reality no botanical distinction.

*Sagittaria natans,* known also as Ribbon Arrowhead, is perhaps the most important of the group to the aquarist. It is of moderate size and is suited to the average aquarium on that account. Multiplying rapidly, growing the entire year, supplying a large amount of oxygen and thriving under varying conditions, it is very valuable. When an aquarium is uprooted on account of Sagittaria or Vallisneria becoming too thick, it will always be found that the sand is not foul-smelling, showing that the roots purify the soil.

Fig. 116. Giant Sagittaria (*Reduced one-half*)

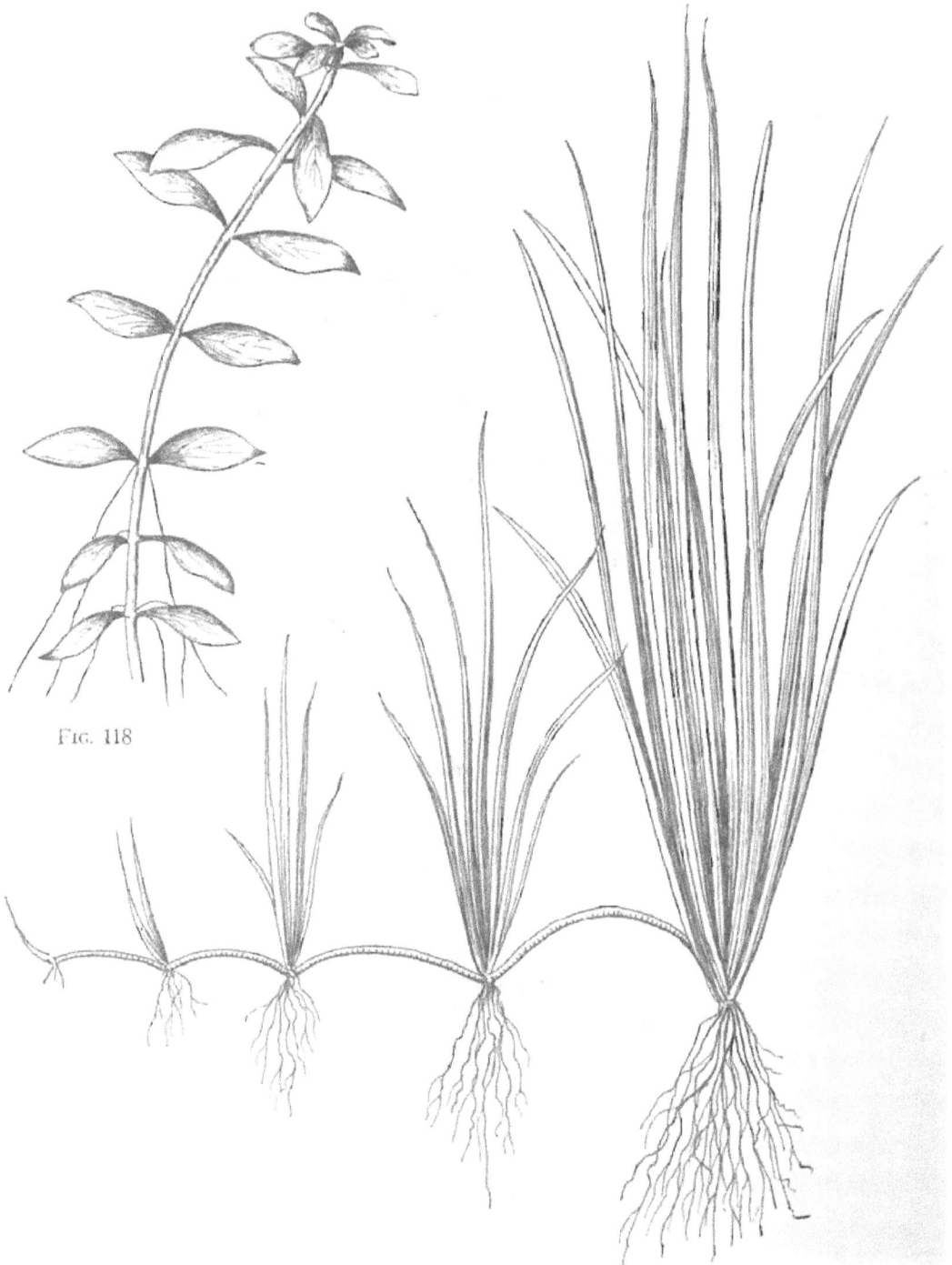

FIG. 117.   SAGITTARIA SUBULATA [*Pusilla*]  (*Natural size*)
FIG. 118.   WILD LUDWIGIA (*L. glandulosa*)

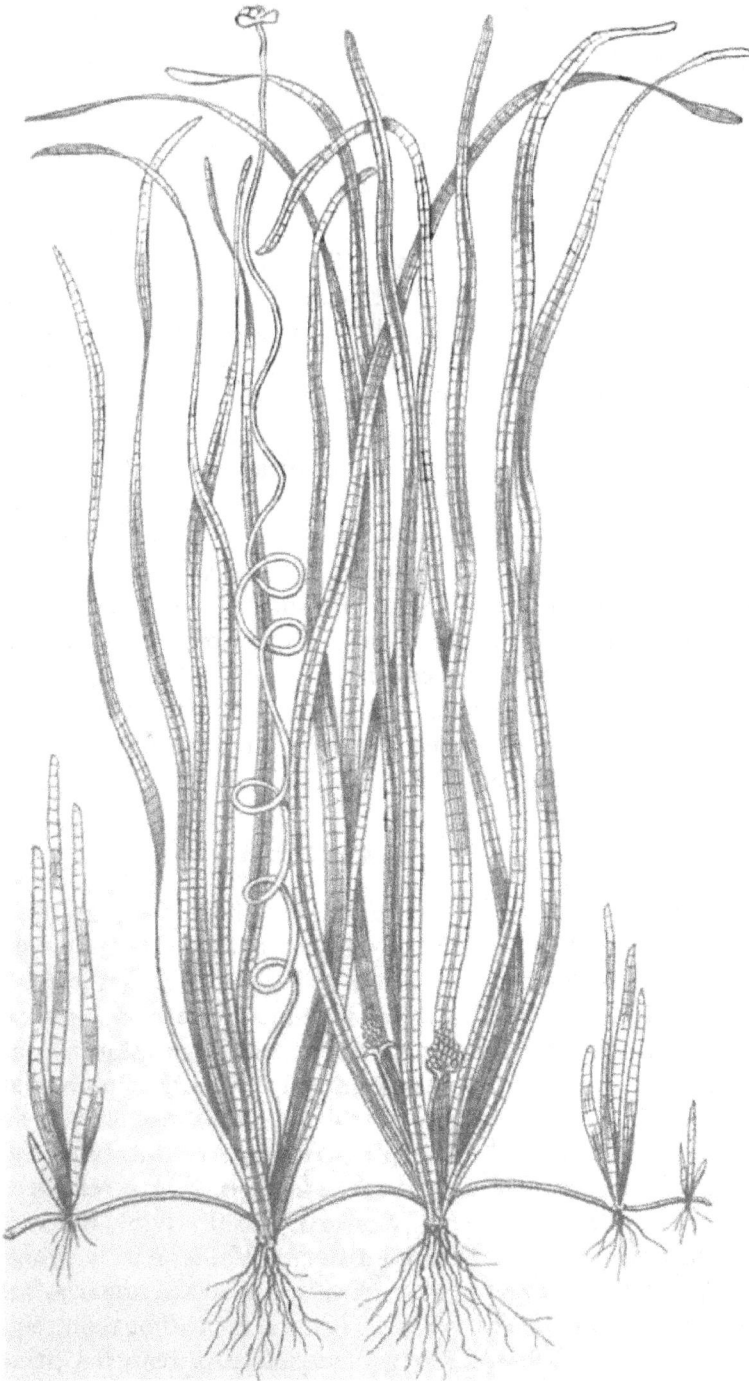

FIG. 119. VALLISNERIA (*Reduced one-half or more*)

*Sagittaria gigantea* is believed to be a cultivated variety of *S. sagittaefolia*. Its leaves are broad and stocky, having a decidedly substantial quality and is one of the easiest plants to succeed with. A healthy specimen is quite light in weight and on this account must be well planted with roots extending in different directions. Once established it holds well and will stand more rough usage from contact with fish-nets, etc., than any other aquatic. Height, 10 to 20 inches. It is better suited in appearance to a large aquarium than a small one, but a single Giant Sagittaria in the centre of a smaller tank, surrounded by some of its lesser cousins makes a good effect. So popular has this plant deservedly become that dealers have difficulty in supplying it, and they are always ready to buy up any surplus stock.

*Sagittaria subulata* has recently come into popularity on account of its small size. Fanciers of tropical fishes, now becoming so numerous, generally use several small aquaria, and in order to produce a symmetrical picture it is necessary to introduce plants of suitable proportion. The leaves are of a rather dark shade of green, narrow and thick through, presenting a strong, wiry appearance. *Sagittaria subulata* grows from 3 to 7 inches, the stronger the light, the shorter the leaves. It multiplies rapidly from runners and soon carpets the bottom of the aquarium, making either a good spawning bed or a miniature thicket in which young fishes may hide from cannibalistic parents. Can be had from some dealers and is collected in the coastwise States from New York to Alabama. It is incorrectly known as *S. pusilla*.

## VALLISNERIA

Vallisneria (*Vallisneria spiralis*) is another of the grass-like plants, having strap-shaped leaves of the same breadth their entire length. It is known as Channel Grass, Eel Grass and Tape Grass. Appearing somewhat like Sagittaria, it has a distinct individuality of its own. The leaves are of a lighter green and have a more translucent quality than Sagittaria. Also the plant tends more to rise vertically in undulating lines, which produces a very pleasant decorative effect, being of a less spreading contour than Vallisneria. The leaves may also be identified by the margins being of a slightly different shade of green. By reflected light the margins appear the darker, but if held up to the light, the centre is the darker when viewed by transmitted light. Vallisneria is probably without a superior as an oxygenator. For use in large aquaria, particularly where artistic effects are striven for, it is without an equal. The aquarium shown in colors as our frontispiece is featured principally by this plant, although printing ink falls far short of giving an adequate idea of the radiant, light silky green color of the leaves themselves.

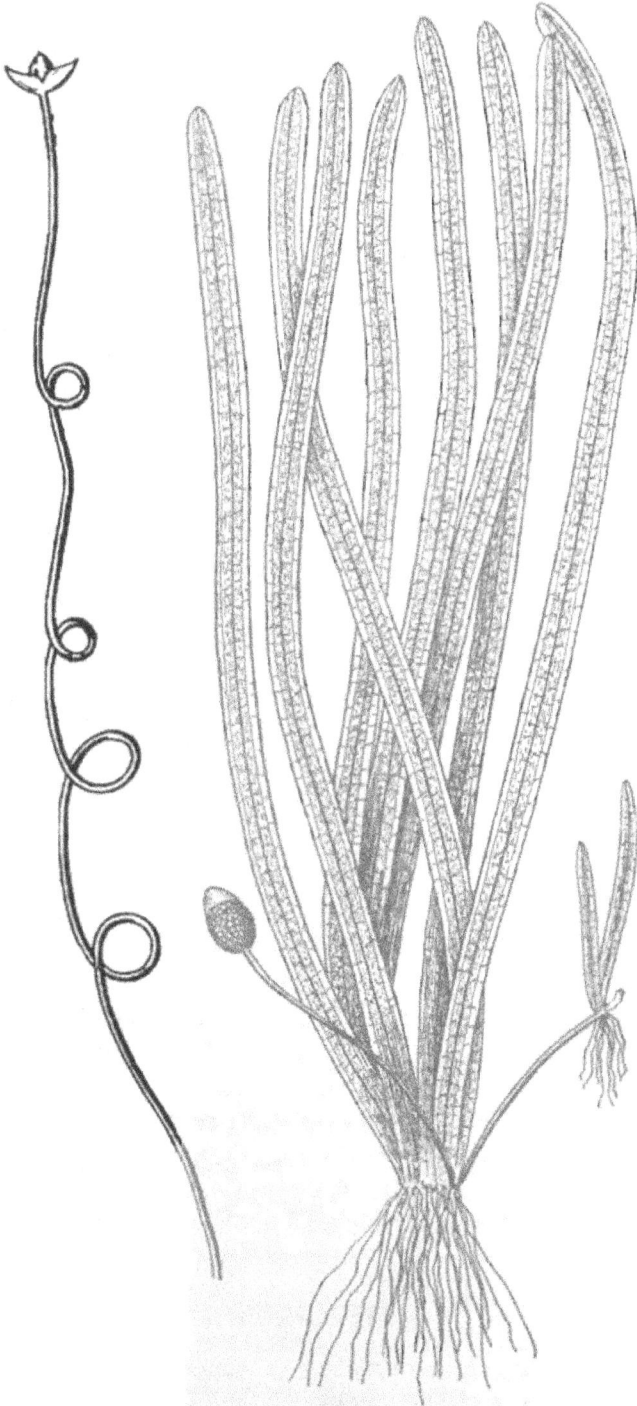

Fig. 120.   Giant Vallisneria (*Reduced two-thirds*)

For some years American aquarists depended upon plants gathered locally from rivers, creeks, mill races, etc. Owing to the long-established habit of dying down to the tuft in winter, the plant had a strong tendency to keep to the schedule, even when kept in a warm aquarium over winter. In order to overcome this difficulty a search was made for a stock growing in a climate without severe winters. This plan was completely successful. In 1910 we were fortunate enough to secure a single small plant from Italy which, by careful propagation and distribution among leading aquarists, has now multiplied itself into the many thousands. There is every reason why it should establish itself in further favor among those having large or fairly deep aquaria. It grows and multiplies constantly and the runners lie close to the bottom, not requiring to be pushed down like young Sagittaria plants. Contrary to the advice of some writers, we advise against deep planting. It is important that the crown be not covered, but just at the surface. The plant is not well suited to small aquaria, as it grows from 18 to 36 inches, according to conditions. If closely confined it is likely to get into a tangled mass whenever a fish has to be caught. Allowed to rise to the surface and then extend horizontally on it for some distance it produces a luxuriant picture. Rising from either end of the aquarium and trained over the surface towards the centre, Vallisneria makes the best of frames to show off the more brilliant beauties of the fishes. The sexes are separate in Vallisneria, fertilization taking place in a peculiar manner. The female flower, small, cup-shaped and white, floats at the end of a long spiral scape on the surface of the water. The male flower on another plant comes only a short distance from the crown. It is a case containing pollen balls. When the case splits the pollen floats to the top, where, by the action of wind, insects or other chance, fertilization is accomplished. Few of these plants in the aquarium start from seed.

For one or two large plants to dominate the centre of the aquarium, nothing is better than Giant Vallisneria, now brought from the Southern States by some of our leading dealers. Its leaves are as wide as those of Giant Sagittaria, but much longer, varying from two to four feet, according to conditions. This variety is also a constant grower. Stocks of Vallisneria or Sagittaria suited to the aquarium do not do well outdoors in direct sun, the old leaves dying and the new ones only developing a few inches in length.

## ANACHARIS

Known to American aquarists as Anacharis and in Europe as Elodea it is also popularly called Ditchmoss, Water Pest, Water Thyme, and Babington's Curse. Some of the rather uncomplimentary titles are due to a

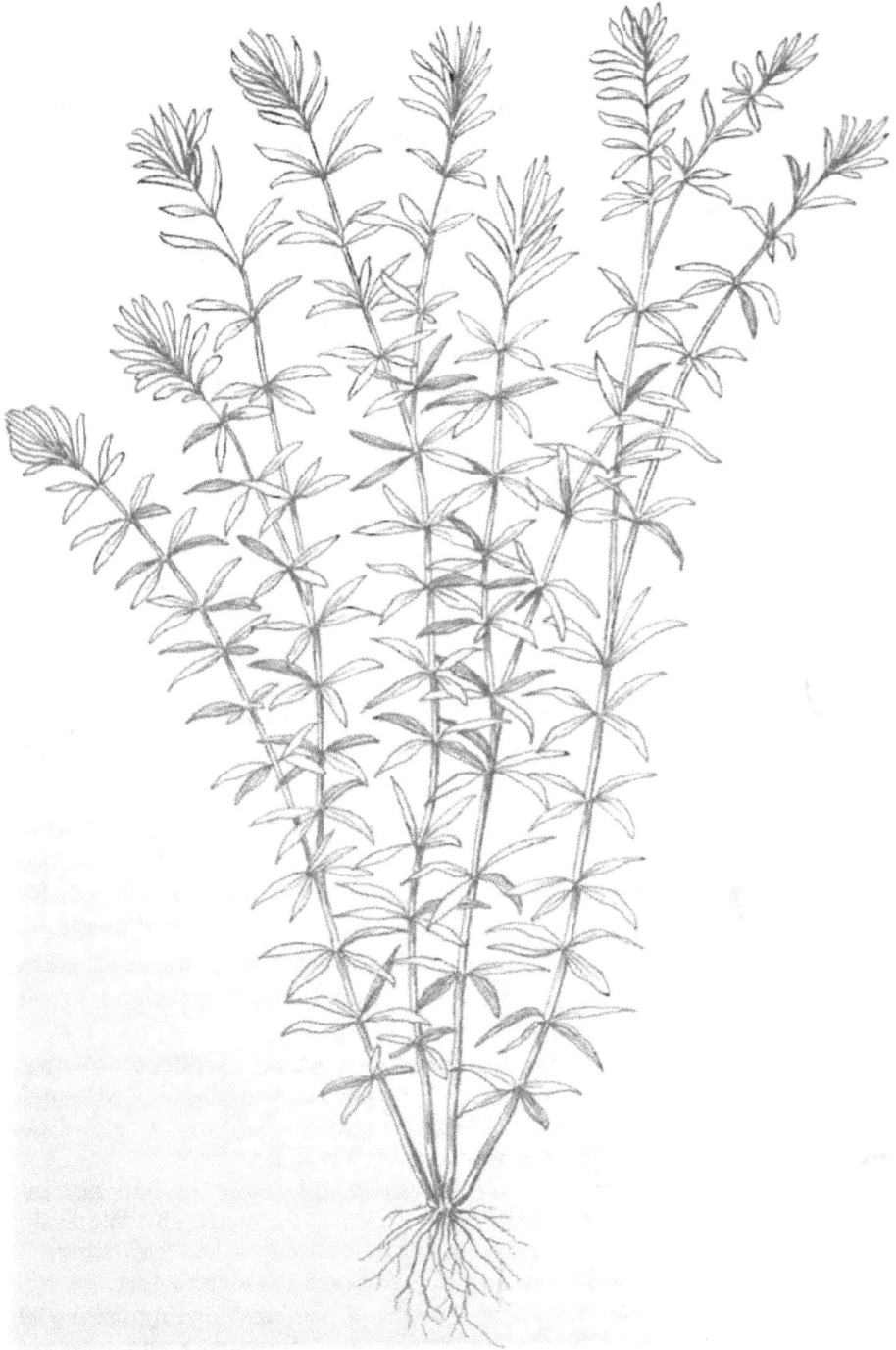

FIG. 121. WILD ANACHARIS (*Life size*)

characteristic which, at least in the aquarium, should be considered a favorable point—that is—rapid growth. It may generally be taken for granted that if an aquatic plant is thriving, it is doing good work for the aquarium. In form it is moss-like, the leaves growing on a fragile stem, the entire plant being completely submerged at all periods. Several species are distributed throughout the United States and Southern Canada. A cultivated variety, probably derived from A. canadensis, is considerably larger than the common local specimens to be found. The closeness of the leaves together depends upon the strength of light in which the plant is kept, the difference being so pronounced that sections of the same plant divided and kept in strong and weak light conditions will soon appear so different as to be scarcely recognizable as the same stock. The plant grows several feet in length, sending off occasional shoots and a few roots at random that reach down into the soil. In the aquarium it is best to only retain from 6 to 15 inches of the newer growth, cutting away the old ends, re-bunching and re-planting. Planting is a matter of little concern to Anacharis. In a well-lighted aquarium, where it will not be nibbled at by large fishes, it will prosper whether planted or not, particularly if not kept too warm. Anacharis is an excellent oxygenator and is a good plant for the beginner or for those who want to add variety to their aquarium vegetation. Allowed to grow into a mass it forms perfect hiding places for young fishes, as it does not grow so close but that they may move about in it. To be had of dealers generally.

## CABOMBA

Commercially there is no doubt Cabomba is the leading aquatic plant. Its finely-cut, fan-like, bright green leaves make a very good first impression, although it does not long look so well in the aquarium. It is brittle and the fishes if active soon pick it to shreds. Even though this does not occur, it becomes long and spindly. Enormous quantities are gathered from ponds, some of them purposely planted, from Maryland to North Carolina.

The plant under natural conditions is a good producer of oxygen, but in the aquarium its activity in this respect is doubtful. Although its use is recommended by many writers, the author's experience and observation lead him to take exception to their views.

*Cabomba caroliniana* is the species usually sold in bunches in pet shops. It is well known as Washington Grass, Fanwort, and Watershield. In habit it is purely aquatic and propagates mainly by branching. The stems under natural conditions attain a length of several feet.

*Cabomba roseafolia* is a species whose principal distinguishing characteristic consists of a distinct reddish hue on the stems and lower sides of the leaves. It too is a handsome plant when first introduced.

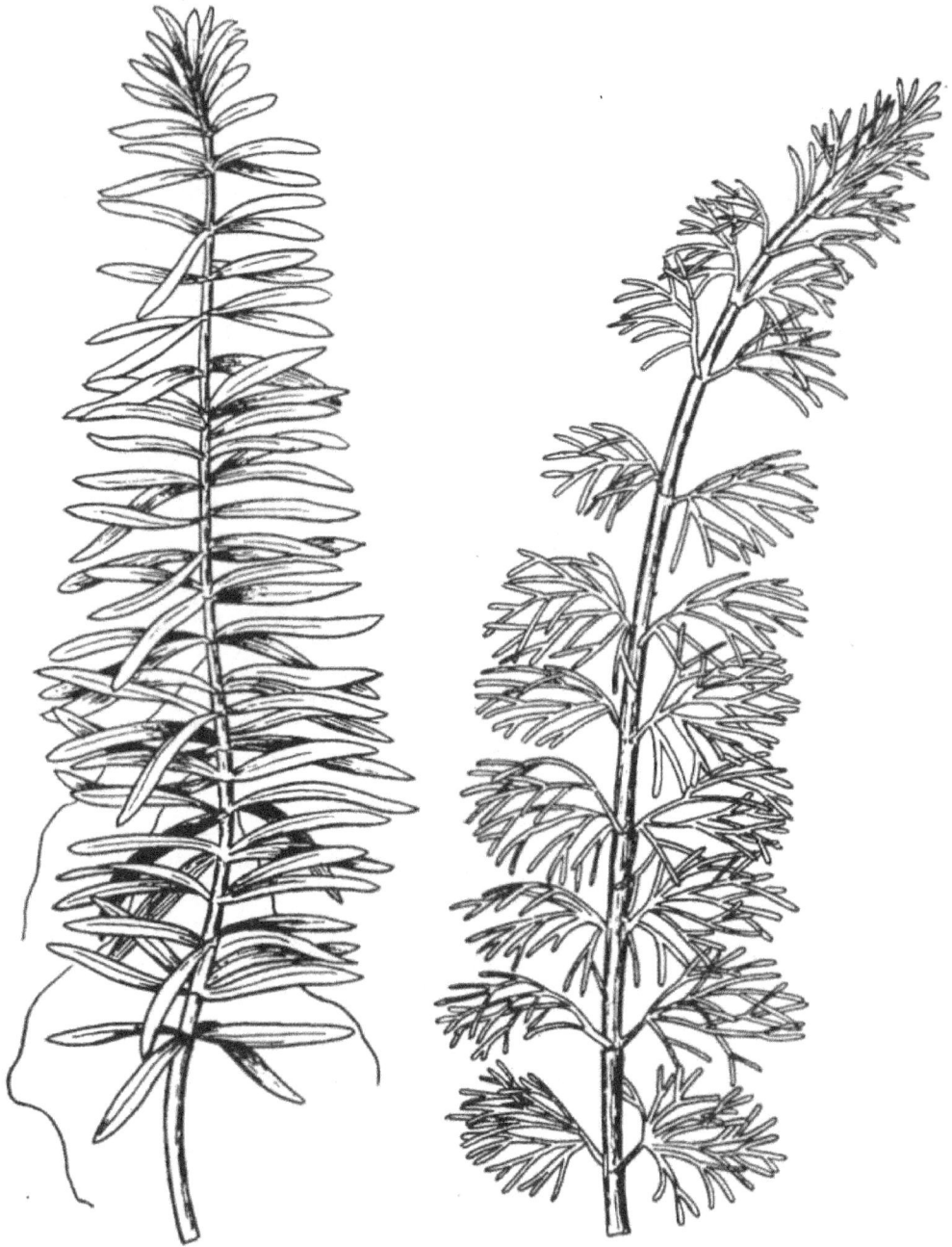

FIG. 122. CULTIVATED ANACHARIS (*Life size*)
FIG. 123. CABOMBA (*Life size*)

## MYRIOPHYLLUM

Here we have another plant which at first looks well in the aquarium but which deteriorates rapidly. It has, however, a strong redeeming feature, the very finely divided hair-like leaves being ideal for receiving the spawn of goldfishes. For this purpose it has grown more and more into favor. It is used either in the bunches as they are sold, or made into a spawning-ring as shown on page 51. As a spawn-receiving plant it has one advantage over Water Hyacinth in that the individual pieces may be spread out so as to give all the eggs a similiar amount of sun, whereas with Hyacinth one side is usually much more protected than the other, making the eggs hatch at different times. Before using Myriophyllum to spawn on it should be well washed off by moving it about in clear water, being careful to remove all insects, snails and snail eggs. When spawning is finished the plant had as well be thrown away.

There are a number of generally distributed species throughout America, all having the same general characteristics, but some are better than others as "spawning grass" on account of closer and longer leaves. They are all popularly known as Water Milfoil.

*Myriophyllum verticillatum.* This is the best American species and is found in both shallow and deep ponds throughout the United States and Lower Canada. Its leaves are dense and crowded, making an excellent spawning plant. *M. nietschei* is a cultivated variety of the same, the leafy filaments developing from 1½ to 3 inches in length.

*Myriophyllum proserpinacoides* or Parrot's Feather is a partially submerged form which should be allowed to creep on the surface of the water, where its blue-green, feathery leaves display a charm exclusively their own. Does well in the greenhouse or established on the edges of partially shaded lakes, where it becomes very robust and looks strikingly beautiful. The roots are not winter-killed. On account of growing so rapidly it requires too much attention in a small aquarium.

## CERATOPHYLLUM

Hornwort, as it is generally known, is mentioned here on account of its resemblance to Myriophyllum, for which it is sometimes gathered. It is an extremely poor aquarium plant, being very brittle and liable to rapid decomposition. Besides its characteristic of being fragile it may also be recognized by having practically no roots, absorption taking place in the leaves.

It is found principally in ponds and slow moving streams, where it washes about freely with the current.

## UTRICULARIA

Many species of Bladderwort are distributed throughout the Temperate Zone. They have somewhat the appearance of the finely-divided leaves of Myriophyllum, but may be identified by the small bladders dotted throughout. Our figure 125 of *U. vulgaris* gives a good idea of the general type. They thrive in the aquarium if given plenty of strong light. The Bladderworts are carnivorous plants, trapping the microscopic lower forms of animal life in their bladders, where they are digested. It has been claimed that they can trap extremely small fishes,

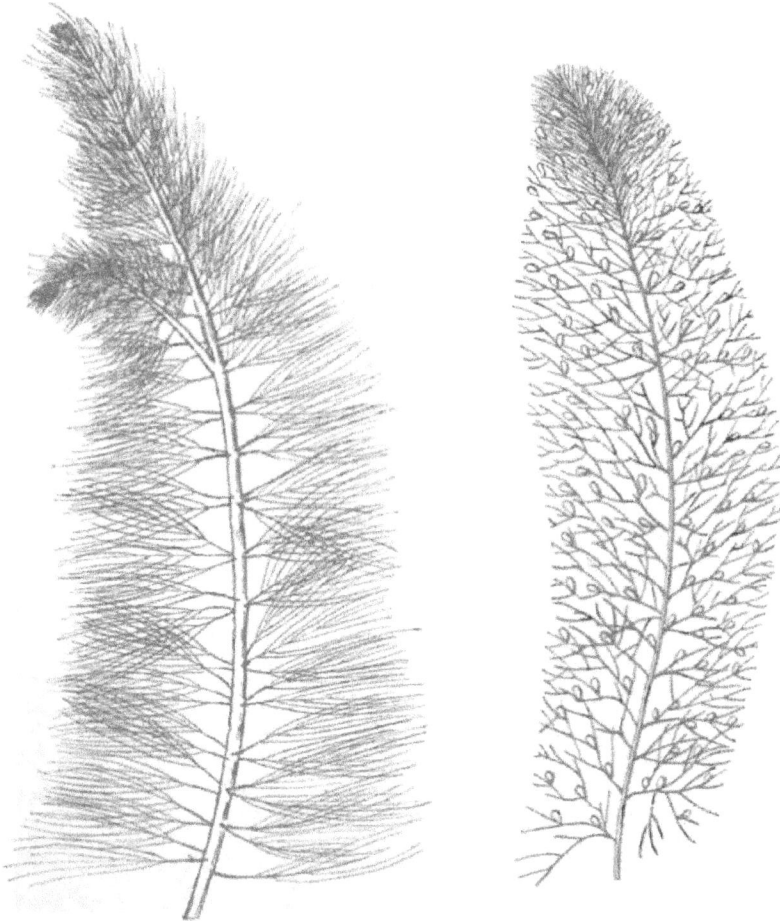

Fig. 124.   Myriophyllum nietschei (*Slightly reduced*)
Fig. 125.   Greater Bladderwort (*Reduced one-third*)

such as the young of Dwarf Gourami, but we do not know that this has ever been definitely proven. There can be no doubt, however, that the plant *does* take living food which would be useful to young fishes, and to that extent is objectionable in the aquarium.

## HAIR GRASS

*Eriocaulon septangulare,* a dainty hair-like aquatic of recent introduction, fills small tropical aquaria in an agreeable manner. It is another
of those plants forming a useful adjunct to the breeding of tropical fishes.
It multiplies rapidly from short runners and is a good oxygenator. Of

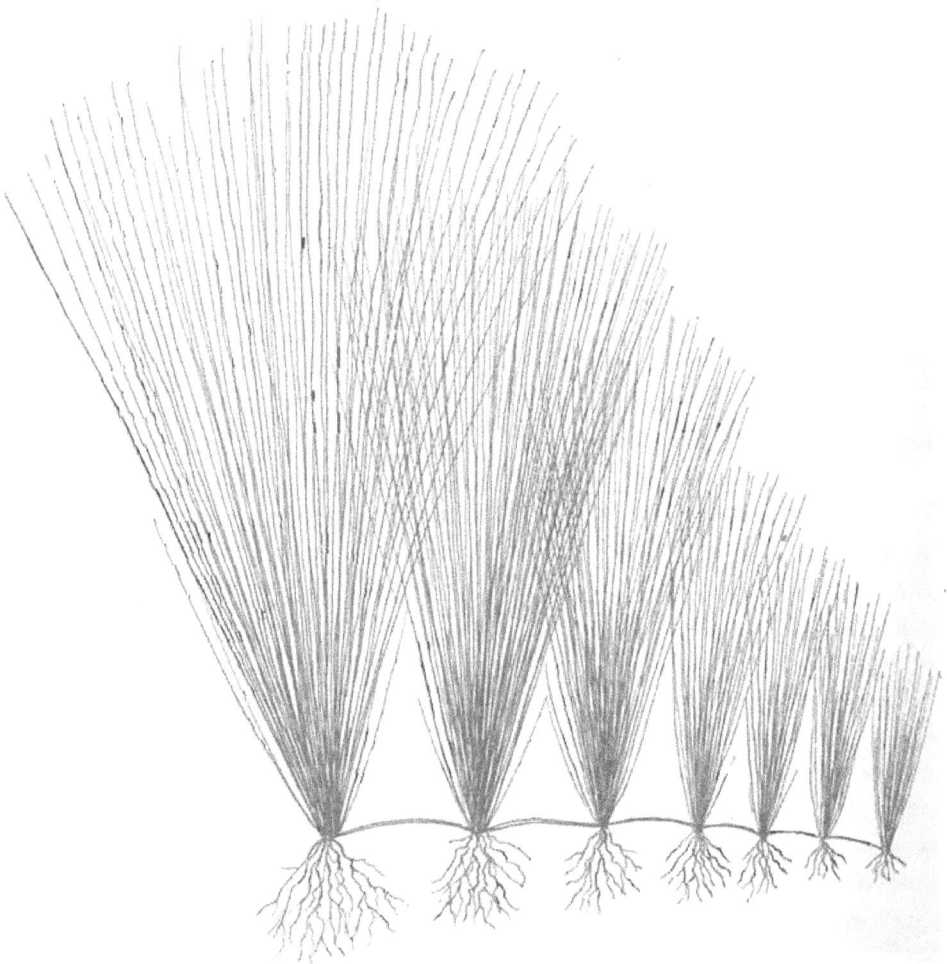

FIG. 126. HAIR GRASS (*Life size*)

a pleasing shade of light green it makes a contrasting group among other
plants in a large aquarium, but it shows to best advantage in a small
aquarium by itself. It grows from 3 to 8 inches and is native to ponds in
the Middle Atlantic and Southern States.

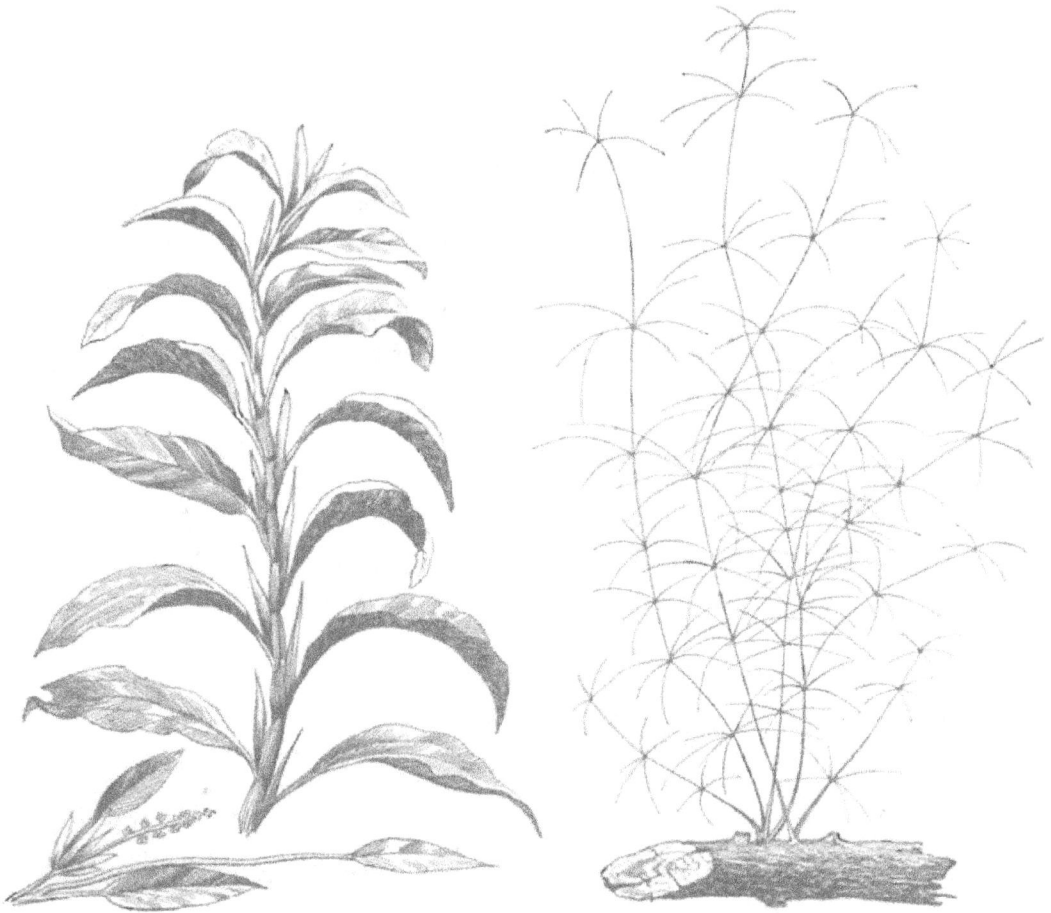

FIG. 127. POTAMOGETON DENSUS (*Reduced one-half*)
FIG. 128. NITELLA GRACILIS (*Reduced one-third*)

## POTAMOGETON

In strong contrast to the foregoing dainty plants is *Potamogeton densus*, or pondweed. As will be seen from figure 127, these leaves are broad and robust. In color they are a bright green. This variety is said to be of European origin but is now common in ponds in the United States. If established in soil in flat pots it flourishes in a well-lighted aquarium. Pieces collected from the wild may be introduced by fastening into the sand. They present a very attractive appearance and will last for quite a time, but should only be regarded as temporary and when the leaves begin to turn yellow should be removed. There are many widely distributed species of Potamogeton, all looking very attractive in a state of Nature, especially *P. crispus* with curly leaves. They look very tempting, but none seem to survive in the aquarium except *P. densus* and that only when established just to its liking.

## NITELLA

Of the slender-leaved aquatics. *Nitella gracilis* is one of the best. Our figure 128 gives a good idea of its dainty form. It is not freely distributed but is found occasionally in ponds and streams in the Eastern States, usually attached to bits of stick or stone. From this it receives its popular name, Stonewort. In removing the plant to the aquarium, it is best to take also the base upon which it roots. If placed in a situation to its liking Nitella prospers wonderfully in the aquarium and is a fine oxygenator. Under the microscope the leaves show the circulation of protoplasm better than any other plant. Requires plenty of light.

## LUDWIGIA

Popularly known as Swamp Loosestrife, this plant in about 25 species is widely and thickly distributed in North America, mostly growing at the edges of streams like Watercress. Although in reality more of a bog-plant than a pure aquatic, it does well in the aquarium, particularly if kept in the earth of the pot in which it was propagated from a cutting. Propagation is very easy in the greenhouse. About 5 short cuttings are placed in a 2-inch pot, having a top-layer of sand. This is not done under water but the pots need to be kept saturated and the air very moist. They soon root and when they have developed about an inch of new growth should be placed in the aquarium.

Ludwigia is one of the more important aquarium plants on account of its decorative value and pronounced individuality. When kept in a strong light the under sides of the leaves become a beautiful red color. Wild stock is not altogether satisfactory. It throws out too many roots to make a pleasing appearance, and in the aquarium becomes attenuated in character. A cultivated variety said to have come from South America is better in every respect and is easily obtained, for it is the kind propagated by dealers in aquatics. As it is sold in the original pots before being plunged into water it can safely be sent long distances. Growing to a length of several feet if untrimmed it is suited to large aquaria but may also be kept small by pinching back. Unlike Anacharis it should not be trimmed at the root end unless the stock has become quite old and no longer prospers. Does best in strong light and may also be propagated in the aquarium from cuttings. A little Ludwigia can be seen in our frontispiece.

FIG. 129.   CULTIVATED LUDWIGIA (*Life size*)

## SPATTERDOCK

Among the newer introductions into the aquarium are the submerged Spatterdocks. The large arrow- or spade-shaped leaves make a very characteristic appearance. Seedling plants gathered from lakes and ponds in the fall will do well in the aquarium over winter. If summer leaves appear and become too large for the aquarium the plant had best be removed. The Southern Spatterdock, *Nuphar sagittæfolia*, does not

Fig. 130. Southern Spatterdock (*Reduced one-half*)

develop aerial leaves, but they gradually lengthen as the warm season progresses. Figure 130 shows the plant in March. Later the stems and leaves will be longer. In October a new growth starts close to the thick, running root or rhizome. The leaves of this Spatterdock are of the brightest green hue and do not darken in strong light. Where the rhizomes have been broken off they have a tendency to rot, eventually killing the plant. This seems to be overcome by planting in sweet soil.

FIG. 131.   JAPANESE SPATTERDOCK (*Reduced two-thirds*)

The Japanese Spatterdock, *Alisma spec.*, has leaves of a considerably darker sage green, broader at the base. It is a continuous grower, has no aerial leaves and multiplies readily at the rhizome. Altogether a satisfactory plant for the large aquarium.

## FONTINALIS

Known as Willowmoss these plants are found attached to stones or other substantial objects. They are of a pleasing dark-green color and have the advantage of doing well in a subdued light, although a moderate amount of direct sun does them no harm.

*Fontinalis antipyretica* grows in long branching form, with leaves closely adhering to the stem. It occurs in cold-water streams and rivers, being very plentiful in some localities but is not freely distributed.

*Fontinalis gracilis* is very much smaller and threadlike, the leaves being so small as to appear like a roughness on the stem. In the aquarium this plant seems to have a faculty of soon becoming covered with sediment. Indeed some aquarists find it useful to clear the water. As soon as the plant becomes well covered it is taken out, rinsed off and returned. As the stems are strong they stand this treatment successfully. A stone containing a thick bunch of *Fontinalis gracilis* is an attractive feature in the aquarium. It is a slow grower. The new leaves are bright green but soon turn to a dark sage color.

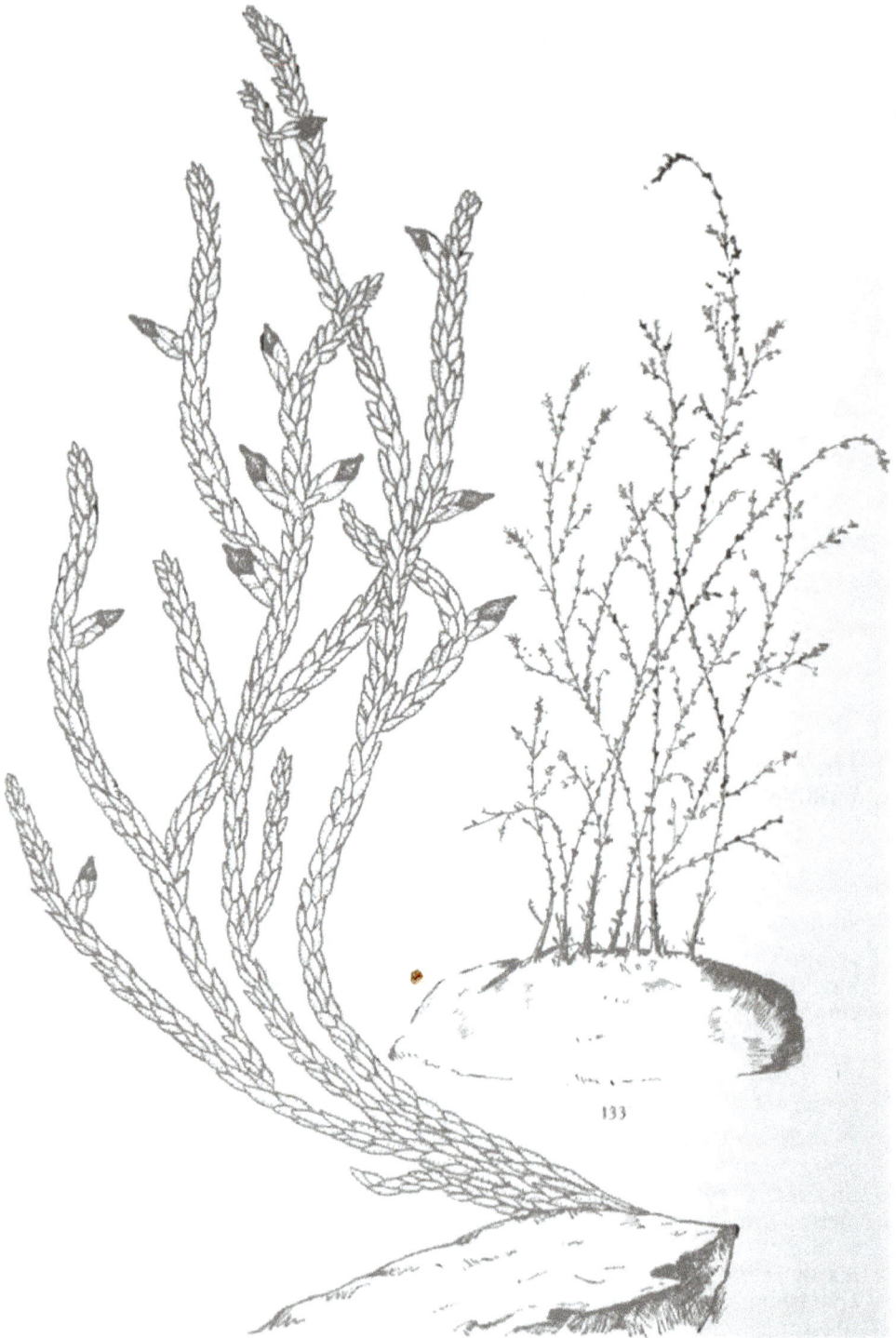

Fig. 132.  Fontinalis antipyretica (*Life size*)
Fig. 133.  Fontinalis gracilis (*Life size*)

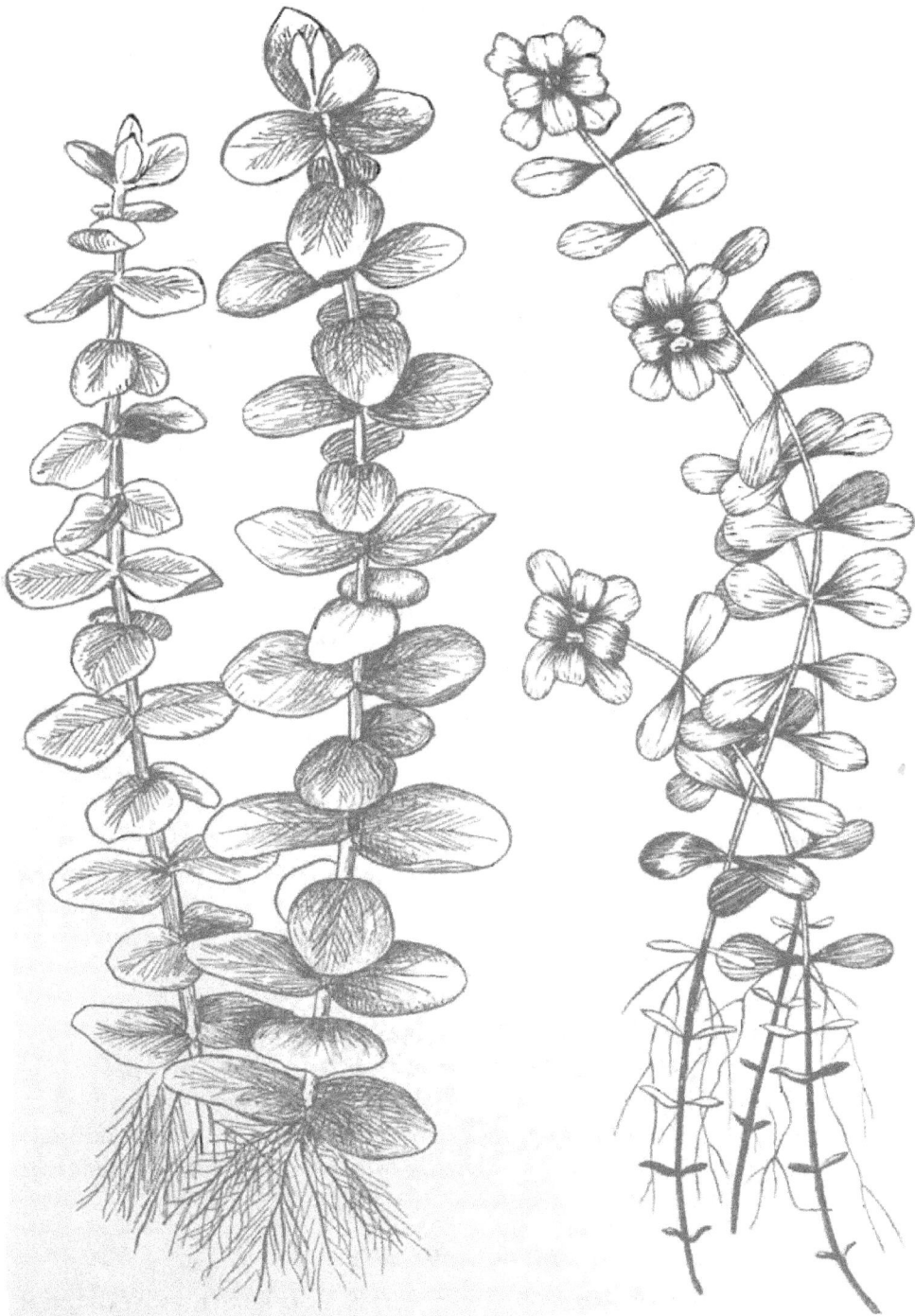

FIG. 134. HERPESTIS (*Life size*)
FIG. 135. SPRING STARWORT (*Life size*)

## HERPESTIS

*Herpestis amplexicaulis* bears a general resemblance to Moneywort, but in essential characteristics is quite different. It is a pure aquatic with thick leaves and a stout stem. Native to the ponds of Southeastern United States as far as Florida. It is one of the best of recent additions to aquarium plants. On account of being a slow grower its introduction is not likely to be rapid, but once established it does very well, holding its bright green leaves a long time. When out of the water it has a pleasant faint odor. Being of Southern origin it will prosper in the temperature of tropical aquaria where some plants will not do so well, although it thrives in cool water also. Incorrectly known as *Bacopa*.

## CALLITRICHE

Floating in small, cool streams throughout the United States and Lower Canada one will find patches of brilliant, light-green small leaves. Examination will show them to be the floating leaves of a long-stemmed plant growing in the mud. These are various forms of Callitriche, or Spring Starwort, sometimes also called Water Fennel. When the plant is loosened we find it disappointing, for the lower leaves are thinner and quite different in appearance. The stems are tangled and difficult to disengage.

*Callitriche verna* is the commonest form, as well as the most easily established in the aquarium, but it shows to best advantage in shallow tanks where a top view can be had of the surface leaves. It should, however, only be kept with tropical fishes unless it is intentionally given to goldfishes to eat, as they are fond of it. The stems and roots when taken are usually swarming with various aquatic insects and crustacea. Although many of these are good fishfood it is best to thoroughly rinse this and all other plants before placing in the aquarium.

## HIPPURIS

Formerly used as an aquarium plant, Mare's Tail has been overlooked of recent years, possibly on account of its tendency to stand above the water. Used in a suitable way this feature could be utilized to advantage. It transplants well and will thrive under varying conditions, but does best in ample light. Occurs in swamps from Labrador to Maine and also the Pacific Coast.

## MONEYWORT

*Lysmachia nummularia* or Moneywort is also known as Wandering Jew, Creeping Jenny and Herb-twopence, the latter name and Moneywort no doubt being derived from the rounded shape of the leaves. It is com-

FIG. 136. MARE'S TAIL (*Life size*)
FIG. 137. MONEYWORT (*Life size*)

mon in all the Eastern States, growing in damp places, usually near or
bordering streams.  Considering that it is scarcely even a bog plant it
does remarkably well in the aquarium, where it grows straight up to the
surface of the water, regardless of where the light comes from.  It is a
fair oxygenator, but if kept submerged the leaves gradually dwindle
in size, so that it is best to gather a new stock once a year, August or
September being the best season to secure vigorous plants.

## QUILLWORT

*Isoetes* is a widely distributed genus of a number of species.  It is
found in the mud and sand at the edges of streams and ponds.  In size it

Fig. 138.  QUILLWORT (*Reduced one-half*)

varies from a few inches to several feet.  The small submerged species
are worth trying in the aquarium, as they are tenacious of life.  The
leaves rise from the centre of a circle or rosette, producing a very pretty
effect.  Quillwort should be placed in a good light.  It is eaten by some
snails and fishes.

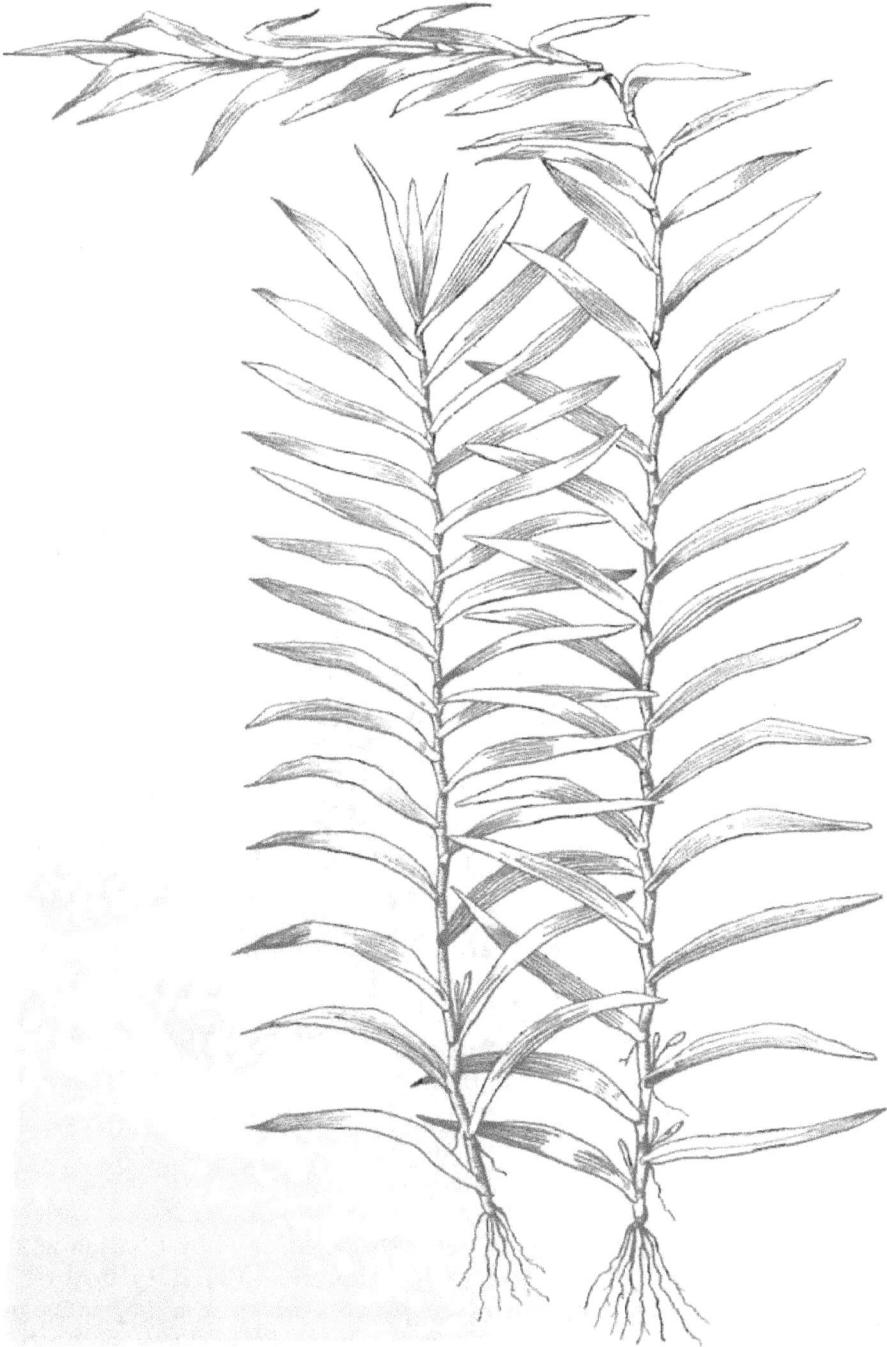

FIG. 139.  HETERANTHERA (*Life size*)

## HETERANTHERA

*Heteranthera zosteracfolia* is a very light green plant, slightly resembling Anacharis, but with longer, more widely separated leaves. It is a rapid grower, soon reaching the top, where it lays limp on the surface of the water. A good oxygenator, but has never become very popular on account of its rambling, untidy habits. Can occasionally be had of dealers.

## LACE PLANT

This extraordinary plant, *Ouviranda fenestralis,* is a native of Madagascar. Its dark-green skeleton leaves appear very fragile, but in reality they are the toughest-leaved aquarium plant we know of. They are slow

Fig. 140.  Madagascar Lace Plant
(*Life size, half-grown*)

of growth and prefer a subdued light. Propagation is by division at the root. This sometimes takes place in the aquarium, but they do best in wooden tanks. At best they are slow growers which in a way is an advantage, for they eventually become rather large. The Lace- or Lattice-leaf plant is used purely for ornamental purposes, its qualities as an oxygenator being negligible.

FIG. 141.  WATER POPPY (*Reduced one-half*)

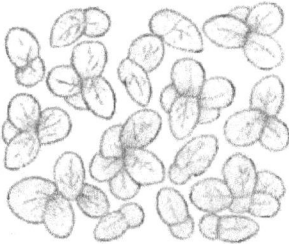

FIG. 142.  DUCKWEED (*Life size*)

FIG. 143.  AZOLLA (*Life size*)

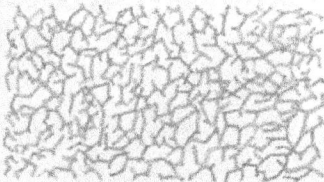

FIG. 144.  CRYSTALWORT (*Life size*)

## WATER POPPY

*Limnocharis humboldti*, owing to its generally satisfactory qualities, has become one of the most popular plants in the indoor and outdoor tank, as well as the large aquarium.  It grows very rapidly and continuously sends out new plants which have groups of buds.  Usually a new bud blooms every day.  The 3-petaled yellow flower with a brown eye or centre only lasts a few hours but is a most pleasing and artistic feature. The parent plant should be potted, preferably not very deeply in the water.  The new plants run at the surface, occasionally sending down strong stems to obtain a fresh rooting.

# Floating Aquatics

### DUCKWEED

This commonest of all floating plants is found in several species in still pools everywhere. From the middle of summer until cold weather many ponds are completely covered with this green mantle, greatly interfering with the work of collecting daphnia for fish food. Duckweed itself is a good food for goldfishes large enough to eat it, and has a laxative effect beneficial to the finer breeds. The form most commonly found is *Lemna minor*. Propagation is by offshoot extensions.

### AZOLLA

*Azolla caroliniana* is one of the less used of small floating aquatics. It is not in any way a brilliant plant but has a rather quaint charm. The leaves are of velvety appearance and range from a dull sage-green to dark red, according to age and the conditions of light. To be had of dealers. Native to the Southern States.

### CRYSTALWORT

*Riccia fluitans* grows in masses in small, angular shapes, resembling crystal formation. It floats just beneath the surface and is valuable in the propagation of small tropical fishes, some depositing eggs in it, and the new-born young of the live-bearing varieties using it for hiding places. Native to the Eastern States and may be had of dealers in aquatics.

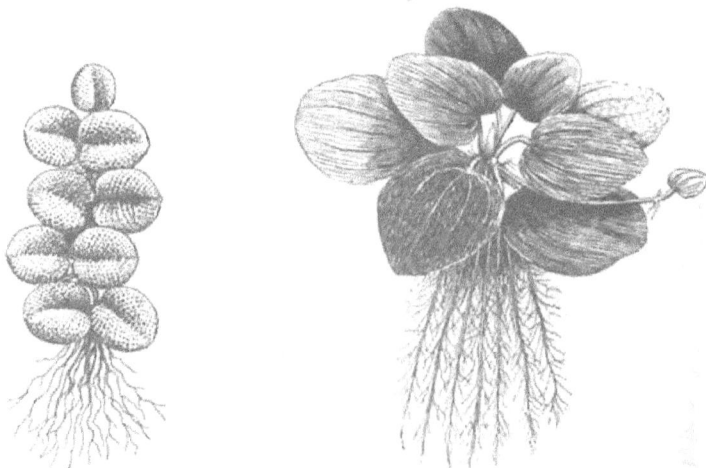

FIG. 145. SALVINIA (*Life size*)
FIG. 146. TRIANEA (*Slightly reduced*)

## SALVINIA

Of the small floating aquatics Salvinia is one of the best. The heart-shaped leaves with bristle-like growth on the upper surface seem like bits of velvet connected by a thread. The roots are naturally long for the size of the plant but fishes usually eat them down to about half length, which interferes with a full development of size. In the greenhouse where they have a moist atmosphere and no interference they develop with amazing rapidity. The variety illustrated, *Salvinia natans*, is native to Europe and is the form commonly used in aquaria and pools.

Although it is claimed that neither Salvinia nor the common wild Duckweed perform any oxygenating function, the author and others have many times seen aquaria completely covered with either of these plants and, with no other plants in the aquarium, the fishes were getting along perfectly well.

## FROGBIT

*Hydrocharis morsus-ranæ*, requiring the same conditions as *Trianea bogotensis*, deserves more attention than it is receiving. Of very pretty appearance when in flower, readily obtained from dealers, there is

FIG. 147. FROGBIT (*Life size*)

no reason why it should not be better known.  As will be noted in Figure 147 it propagates from runners, but the seeds also germinate under favorable conditions.  The plant is of European introduction.

## TRIANEA

*Trianea bogotensis* is an attractive, small floating plant with thick, heart-shaped leaves.  It needs a moist warm atmosphere and not too much direct sun.  Under these conditions it thrives and is a valued feature in the summer pool or greenhouse tank.  It is not found locally in temperate climate but may be had of dealers.

## WATER FERN

Not looking particularly fern-like, the Water Fern, *Ceratopteris thalictroides*, is the only truly aquatic species of the fern family.  It is of comparatively recent introduction into the aquarium and indoor pool,

FIG. 148.  WATER FERN (*Reduced*)

it being more suited to the latter.  In a partially shaded position in the greenhouse it grows into floating masses a foot or more in diameter, piling up to some height on account of its peculiar means of reproduction, the new plants springing directly out of the parent leaves, as is shown in Figure 148. Ordinarily the plants are about 6 inches in diameter and are of very pleasing appearance. Native to the Tropics around the world.

## WATER LETTUCE

*Pistia stratiotes* is a floating plant with fluted, light-green velvety leaves, forming a rosette. It likes plenty of heat, a moist atmosphere and protection from the sun. Under favorable conditions it grows to a

FIG. 149. WATER LETTUCE (*Reduced one-quarter*)

diameter of about 4 inches or more and is decidedly pretty. The roots sometimes attain a length of 18 inches, but they are not sufficiently dense to use for spawning purposes. Multiplies rapidly in a congenial environment.

## WATER CHESTNUT

Probably obtaining its popular name from the serrated edges of the leaves somewhat resembling those of the Chestnut tree, *Trapa natans* forms one of the pleasing varieties among floating aquatics. It is an annual doing well in exposed out-door positions. New plants are pro-

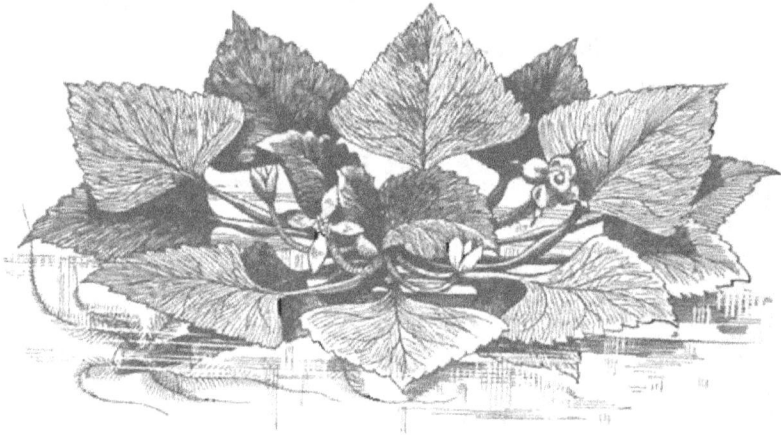

FIG. 149a.   WATER CHESTNUT

duced each year from large, hard seeds.   The big, black, two-horned seeds sometimes sold in Chinese stores are of a closely related species of *Trapa*. Can be had of dealers after May 15.

## WATER HYACINTH

Although Water Hyacinth, *Eichhornia,* is considered a pest in its native habitat on account of clogging up rivers and lakes, it is none the less a favorite with the aquarist, especially the breeder of goldfishes.   Its long, finely divided dense roots are admirable for receiving the eggs of any fishes that spawn on plants.   The pale purple flower-spike only blooms for a single day but is quite beautiful, having the general form of its namesake, the Hyacinth.   Propagation is by runners at the surface of the water.   Figure 150 clearly shows this.   Water Hyacinths do best if their roots can root or drag in soil.   Outdoors they do not like to be blown about nor to strike against the sides of a tank, although apparently not minding how closely they are crowded together.   This plant does well in a warm greenhouse the year round.   Unless supplied with plenty of light and heat during the winter they degenerate very much.

FIG. 150. WATER HYACINTH, SHOWING DETAIL OF FLOWER AND THE
FORMATION OF A NEW PLANT

FIG. 151. HARDY WHITE WATER LILY (*Tuberosa richardsoni*)

## WATER LILY CULTURE

All fish pools or large tanks standing in the sun should have water lilies growing in them. They are of easy culture and not only give protection to the fish but add greatly to appearances. Small or large varities may be had, according to the needs of the space. Water lilies are divided into the tender and hardy varieties. The tenders are more free-blooming and the day-blooming tenders are the most fragrant, as well as presenting the greatest range of color. They usually open in the fore part of the morning and close in mid afternoon. The night bloomers open in the evening and close about nine in the morning. They are not fragrant nor as elegant as the day-bloomers, but they are called the business man's water lily because he can see them in bloom in the evening and in the morning.

Water lilies need extremely rich soil. A mixture of half clay and half cow manure suits them very well. An inch top layer of sand will prevent any of this soil from getting into the water. The crown of the plant should not be covered and ought to be about 12 to 14 inches below surface of the water. They need an abundance of sunlight.

Before freezing weather sets in the tender plants should be taken up. Close to the main root will be found a few tubers about the size of shellbarks. These are the starts for next season's plants. They are to be broken off and kept in cool water or moist sand. In April they may be laid in shallow, warm water until sprouted, then placed in submerged pots and later permanently planted out in June.

Hardy water lily roots only need be kept moist and from actual freezing. In a pond they may be left out. In early Spring they form a number of new crowns. The parent root should be cut up into pieces, allowing a crown to each piece. Plant only one crown to a pot. Let all water lily pots be as large as space will permit. Most tenders will grow and bloom in a 7-inch bulb pan in an ordinary tub, but they are dwarfed from lack of space. They will do better in a box about a foot deep by thirty inches square, or in a hole 18 inches wide and 20 inches deep, as shown in Figure 163. Tropical water lilies have a surprising degree of intelligence in adapting themselves to the size of the pool they are in. The ordinary hardy water lilies if given as much space as they can use will have a surface diameter of about 4 feet. The usual tropicals vary from 10 to 15 feet, but will do well in pools of 6-foot diameter.

In the maze of offerings and alluring descriptions of water lilies, the beginner is at a loss to know what to select. We present a list of the most satisfactory varieties in each class. Most of them sell at moderate prices and can be had of either of the two leading dealers, Dreer's at Riverton, N. J., or Wm. Tricker, Arlington, N. J.

### Hardy

WHITE: Gladstoniana, Marliacea albida, Richardsoni.
PINK: Marliacea rosea.
YELLOW: Marliacea chromatella.
RED: Paul Hariot, Gloriosa, Aurora, James Brydon.

### Tender Day-Blooming

WHITE: Gracilis.
PINK: Mrs. C. W. Ward.
BLUE: Pennsylvania, Wm. Stone, Pulcherrima.
PURPLE: Zanzibariensis.

### Tender Night-Blooming

WHITE: Dentata magnifica.
PINK: O'Marana.
RED: Rubra, Devonensis.

### Winter-Blooming (Indoor)

BLUE: Mrs. Woodrow Wilson, Panama Pacific.

### Small Hardys

Pygmaea (white), Pygmaea helvola (yellow), Laydeckeri lilacea (rosy lilac), Laydeckeri rosea (pink to red).

## OTHER POND PLANTS

### Lotuses (Nelumbiums)

Album grandiflorum (white), Luteum (yellow), Speciosum (rose), Pekinensis (red).

The culture of Nelumbiums requires more root-space than for water lilies. Planted in a shallow pond where they have plenty of space for the strong roots to branch out and travel, they prosper amazingly. They are hardy over winter, and if it is desired to confine them to a certain space or locality they should be boarded in or otherwise divided from the rest of the pond. The roots go several feet deep. The Lotus is one of the most beautiful of all decorative plants. Its magnificent leaves and flowers swaying majestically in the summer breezes give us an inkling of why the ancient Egyptians considered the plant sacred.

Among the best of the bog and pond plants are Variegated Sweet Flag, Cape Pond Weed, Marsh Marigold, Umbrella Plant, Cyperus Papyrus, Water Arum, Pickerel Weed, Sagittaria japonica, Sagittaria montevidiensis, and Lizard's Tail.

Water Snowflake is one of the most charming of the small floating aquatics. White, star-like flowers of 1-inch diameter are freely borne above the water. Parent plant should be rooted in soil near surface.

FIG. 152. NELUMBIUM SPECIOSUM

The Sacred Lotus of the Orient, from 4 to 7 feet in height, is easily
the most magnificent of the aquatics with leaves and flowers above the water.

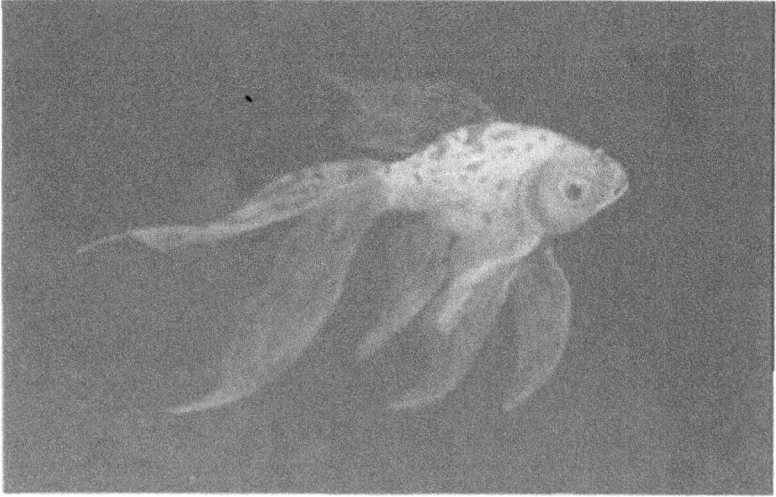

FIG. 153.   PRIZEWINNING CALICO COMET GOLDFISH

FIG. 154.   PRIZEWINNING LIONHEAD GOLDFISH

These two specimens show perhaps the greatest possible divergence of extremes in the accomplishments of fancy fish breeders. It is almost incredible that they are both derived from the same root stock.

**Enemies of Aquatic Plants.**  The most serious enemies are musk-rats. These eat the roots of several hardy aquatics, particularly over the winter season.  They are partial to the roots of the small yellow water lily, *Pygmaea helvola*.

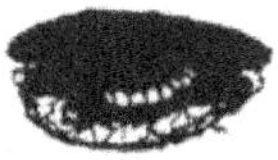

FIG. 155.   AQUATIC CUT-WORM

A leaf-cutting worm (*Hydrocampa*), sometimes becomes quite a nuisance.  It cuts a piece from the edge and, laying it on the leaf, attaches the two together and uses the two pieces as a cocoon.  Loose bits of water lily leaves, Sagittaria, etc., observed floating around will, if pried apart, often be found to contain this white worm.  The accompanying illustration is of life size.

*Chapter Sixteen*

———

# Photographing Fishes

## PHOTOGRAPHING FISHES

Achievements of modern photography have done much to lessen the difficulties of photographing living fish, although a picture good in every respect demands all the patience and care at one's disposal. Exact photographic records are extremely interesting to the fancier, valuable to the scientist and form the only certain basis for noting the changes in the fancy breeds of goldfish.

A high-grade lens that will work at F 6 or better and a shutter that will give an exposure of 1-25 second should be used. Sufficient length of bellows is needed so that the fish may be photographed about two-thirds life size. Sharp negatives can be had in this way and those which turn out well can be enlarged. Direct photography at life size is not practicable, as the depth of focus and power of the light are very much cut down at this close range. The chances of blurring by movement are greatly increased by attempting to photograph at life size. A photographic plate size 5 x 7 is quite satisfactory for photographing goldfish. For the most of the tropicals, 4 x 5 is sufficient. The Graflex camera is very convenient, allowing one to focus up to the instant of exposure.

To properly carry out this work a special photographing aquarium should be prepared. It should be seven inches deep, seven inches wide and two and one-half inches through from front to back. The front should be of ⅛-inch plate glass. This is important. A white background for photographing dark subjects and a black for light ones will be needed. A piece of cardboard folded twice and stood on end immediately in back of the aquarium will be found to be satisfactory. The back may be painted with flat black to serve for the alternate background. If this is done the two creases should be stripped with tape so the board will not separate when the fold is reversed. To carry out the background effect completely, cut a piece of glass the size of the inside bottom of the aquarium. Paint one side white and the other black, using either as required. The fish will frequently sink to the bottom, and if the background is of the proper color throughout, the photograph can be as well made there as higher in the water.

A very important item is to have a movable glass partition so that the fish may be forced near the front glass and thus kept in focus. Thin brass forms to snap on either top end of the aquarium and leaving notches filed to hold glass partition in position will be found most convenient.

FIG. 156.  PHOTOGRAPHING AQUARIUM

This aquarium was used in making all the photographic reproductions of fishes shown in this volume.  Note glass partition for keeping subject in focus.

FIG. 157. PRIZEWINNING CELESTIAL TELESCOPE GOLDFISH

As well as being one of the most extraordinary appearing of goldfishes, the Celestial is also the most difficult to breed and keep alive.

All the camera except lens should be covered with a black cloth at time of exposure to prevent its own reflection in the aquarium. The author believes that sunlight furnishes the best illumination, giving better color values and modelling than flashlight. Exposures should be made only on very bright days from eleven until two o'clock, and in the period, if possible, between April 10 and September 1. At other times flash-powder will be better, using a liberal supply. Care should be taken not to allow the dust from flashlight to settle in the aquarium, as it contains metallic salts injurious to fishes. Keep the sun on the subject and directly behind the camera. The water should be as free as possible of all particles, as they show in the picture with annoying distinctness. Much patience is sometimes required to get a fish into a satisfactory "pose," but when a good picture is obtained, it is well worth all the trouble it costs.

The photographing aquarium shown herewith was constructed by pouring cement in a form surrounding the four uprights. Just after the cement is poured, quarter-inch square sticks of wood should be pressed in where the glass is to stand. These are removed when cement is dry. Waterproof the base as described on page 216, then fill all four depressions and posts with aquarium cement and insert glass. Owing to small size of aquarium it is best to do all cementing before any glass is inserted for it is impossible to satisfactorily reach inside. Only the front needs to be of plate glass. This should be inserted first and all surplus cement neatly cleared away. It will be noted that this style of construction has no bottom metal frame to interfere with photographing when the subject happens to be low, which is often the case. One part of cement to two of sand is a good proportion. White cement makes a pretty effect and when using a white background, no other inside reflector is needed. This aquarium was used in making the photographic illustrations of fishes in this volume.

Unless the base immediately in front of the glass is of a dull black it will be desirable to cover it with a dull black or red cloth. Black is better.

*Chapter Seventeen*

———

# Construction of Aquaria, Tanks and Ponds

## AQUARIUM CONSTRUCTION

The amateur aquarist with a little talent for things mechanical can find profit as well as pleasure in making an aquarium according to his own ideas and requirements. The few necessary tools either are, or ought to be, a part of every household equipment.

Naturally the first consideration is that of the space to be occupied by the aquarium. In determining this it is well to be influenced, as far as conditions will permit, by the needs of the aquarium inmates. As to proportions, it will be found that most aquarium fishes do best in shallow aquaria with plenty of water surface. However, for artistic arrangement and symmetrical plant growth we must have a certain amount of depth. Twenty inches deep is sufficient even for large aquaria. In the smaller sizes, plants of suitable height can be secured. For all-round purposes, bearing in mind both the artistic and the useful, a good general rule is to make the aquarium in the form of a double cube. That is, the width and height identical, and the length twice that of either. Unless an aquarium is to be viewed only from the top, it is not advisable to make the width over 25 inches, as even a slight cloudiness of the water considerably obscures the fishes when there is so much of it to look through. Within reason, make the aquarium as large as possible, but nothing over a 70-gallon size is to be recommended for the household. An accidental breaking of the glass, even at this size, is too great a catastrophe to contemplate with composure. Since it is very little more trouble to keep a large-sized aquarium than a small one, and the results are so much better, at least with goldfishes, we would unhesitatingly say to those weighing the merits of two sizes, *take the larger.*

For a large variety of tropical fishes, a number of small aquaria will be found preferable. These will be treated of hereafter in the present chapter.

After the considerations of size and proportions, which we have already touched upon, we will now take up in order the points of construction, laying particular emphasis on the factor of safety.

**Bases.** The best material for general use in aquarium bases is slate. It is inexpensive, durable, easily worked, free from cleavage cracks, and in every way reliable. The requirements for thickness are from ¾ inch for sizes up to 30 gallons, to 1¼ inches for 130 gallons. Polished Tennessee marble makes a handsome and durable base. White marble is too glaring and besides is easily chipped in moving an aquarium about. Also when brought into contact with aquarium cement it absorbs and spreads the oil, making a bad appearance.  Bases of heavy white pine, strongly cross-battened, have been used with success, but the wisdom of using a wooden base is open to serious question, especially as wide, thick pine boards can scarcely be had any more, even at high prices.  The ever-present danger of warping either from a leak or the weather, or again from bending due to continuous heavy pressure are considerations weighing against the wooden base.  If an all-wood frame is used, it is desirable to line the bottom with a sheet of glass, preferably wired, embedding it in soft aquarium cement at the edges, and at several supporting spots near the centre.  The same plan is to be recommended in aquaria with solid metal bases, in order to keep iron rust out of the water.

Aquarium bases usually extend from one to one and one-half inches beyond the frames on all sides.  Slate or marble bases ought to be bevelled sufficiently on the upper edges and corners to take away the sharpness.  The necessary holes through which the frame is to be clamped on can be drilled with an ordinary metal drill, but it costs very little extra to have the slate-worker do this when he is finishing the base.  Aquaria up to 10 gallons require 4 bolts, 20 gallons 6, and for the larger sizes they should be placed about 10 inches apart.

**Frame Metals.**  Angle brass, iron or aluminum form the best metal aquarium frames.  For the amateur worker, brass offers the best advantages.  It is easily sawed, drilled and soldered, besides making a handsome appearance when polished and lacquered or nickel-plated.  If nickeled it should be heavily coated.  Angle iron is not so attractive in appearance, but is undoubtedly more rigid.  It cannot be soldered.  Consequently the four corners of the upper and lower frames have to be riveted through connecting elbow pieces on the inside or special castings on the outside, and then the whole riveted to the uprights.  Aluminum has seldom been used, but makes an attractive frame.  As the soldering of this metal is of doubtful durability it is safer to rivet the same as with iron.

For aquaria up to 25 gallons, $\frac{5}{8}$-inch angle metal is suitable; up to 50 gallons, $\frac{3}{4}$ inch; up to 75 gallons, 1 inch; up to 125 gallons, $1\frac{1}{4}$ inch.  The author prefers seeing as little of the frame as possible and for ten years has successfully used a 60-gallon aquarium constructed with only $\frac{5}{8}$-inch angle brass, but he would not care to make this as a general recommendation.  It is mentioned so that if others have the same idea they will know that it is a mechanical possibility.

Unless constructed of heavy angle iron it is best to carry a light rod across short dimension of the centre of top frame of aquaria over 30 inches in length, to prevent bulging by water pressure.

**Frame Construction.** A hack-saw with fine teeth for metal-working will be needed to cut the proper lengths of angle metal. After carefully determining proportions desired, cut the four uprights and then the material for top and bottom frames. If working in brass the latter should

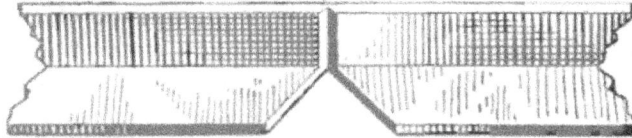

FIG. 158. CUT, PREPARATORY TO BENDING ANGLE BRASS

each be left in one piece. By accurately bevelling the two ends and preparing right-angle cuts at three points as shown in figure 158, the whole can be bent into a frame that will produce very neat corners and make soldering easy. The right-angle cuts should be finished with a square file and carried within about 1/32 inch of going through. This leaves the bar very weak at these points and considerable care is necessary in handling in order that some accident does not break them apart before it is time to bend. If one breaks it is not a very serious matter, only the corner will not have quite such a neat appearance. In practise we find it best to bend each cut as soon as finished and roughly fasten with solder. When all

FIG. 159. FRAME SECURED AROUND WOODEN FORM. NOTE RE-INFORCEMENT IN ONE
CORNER

three bends have been completed, place within it a wooden form as shown in figure 159. Except for the corners being cut off (to allow for soldering) the edges of form should be perfectly rectangular and fit closely. Now secure quite firmly with stout twine. After all corners are trued up with the board, apply the permanent solder. Melt solder from any corner that does not stand true without forcing. In the upper-right corner of our illustration will be noted a right-angle flange reinforcement, cut from a flat piece of 1/16-inch brass. It is advisable to use these. They add greatly to the strength and actually make the work of soldering easier. After preparing the surfaces with solder-flux it is only necessary to place solder on the frame, lay the flange on top of it and apply torch beneath. When solder melts, press flange down and into exact position with a small stick of wood. It is better to have flanges sufficiently narrow to allow the uprights to fit in back of them.

The same form can be used for upper and lower frames. Should there be any irregularity in shape they will both be alike, and so far as strength is concerned, it will only be necessary to keep corresponding defective corners parallel with each other, so as not to make any twisting strain on the glass—a force which, sooner or later, will cause it to break. If the frame is too large for a board, it may be trued by lines drawn to lay it over. The use of forms, however, is so desirable to the amateur that we recommend having boards rabbited together in order to secure sufficient width.

To test the squareness of upper and lower frames, lay them on the floor, make marks at the corners and turn completely over, trying both length and width in this way. Tests by squares at corners are only approximate, as the angle metal is seldom perfectly straight, especially lighter brass. Before leaving the subject of bending the frames to right-angles we strongly suggest that an experimental bend first be made with a waste piece of angle brass. A little practise will be necessary to learn just how thin a particular lot of brass must be filed in order to make a good bend.

The next step is to bore holes in the lower frame where it is to be bolted through the base, countersinking for depression of bolt or rivet head, and allowing enough room not to interfere with the glass. Now solder in uprights at perfect right angles to inside of top and bottom frames, being careful not to use enough heat to melt former soldering.

It will be observed that the glass will be supported by the upright posts but not by the top nor bottom frames. This is corrected by soldering, about every eight inches, a small piece of brass (cut from the same material) to the horizontal frames next to where the glass is to come, thus giving it even support on all four edges. The pieces are soldered down perfectly flat and if high should be filed down. Before the glass is finally inserted it must be laid in the frame to see that the points of contact are even. Deficiencies can be made up by a drop of solder on the brass, and filed down as required.

The frame being trued up it is now bolted through the base, aquarium cement being liberally supplied in the bolt holes and between the frame and the base, all surplus being immediately wiped away.

**Soldering.** The ordinary amateur is equipped neither with the facilities nor the experience to use a soldering iron to advantage. The author has engaged in considerable aquarium construction and has usually been able to get along very well without an iron, its main use being to clear surplus solder away more quickly than can be done with a file. Before soldering, the surface is properly prepared by scraping and the application of a flux composed of hydrochloric acid which has dissolved as much zinc as possible. An alcohol blow-torch is satisfactory for small work, but for the heavier construction a gasoline torch is better. When the heat is applied and the liquid of the flux has boiled away, touch the heated surface occasionally with soft solder wire. Apply a little more heat after first sign of melting, withdraw flame and proceed to quickly solder. Where work is in a position so that it is difficult to hold the pieces steadily in place while solder cools, an assistant can instantly "set" it by pouring on a little water. If acid flux darkens the hands where it touches, the stain can be removed by dilute ammonia water.

**Small Aquaria.** Very compact, neat and substantial aquaria can be made in the foregoing manner, but without projecting base—in fact without slate at all. The bottom is self-contained concrete. The top frame and upright corner posts are of ½-inch angle brass, and the bottom frame of 1-inch size. In the inside edges of this are soldered a few brass screws. Now prepare a mixture of one part of Portland Cement to two of clean sand, brought to a thick, mushy consistency by addition of water. Lay the frame on a good, flat piece of glass and pour in the cement to a depth of ¾ inch, seeing that it lays smooth, particularly where the glass is to rest.

After the cement is poured and smoothed it should be covered to be allowed to dry slowly. In about two days the frame and base can be slid off the glass. The screws soldered on inside will always hold the base securely in place. To prevent free chemicals washing out of cement into the aquarium water it is well to waterproof the inside of base before setting glass in. This may be done by melting chips of paraffine under the alcohol blow-torch, or by pouring on a mixture of paraffine dissolved in warm gasoline. To prepare this mixture place a quart bottle of gasoline in a butcket of warm water. Add two ounces of paraffine chips and stir until dissolved. Keep the solution warm and saturate the base with it. When dry, place in glass as in an ordinary aquarium.

(The foregoing mixture of gasoline-paraffine will waterproof wood, concrete, brick, fabrics or anything that will absorb it. For fabrics to be used or bent, use only one ounce of paraffine.)

After making one of these aquaria the knack becomes very easy. A row of them of uniform size presents a neat appearance and can be used in small space, since there is no projecting base. This style of construction is suitable for aquaria with bases up to eleven by eighteen inches. In larger sizes the uprights and top angles ought to be from five-eights to three-quarter inch metal, while heavy wire screen should be embedded in the cement for re-inforcement.

If the frames are to be nickeled this should be done before pouring the cement base.

**Glass for Aquaria.** Although double-thick window glass may be used for aquaria up to the 25 gallon size, plate-glass is so much handsomer and costs so little more, it seems like a wise investment. If window-glass is used, the imported kinds will be found best. Plate-glass is now made in 3-16 inches thickness. This is suitable for aquaria under 50 gallons. For those for 50 to 75 gallons, the best thickness is $\frac{1}{4}$ inch, and for the still larger sizes up to 120 gallons, $\frac{3}{8}$ inch. The author and others have occasionally picked up bargains in plate-glass from plate-glass insurance concerns, who often have on their hands large remnants of bulk-windows.

**Setting the Glass.** The edges of the glass should be carefully cleaned with whiting, ammonia or alcohol to remove any grease. It is well to first coat the edges which are to come into contact with the cement with gold size, allowing this to set for a day or two. This is more particularly needed with large plate-glass aquaria. Apply a liberal coating of aquarium cement to the inside of frame, and a thin but well covered coat to the contact edges of the glass. Press into place slowly but firmly, cleaning away at once all surplus cement. Light sticks cut of a length to brace across inside of aquarium will maintain an outward pressure on the glass for several days until it is fairly set. After the glass is well set it is advisable, especially with the larger sizes, to run a line of aquarium cement up the inside corners and along the bottom edges, covering with a narrow strip of glass, or, better, embedding a glass rod of from $\frac{1}{4}$ to $\frac{3}{8}$-inch diameter in it, pressing in as far as possible and wiping away the surplus cement.

Fill slowly in about a week and change water several times in two weeks before putting in fishes.

Large aquaria nearly always leak a little at first, or after moving them, or even after emptying without moving. This usually corrects itself within a few days, but, as elsewhere directed, it can nearly always be stopped by making the water very muddy. The particles of dirt get into the leak and choke it up.

**Aquarium Cements.** The prime requisites of an aquarium cement are resistence to water, adhesiveness, moderately quick setting without ever becoming stone-hard, and being non-poisonous. A cement combining these qualities is composed of one pound of litharge, one pound of Plaster of Paris, two ounces of powdered resin and one-half pound of glazier's sand; mixed with boiled linseed oil to a consistency of putty suitable for glazing. This cement has been found to be good for both fresh and marine water aquaria. A durable cement for those who cannot obtain very fine sand is made of equal parts by weight of zinc white, whiting and litharge, mixed with boiled linseed oil to a firm but tacky consistency.

Cement for Marine Aquaria. A cement used for large, city marine aquaria is composed of 3 parts by measurement of Portland Cement, 3 parts fine white sand, 1 part powdered resin; mixed with boiled linseed oil.

Cement for Wooden-Framed Aquaria. The best cement for small wooden-framed aquaria is made of 1 part of gutta percha and 4 parts of pitch, boiled together and applied warm, first heating the glass somewhat. It is difficult to handle this quickly enough on large aquaria, for which the following will be found better: 3 parts Portland Cement, 2 parts zinc white, 3 parts fine sand, 1 part powdered resin, made into a firm paste with boiled linseed oil.

## CONCRETE AQUARIA

The making of concrete aquaria opens a new and an unlimited field. Those who have felt that the metal-frame aquarium is hopelessly restricted and commonplace can here find more room for individual expression, design and achievement. The illustration facing title page gives an idea of possibilities along this line. The aquarium shown is one designed and built by Mr. L. M. Dorsey and probably represents the highest development, up to this time, of artistic ideas as applied to a household aquarium. In the Philadelphia Aquarium Society annual competition Mr. Dorsey was awarded the prize cup three times, thereby becoming its permanent possessor.

As individual ideas will vary so widely in the design of concrete aquaria, only a few (yet important) directions can be given. Cement should be of the highest grade, fresh and free from lumps. A mixture of one part cement to two of clean, sharp sand is about right. Wooden forms ought to be soaked with water just before using, or else thoroughly paraffined. Cement mixture should be wet enough to just pour, and needs to be well tamped to avoid bubbles. Re-inforcement rods (¼ inch diameter) are essential, especially around the top edge, where a continuous band should be formed. Over the bottom the bars should be wired together, forming 4-inch squares. Do not be in a hurry to get the forms off. The whole job should be moistened for a day and allowed to stand for two more days if their removal is going to cause any strain. Glass must not be embedded directly in the concrete, but provision made for later setting it in with ordinary aquarium cement. If sides do not support the glass evenly they should be cut away or built up until they do. Otherwise glass is sure to crack when the soft aquarium cement yields to the water pressure. After base is finished it is well to paraffine it as described on page 216. All cement pouring should be done at one operation.

## CONSTRUCTION OF WOODEN TANKS

Many expert fanciers are of the opinion that for the welfare of fishes there is no receptacle equal to a well-seasoned wooden tank. For breeding purposes they are especially valuable, but in no case should tanks be used before numerous changes of water have been made over a period of several weeks.

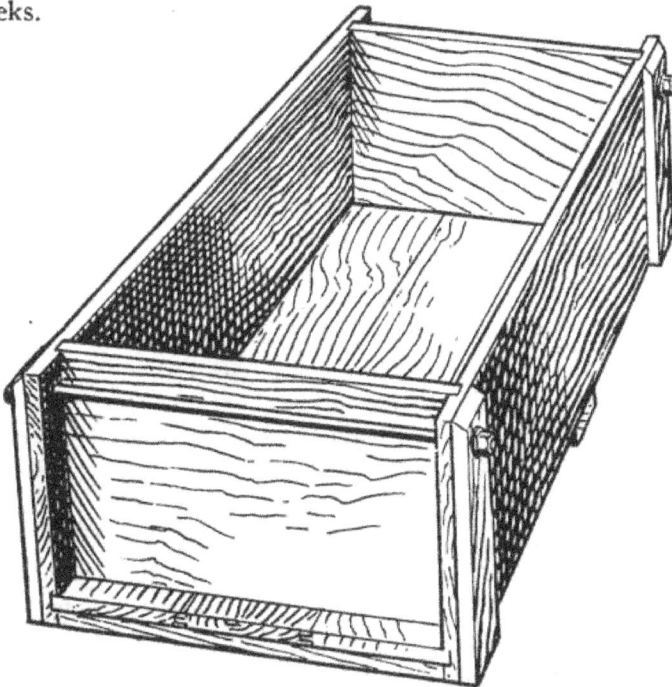

FIG. 160. WOODEN BREEDING TANK

The best wood for tanks is well-seasoned cypress, the natural habitat of the tree being in wet places. Any size tank may be made, but there are two sizes found quite convenient and which cut to good advantage out of the lumber. The larger measures 16 inches high, 30 inches wide and 48 inches long. The smaller one measures 9 inches high, 24 inches wide and 32 inches in length. For the larger size 1¼-inch lumber is used, which is about 1⅛ inches when dressed. Here a board 16 inches wide is used, avoiding seams in any of the sides, and being but one in the bottom. The side and bottom boards are rabbeted to ¼ inch deep and 1½ inches from edge to receive the ends. Bottom boards are tongued and grooved. All joints should receive a preliminary coating of white lead paint. After this is dried a thicker coat should be applied just before putting joints together. The tank is then clamped and 1¾-inch screws inserted through the sides into the bottom and ends, and through the bottom into the ends. Cleats 3 inches wide are placed across centre of bottom and all the way around the ends. Through the top of latter is passed an iron rod ¼ inch thick, then secured and tightened with washer and nut at ends. The smaller tank is constructed in the same manner, except that cleat across centre bottom and the iron rods are omitted.

While painting the outside improves the appearance, it has more of a tendency to rot a tank than preserve it, as the paint prevents the evaporation of the moisture naturally gathered from the inside. Leaks will usually correct themselves in a few days, but should they not do so, a few handfulls of earth stirred in the water and allowed to stand a few hours will make the job tight. Occasional stirring of the dirty water helps. The white lead should be allowed a day to harden before filling with water.

## CONSTRUCTION OF TANKS AND POOLS

For outdoor purposes it is better to dig holes in the ground and puddle them with clay rather than make poorly constructed concrete basins or pools of any size. Unless the work is properly done the frost is certain to crack it, and even the weight of the water may be sufficient to bring about this result. Repaired work is never satisfactory, and the next winter will open more seams, making continual expense, dissatisfaction, loss of water and of fishes. With indoor concrete tanks too, thorough construction is a good investment.

The main points in the construction of such work are good foundations, thorough reinforcement, good cement properly mixed, and one continuous job of the finishing coat. The concrete centre ought also be poured within the space of one day. There is some difference of opinion as to the necessity for a base of cinders. The author favors them. If used they should be the hard kind, wetted down and packed solid to a depth of one foot or more. For tanks of moderate size—say **11 x 22** feet—reinforcement should be by use of ¼-inch steel rods, crossed on squares of 8 inches. The bottom needs two layers of these bars, one near the upper and one near the lower surface. This protects against both

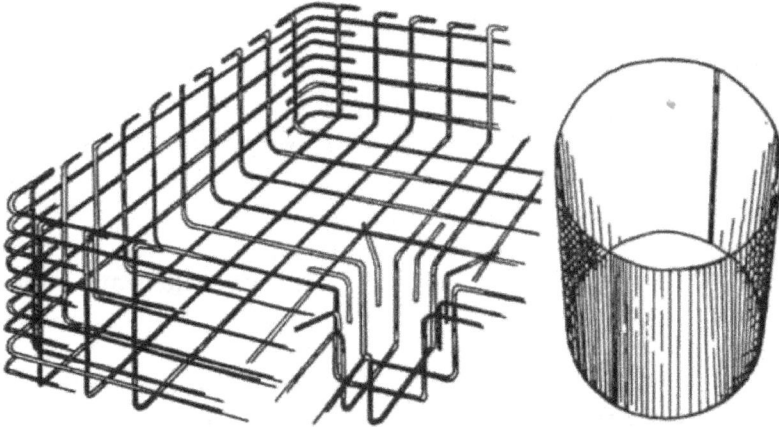

FIG. 161. CORRECT ARRANGEMENT OF REINFORCING STEEL, AND GALVANIZED IRON FORM FOR WATER LILY POT

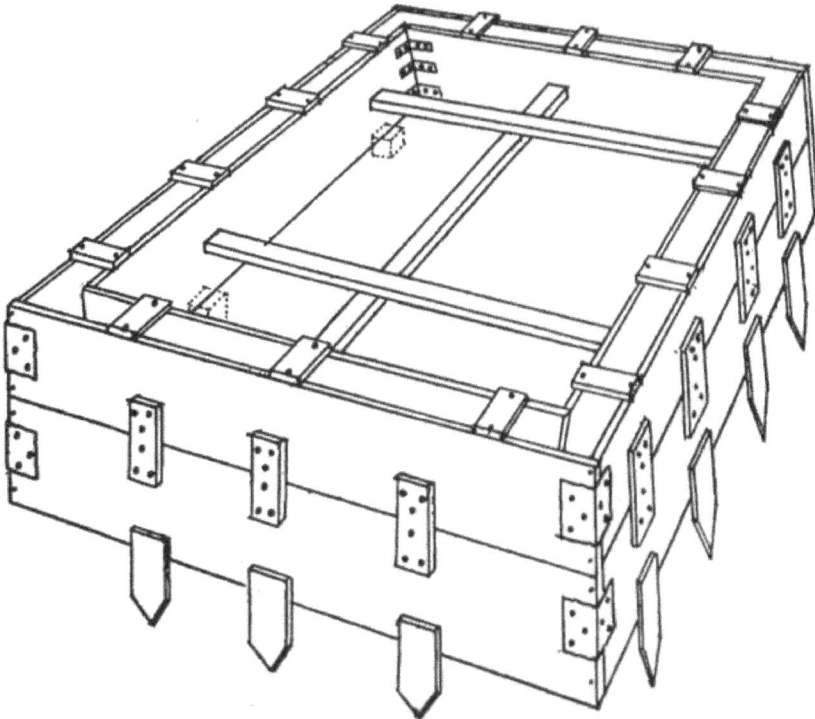

FIG. 162. WOODEN FORM READY FOR CONCRETE POURING

The dotted blocks represent bricks or stones to hold inside form to same height as the outside. Note slope of inside form.

inside and outside pressures. The lower frame of bars is bent up at the ends to form a cradle, thus reinforcing the side walls. The ends are finally again bent over at right angles, running in the direction of the wall, and laced together. Above this are two continuous bands of the steel. Figures 161 and 163 will indicate these points. The corners are always the weakest points. As the concrete is poured, lay in extra right-angle pieces of 12 inches total length.

The pouring of the concrete makes a great strain on the forms. These need to be thoroughly braced in the beginning, for it is impossible to improvise means of looking after these points, once the work has started and the walls have bulged or the corners sprung. The outside bottom stakes are merely driven into the ground and not otherwise fastened. Outside corners in addition to being nailed are secured by pieces of tin, nailed through. Inside corners are held by iron elbows (to be had at hardware stores). They are secured by screws. The nails fastening side-cleats should be driven through and turned over. Concrete walls had best be thicker at the bottom, putting all the slope on the inside. A good inside depth for ordinary purposes is 15 inches, filling to 13½ inches with water. If an overflow is to be made through side, make a core of soft wood and saturate it with water so that it will contract upon

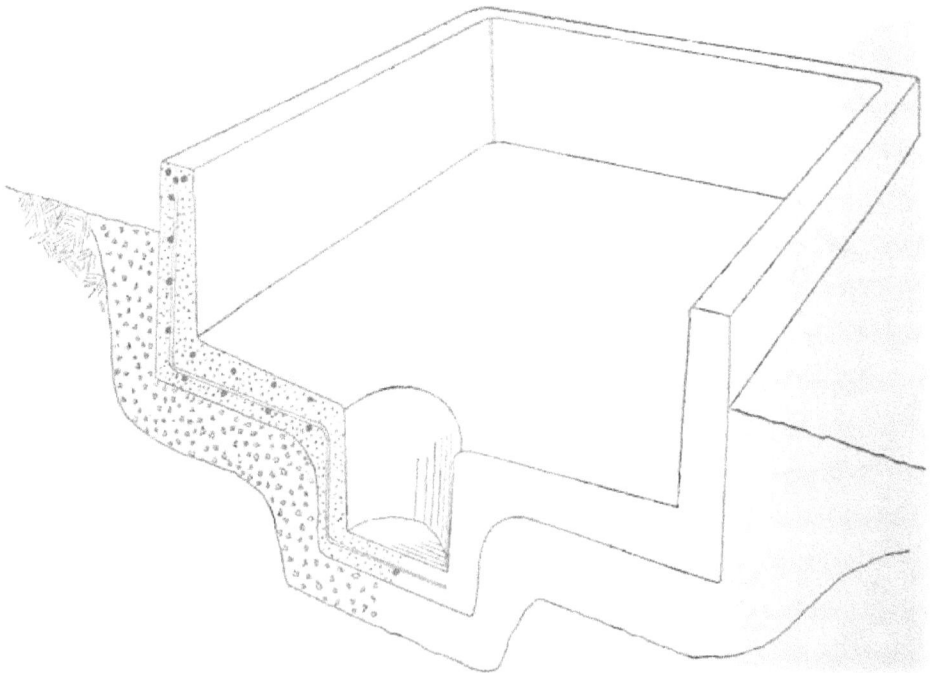

FIG. 163. CROSS-SECTION OF FINISHED POOL
The lowest layer represents cinders. We have indicated here the upper layer of re-inforcement in the base, impossible to show in Fig. 161.

drying. For outdoor pools an inside slope of 2 inches is about right. This would be, for a 7 x 9-foot pool, a top thickness of 4 inches, with 6 inches at the bottom. Base, 6 inches thick. For larger sizes add 1 inch of thickness to walls and base. Indoor pools require no slope. In making all calculations, allow ⅜ inch for thickness of finishing coat. The forms should be levelled up and made absolutely true in the beginning. It is a bad plan to depend upon the finishing coat to correct inaccuracies. It seldom does it. Some considerable care is necessary to establish the four corners at perfect level. Select one corner and measure each of the other three from that. If the spirit-level is attached to a board, its trueness should be tested by reversing the ends. In any case the level should be reversed on each test.

The concrete is mixed 1 part cement, 2 parts sand, 4 parts ¾-inch crushed stone or round stone. This is poured to within ½ inch of top of form, beginning with the base and must be well tamped to avoid bubbles and open spots. Those wishing to secure the best possible results first place a thin skin of cement over the cinders so the water in concrete will not seep into the cinder base, it being desirable that all concrete work dry slowly in order to crystallize perfectly. This preliminary skin is as thin as possible and is applied the day before. It is composed half each of sand and cement. If this is used, the lower layer of re-inforcement may be laid directly upon it.

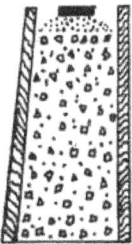    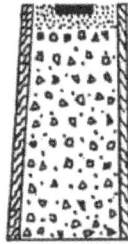    

FIG. 164                        FIG. 165                        FIG. 166

Fig. 164. Tile Set on Cement Mound.    Fig. 165. Top Finishing Coat Brought to Level of Form.    Fig. 166. Guide-board in Position for Inside Finishing Coat (Whether or not tiles are used, this is the best method of finishing)

Finishing coat should be applied within 24 hours, and is made 1 part cement, 2 parts sand. Finish one side at a time, top edge first, inside surface next, then outside, and the bottom after 4 sides are complete. Begin by filling to top of form. Now take off inside form *from one side only.* Lay a piece of perfectly straight board along top edge. This makes an infallible gauge for thickness and straightness of finishing coat (Figure 166). Here we might say that it is advisable to have an experienced finisher do this work, but a resourceful amateur can do it. Now do the outside in the same manner, the idea here being to have the top bind with the sides while fresh. The outside being done last is less likely to be kicked. Try to protect the job from rapid drying in the sun.

It is very nice to sink a hole in the centre for the reception of a water lily plant. This adds considerably to the planning and labor, but the result is worth it in satisfaction if one is fond of beautiful aquatics. At the same time the bottom can be drained towards the centre, a good point when it comes to the annual cleaning-out. Figure 163 shows this. The hole ought to be about 18 inches wide at the top, 15 at the bottom and 17 deep. The galvanized iron form is removed by bending it inwards at one point. This form is of *thin* metal and has no bottom, it being impossible to withdraw a bucket on account of suction.

Another added attraction for those caring for the aesthetic side is the addition of tiles in the edges. To try to push these into the finishing coat is to court certain trouble and a botch job. As soon as the concrete is poured the tiles should be set on little mounds of cement as indicated in Figure 164, seeing that they come to exactly the right level, fixing the four corner ones first. Next day the finishing coat is filled around them and they help to establish the correct level. The cement will slop over on them a little, but this is no matter. Most of it can be wiped off with water and the balance after drying, with dilute hydrochloric acid.

The author is not partial to drain-pipes. They may become dislodged and let the tank run dry, or, on the other hand, they may get sand in them and not go back into place. However, this is a matter of personal preference.

In two days after the finishing coat is applied, a little water may be run in. On the fourth day fill completely. All cement containers should be seasoned before the fishes are introduced.

This can be done by changing the water six times over a period of two weeks. This is not thorough and a longer time is better. Seasoning can be accelerated by different chemical processes. The safest is to fill the pool and slake a large piece of lime in it. In a pool 8 x 12 feet, slake about half a bushel. There is no danger of using too much. After slaking, stir every few hours and clean out thoroughly in two days. Another method is to place a piece of blue litmus paper (obtainable in drug store) in the water after it has stood a day and been stirred up. Then slowly add and stir in commercial sulphuric acid until the paper shows a faint pink hue. Allow to stand another day and if the paper goes back to blue, repeat addition of acid. When the pink shade remains draw off water, clean thoroughly and use. Enough acid to turn the paper a distinct pink or red should not be used. Always stir water well before determining color of paper. This test is only for the acid process.

**Aquarium or Tank Capacity.** To ascertain the gallon capacity of any rectangular tank, multiply the length, breadth and depth together in inches. Divide by 231. The result will be in gallons.

A gallon weighs 8 1-3 pounds.

FIG. 167.  FINISHED POOL, SHOWING SUNKEN LILY POT AND OVERFLOW

FIG. 168.  SAME IN USE, WITH TROPICAL AND PIGMY LILIES IN BLOOM

FIG. 169. "QUEEN LIL," A MANY-TIME PRIZEWINNING SCALELESS TELESCOPE
GOLDFISH

*Chapter Eighteen*

———

# Aquarium Appliances

## AQUARIUM APPLIANCES

**Nets.** The most important device in aquarium work is a net with which to catch the fish, yet in most instances it is of faulty construction. The scales of a fish are easily knocked off by the hard knots in the coarse

FIGS. 170 AND 171. PROPER NETS FOR GOLDFISHES AND YOUNG TROPICALS

threads composing nets usually sold. This is very bad for the fish. A far better material is Brussels netting of a mesh such as is used on window curtains—not too fine.

When fish have to be caught from a globe, a round net is convenient, but for a straight-side aquarium, a square or oblong net is very much better. Usually these cannot be purchased, but to make one is a simple matter and well repays for the effort. Perhaps the easiest way is to purchase a round net, remove netting, bend wires to an oblong form and re-cover with Brussels netting.

**Glass Cleaners.** The best device for cleaning the inside glass of straight aquaria is a safety razor blade secured in a stick and riveted through. First rivet or wrap end of stick with fine copper wire to prevent

FIG. 172. SAFETY RAZOR BLADE AQUARIUM GLASS CLEANER

splitting, place razor blade firmly in iron vise and drive down stick to proper point. A blade may be used directly in the hand, but in this case it is better to dull one edge first in order to avoid cutting the fingers.

A dime rubbed flat against the glass will clean it. For cleaning globes a piece of thick felt is very good, although any piece of clean fabric will do.

**Dip Tube.** Sometimes particles of food remain too long after feeding. Also dirt collects in spots. Such places can easily be cleaned by use of a dip tube. Any tube of from one-quarter to three-eighths inch inside diameter and about six inches longer than the depth of the aquarium will do. Glass is preferable. Hold the thumb firmly over one end, place other end near particles to be lifted. Remove thumb, allowing water and particles to rush into tube. Replace thumb, lift out and empty. The capacity of the tube can be considerably increased by heating the centre over a Bunsen flame and blowing a sort of belly.

**Siphon.** When much dirt needs to be removed or the aquarium emptied, a siphon should be used. This consists simply of a hose sufficiently long to reach from the bottom of the aquarium, up over the edge and down again to a point near the floor. The longer the drop, the more rapid the flow. Fill tube with water, close both ends by finger pressure, insert one end in the aquarium and hold the other as low as possible. Release the ends of tube and the water will flow as long as there is water in the aquarium at a higher point than the discharging end of tube. Care should be taken not to draw in fish or snails.          .

**Forceps.** A pair of forceps for aquarium work forms a most handy tool. Their construction is very simple. Take a piece of ⅛-inch brass wire thirty inches long and bend to shape shown in Figure 173. Where the wire crosses, hammer out a small flat space through which a rivet

FIG. 173.  AQUARIUM FORCEPS

can be fastened. A small section of brass wire or a copper tack can be used as a rivet. When the forceps are otherwise completed, flatten out the ends by hammering on an iron vise or other firm surface. The jaws of the forceps automatically remain open. Pressure on the upper loop closes them. They will be found quite handy in adjusting plants and lifting out snails, stones or other small objects.

**Planting Sticks.** To secure the roots of plants in sand would seem a very simple matter, but when the aquarium is filled it is most difficult to set them without the help of one or two planting sticks. These are as simple as they are useful, being merely thin sticks with a dull

FIG. 174.  PLANTING STICK

notch in the end. About three-eighths of an inch is a suitable size diameter for the sticks. The notch should be slightly rounded on the edges to avoid cutting the roots as they are forced into the sand. Two sticks are better than one. Plants like Giant Sagittaria should be pressed down from two sides. After the plant is placed to the proper depth, it should be held with one stick while the other is used to push sand over the roots and to press down straggling roots which have not been covered. Aquariums should not be planted while filled, but sometimes a few plants ride loose on the first filling or some are added later. For such occasions planting sticks are most handy. A pair of rulers will do for an emergency. Almost anything is better than the fingers.

**Scissors.** A pair of scissors with a 15-inch rod securely wrapped to each handle is useful for trimming dead leaves from plants. With this

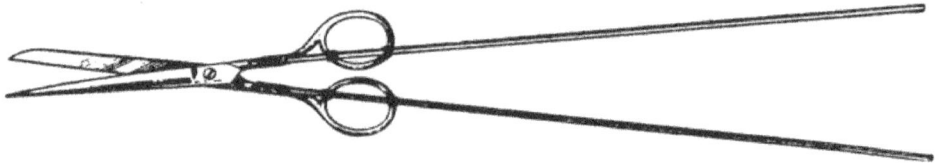

FIG. 175. AQUARIUM SCISSORS

tool plants can be reached without disturbing anything, and one can get a better view of what is to be done than when working elbow-deep in the water.

**Live-bearing Jars.** With most varieties of viviparous (live-bearing) fishes it is desirable to promptly separate the mother and other fish from the young in order that they will not be eaten. One simple method is to take a glass funnel about six inches across the top, file a nick where base joins tube, break off tube and place a small piece of U-shaped wire

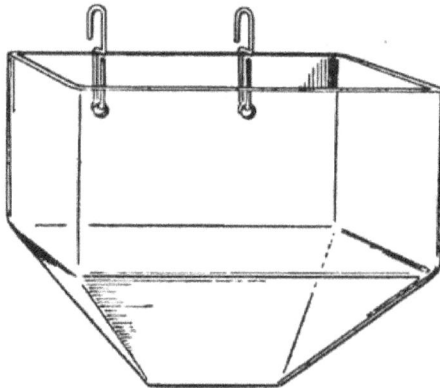

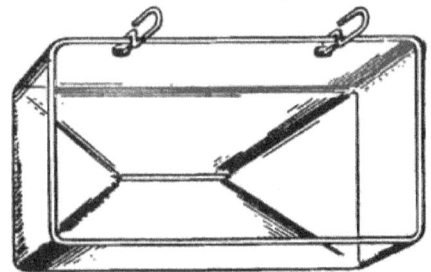

177

FIGS. 176 AND 177. SIDE AND TOP VIEWS OF ALL-GLASS BREEDING JARS, SHOWING ESCAPE SLIT

in the opening so that the wire divides the hole in half. The funnel is then placed in a bell jar or other aquarium of a size that will suspend it by the edge, bring the water as high as possible in funnel, place female fish in funnel and cover over with screen. The wire will prevent the mother fish from becoming jammed in the outlet, but will allow the young to pass through and collect in the lower portion of jar.

Very excellent breeding glasses come from Germany. These have a long narrow slit in the bottom and may be hooked on the inside of any receptacle. See Fig. 177.

**Spawning Net.** In the spawning season aquarium space is often limited, particularly among amateur breeders who have perhaps a single aquarium. The breeding fish should be separated from the others, as the idle fish would eat the spawn. An easy way over this difficulty is the

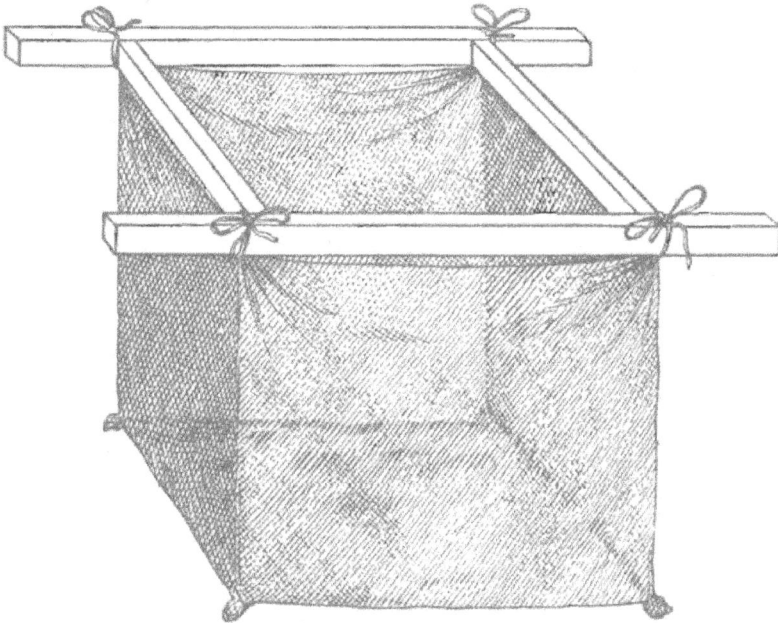

FIG. 178. SPAWNING NET

use of the spawning net. This is simply a square bag of cheesecloth suspended in the aquarium. Figure number 178 will clearly show how this may be done. The four corners should be weighted down with bits of lead or stone sewed in. The plants and spawning fish are simply transferred into the net. Confined in this comparatively small space the chances of the eggs becoming fertilized are increased, while the netting is sufficiently open to allow the aquarium water to flow slowly through it and prevent suffocation. In this way the large amount of dirt usually stirred up in an aquarium at spawning time, and which can do the adhesive eggs no good, is entirely avoided. The size of the net will depend somewhat on the proportions of the aquarium, but the capacity of net (portion in water) should be about twelve to eighteen inches long, ten inches wide and ten inches deep. In constructing, allow extra material for space between top frame and surface of water.

**Constant Aquarium Filter.** This device is for use in connection with the air pump referred to on page 10. It is capable of a number of variations, once the principle is understood. There are two columns of water in the tubes, one solid and one punctuated by air bubbles, thereby making it the lighter. This causes it to rise and therefore establish circulation as long as air is supplied. A ⅜-inch diameter glass surgical drain is shown at A. This should contain about eight small openings and be suspended two inches above the sand. This is connected by a short piece of rubber tubing to the rest of the system, which is of glass tubing from 5/16 to ⅜ inch inside diameter. The dark sections represent rubber joints, making the system more flexible, less liable to breakage, less expense in case of break and makes cleaning of each section easy. (The tubes require an annual cleaning.) Air is injected under pressure at C, which should be five inches above lowest point of pipes. This starts the flow, which is discharged into D, a small filter suspended in the corner of the aquarium, and just above water level. It may be made of glass, aluminum, porcelain or eathenware, and should approximate in size five inches in diameter by two deep, the bottom having a few perforations. The best filtering medium in this work is absorbent cotton, which should be laid on a few pebbles, glass bars or bits of charcoal for good drainage. The force of air and the distance between C and the surface of water determines the speed at which the water travels. The lower the point at which air is injected, the greater the speed. To start the system, disconnect at B, suck with the lips to start siphon, re-connect while water is running. After water in rise tube has reached aquarium level, turn on air-cock at C. This cock should always be closed when air is not wanted and pump not working, in order to prevent water backing up into air pipe. All rubber joints should be tightly secured by wrapping with thread or narrow strips of electric tape. Rubber cement spread on connecting surfaces helps make a good job. If there is danger of glass tubes being broken it is best to use pipe of block tin. For salt water, use glass or lead.

Instead of filtering at top of aquarium it is possible to pass the water through a big, large-necked bottle of sand at the lowest point of dip. Both tubes pass through a rubber cork, the dirty water being carried to bottom of bottle, discharged in a layer of pebbles, brought upwards through fine sand and taken off by rise pipe just inside of cork. The sand should not quite fill bottle. Cork must be securely tied down. This is a nice arrange-

ment, but was abandoned by the writer owing to the trouble of discon-
necting everything and washing sand every ten days, which was necessary
owing to clogging.  In top filter the cotton must be changed every two
days, but this can be done in a few seconds.

This arrangement both filters and aerates the water.  If filtering is
not needed, the filter can be removed and aeration will go on.

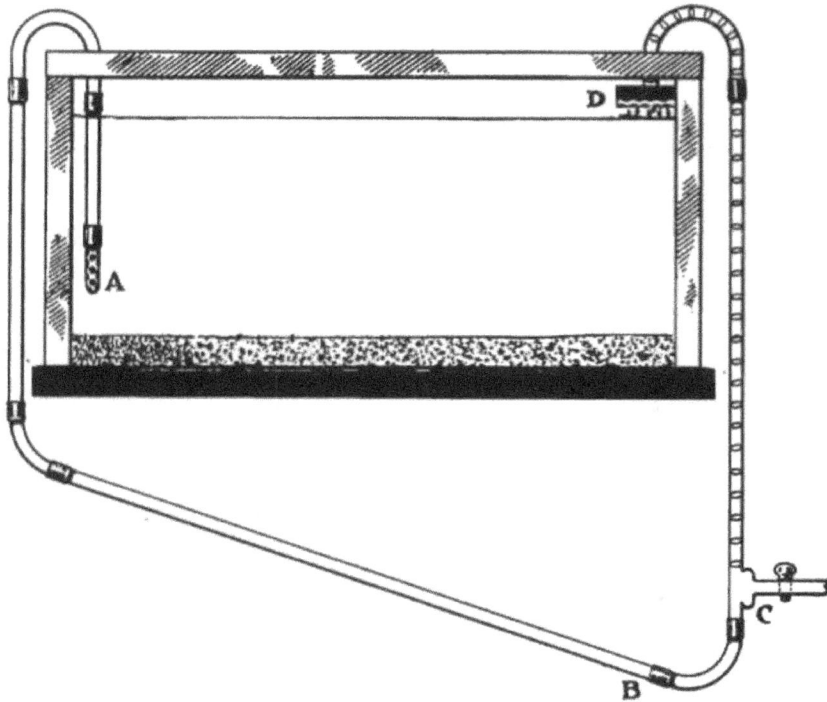

FIG. 179.  WATER CIRCULATION BY AIR PRESSURE

Water can be raised by this method from fifteen to twenty-five inches
above level.  To secure the greater height, use ¼-inch inside diameter
tube, take plenty of drop and allow eight inches from lowest point to C.
By this means and a little ingenuity a return fountain can be made.  To
secure a uniform flow it would require a small tank to receive the discharge from the pipe, and from this an overflow to aquarium in case the
water supply comes too rapidly for discharge rate of fountain.

It is not necessary to carry pipes over edge of aquarium as shown in
diagram;  they may be carried through the bottom, carrying dirty water
directly down.  The rise tube should be brought up through inside, over
edge of filter.  Short pieces of tubing long enough to reach above the
sand and to extend an inch below the aquarium base should be used for
passing through the slate.  A very effective means of securing these in

permanent position is to melt by alcohol blow-torch some chips of gum shellac. This melting is done in the aquarium directly around the tube and is continued until a small mound is formed. A piece of wet cardboard will protect nearby glass from the heat. Gum shellac has perfect resistance to water. It will adhere to almost anything and is of especial value in connecting glass to metal. When cool it is quite hard.

*Chapter Nineteen*

———

# Forty Don'ts

## FORTY DON'TS

Don't overfeed.

Don't overstock.

Don't inbreed too long.

Don't use very deep aquaria.

Don't delay treating sick fishes.

Don't start with expensive fishes.

Don't allow dead leaves to accumulate.

Don't use fishglobes except temporarily.

Don't attempt to move filled large aquaria.

Don't neglect to look fishes over carefully.

Don't fail to replace covers on tropical aquaria.

Don't use oil stoves if anything else can be had.

Don't keep very large and small fishes together.

Don't always blame the dealer if your fishes die.

Don't use coarse nets.  Brussels netting is better.

Don't keep any aquarium in a very subdued light.

Don't introduce plants without thoroughly cleansing.

Don't fail to give the fishes an occasional pinch of salts.

Don't fail to sterilize a net after lifting a diseased fish.

Don't put the fish outdoors the first warm day of Spring.

Don't be too sure the family cat won't fish in the aquarium.

Don't entrust the feeding to another if this can be avoided.

Don't as a beginner disregard the greater experience of others.

Don't sell surplus stock for a song.  It had better be given away.

Don't feed large earthworms.  They should be chopped and rinsed.

Don't slide all-glass aquaria.  Scratches may cause them to break.

Don't forget that most fishes enjoy an occasional variation in food.

Don't assume that ordinary artificial light is a substitute for daylight.

Don't experiment with rare tropicals to see how cool they may be kept.

Don't suddenly change the temperature of the water, either higher or lower.

Don't allow unconsumed food to remain in the aquarium.  Remove with dip-tube.

Don't use unmixed raw water from the faucet. The excess of oxygen is undesirable.

Don't fail to join an aquarium society, either as an active or a corresponding member.

Don't place daphnia in the aquarium without first looking carefully for insect enemies.

Don't fail to thoroughly disinfect an aquarium in which there has been a contagious disease.

Don't tear up the plants in trying to catch a fish. A little patience will avoid later regrets.

Don't be stingy, but give away a few interesting fishes to those who might become fanciers.

Don't keep goldfishes and tropicals together. They may not quarrel, but the appearance is not good.

Don't throw away dead rare fishes. Preserve in alcohol. Scientific institutions are glad to have them.

Don't always use chemicals on a fish a little out of condition. A change of aquarium or of food may be all that is necessary.

## ILLUSTRATIONS AND THEIR SOURCES

Frontispiece. Original Photograph (*colored*) by the Author, Mr. L. M. Dorsey's Prizewinning Concrete Aquarium.

## BIBLIOGRAPHY

An Account of the Fish Epidemic in Lake Mendota. S. A. Forbes, 1890
A Guide to the Study of Fishes. David Starr Jordan.
A Manual for the Study of Insects. J. H. Comstock, 1895
A Manual of Fish Culture. U. S. Com. of Fish and Fisheries, 1900
American Fishes. G. Brown Good, 1888
American Fish Culture. Thaddeus Norris, 1868
Aquarium Fish. Dr. E. Bade.
Aquatic Insects in the Adirondacks. Jas. G. Needham, 1901
Das Süswasser Aquarium. Dr. E. Bade.
Das Zimmer Aquarium. Dr. E. Bade.
Der Schleierschwanz und Telescopschleirschwanz, &c. Dr. E. Bade, 1900
Die ausländischen Zierfische. Reuter.
Domesticated Fish. W. L. Brind.
Entomological News
Feeding and Rearing Fishes, particularly Trout, &c. Wm. F. Page, 1895
Fish Culture. William E. Meehan.
Fish Culture on the Farm. J. J. Stranahan in Trans. Am. Fisheries Society, 1902
Fish Hatching and Fish Catching. Seth Green and R. B. Roosevelt, 1870
Fish Parasites, collected at Wood's Hole in 1898. Edwin Linton, Ph.D.
Flora of the Northern United States. Britton and Brown, 1898
Fresh-water Aquaria. Rev. G. C. Bateman, 1902
Fungi Affecting Fishes. Samuel Lockwood, 1890
Gas Bubble Disease of Fishes and Its Cause. F. P. Gorham, A.M., 1900.
Goldfish Breeds and Other Aquarium Fishes. H. T. Wolf, 1908
Handbook of Nature Study. A. B. Comstock
Histoire Naturelle des Dorades de la Chine. M. de Sauvigny, 1780
Histoire Naturelle des Poissons. M. le B. Cuvier and M. A. Vallencienes, 1842
Histoire Naturelle des Vegetaux Parasites. Charles Robin, 1853
Inherited Modifications in the Japanese Domesticated Golden Carp, &c. John A.
    Rider, 1893
Insects. Vernon L. Kellogg.
Insects; Their Structure and Life. G. H. Carpenter, 1899
Invertebrates of Massachusetts. August A. Gould, 1845
Leitfaden für Aquarien und Terrarienfreunde. Dr. E. Zernecke, 1897
Life in Inland Waters. Needham and Lloyd
Modern Fish Culture in Fresh and Salt Water. Fred'k Mather, 1900
Notes on Fish Culture in Germany. S. Jaffé, 1895
Notes on the Mosquitoes of the United States. L. O. Howard, 1900
Notes on Trematode Parasites on Fishes. Edwin Linton, 1898
Notice of the Occurrence of Protozoan Parasites on Fishes in Ohio. Edwin
    Linton, 1897
Observation on a Fungus infesting the Fish. G. P. Clinton, 1894
Observations on the Aquaria of the United States Fish Commission. William P.
    Seal, 1890
*On Entomostraca. Emil Weeger, 1890
On the Caudal and Anal Fins of Goldfishes. Dr. S. Watasa, 1887
Parasites. T. Spencer Cobbold, 1879

Photography of Live Fishes. R. H. Shufeldt, 1899
*Popular History of the Aquarium. G. B. Sowerby
Praxis der Aquarienkunde. Dr. E. Bade, 1899
Praxis der Terrarienkunde. Dr. E. Bade.
Reports and Bulletins of the New York Zoological Society
Rotatoria of the United States. H. S. Jennings, 1900
Sea Shore Life: The Invertebrates of the New York Coast. A. G. Mayer
Seaside Studies in Natural History. E. C. & A. Agassiz, 1865
Some Observations concerning Fish Parasites. Edwin Linton, 1894
The Care of Goldfishes. C. H. Townsend in Bulletins of the New York Zoological
    Society, 1907
The Care of Home Aquaria. R. C. Osburn
The Cultivation of Fishes in Natural and Artificial Ponds. C. H. Townsend, 1907
The Aquarium; a Brief Exposition of its Principles and Management. Wm. P.
    Seal, 1887
The Aquarium. Mark Samuels, 1898
*The Aquarium. J. E. Taylor, 1876
*The Aquarium. P. H. Gosse, 1854
The Aquarium as an aid to Biological Research. Wm. P. Seal, 1883
The Aquarium of the U. S. Fish Commission at the World's Columbian Exposition.
    S. A. Forbes and others, 1894
*The Book of the Aquarium. Shirley Hibberd
The Crustacea of the Fresh Waters of the U. S. Sidney Smith, 1872
The Destruction of Trout Fry by Hydra. E. A. Beardsley, 1903
The Family Aquarium or Aqua-vivarium. Henry D. Butler, 1858
The Fishes of Illinois. Forbes and Robertson.
The Fishes of New Jersey. Henry W. Fowler.
The Fishes of North Carolina (Bulletin of the N. C. Geological Survey).
    Hugh M. Smith.
The Fish Notebook (Nature Notebook Series). George C. Embody
The Fishes of Pennsylvania. Tarleton H. Bean, 1893
The Fishes of Pennsylvania. E. D. Cope, 1881
The Fishes of North and Middle America. Jordan and Evermann, 1896
The Fish of the Fresh and Brackish Waters in the Vicinity of New York. Eugene
    Smith, 1897
*The Fresh and Saltwater Aquarium. Rev. J. G. Wood
The Freshwater Aquarium. Eggling and Ehrenberg.
The Home Aquarium and How to Care for it. Eugene Smith, 1902
The Insect Book. Leland O. Howard, 1901
The Sea-Beach at Ebb-Tide. Augusta F. Arnold, 1901
The Trematodes. H. S. Pratt. American Naturalist, 1900 and 1902
*The Vivarium. Rev. G. C. Bateman, 1893

## AQUARIUM AND FISH-CULTURE PERIODICALS

Aquatic Life. Philadelphia.
Blätter für Aquarien und Terrarien-Kunde, Magdeburg
Bulletin. Brooklyn Aquarium Society.
Cyclopedia of American Horticulture. L. H. Bailey, 1900
Forschungsberichte aus der Biologischen Station zu Plön
*L'Acclimatation, Paris
L'Aquarium, Paris
Wochenschrift, Hamburg.

# CROSS INDEX

*Illustrations are marked by asterisk (\*).*

www.ingramcontent.com/pod-product-compliance
Lightning Source LLC
Chambersburg PA
CBHW080513090426
42734CB00015B/3040